The Mysteries of Bilingualism

The Mysteries of Bilingualism

Unresolved Issues

François Grosjean

This edition first published 2022

Registered Office(s)
John Wiley & Sons, Inc., 111 River Street, Hoboken, NJ 07030, USA
John Wiley & Sons Ltd, The Atrium, Southern Gate, Chichester, West Sussex, PO19 8SQ, UK

Editorial Office
9600 Garsington Road, Oxford, OX4 2DQ, UK

For details of our global editorial offices, customer services, and more information about Wiley products visit us at www.wiley.com.

Wiley also publishes its books in a variety of electronic formats and by print-on-demand. Some content that appears in standard print versions of this book may not be available in other formats.

Library of Congress Cataloging-in-Publication Data
A catalogue record for this book is available from the Library of Congress

Paperback: 9781119602378; epub: 9781119602415;
ePDF: 9781119602408

Cover image: © graphicwithart/Shutterstock
Cover design: Wiley

Set in 10/12pt WarnockPro by Integra Software Services Pvt. Ltd, Pondicherry, India

10 9 8 7 6 5 4 3 2 1

Contents

Author Biography

François Grosjean is Professor Emeritus of Psycholinguistics at Neuchâtel University, Switzerland. His publications on bilingualism include many articles and chapters as well as seven books: *Life with Two Languages: An Introduction to Bilingualism* (1982), *Studying Bilinguals* (2008), *Bilingual: Life and Reality* (2010), *The Psycholinguistics of Bilingualism* (with Ping Li; 2013), *The Listening Bilingual: Speech Perception, Comprehension, and Bilingualism* (with Krista Byers-Heinlein, 2018), *Life as a Bilingual* (2021), and *Parler plusieurs langues: Le monde des bilingues* (2015). He is a Founding Editor of the journal *Bilingualism: Language and Cognition* and was its first Coordinating Editor. In 2019 he published his autobiography, *A Journey in Languages and Cultures: The Life of a Bicultural Bilingual.*

Introduction

Every field of study has issues that remain unresolved, and the field of bilingualism is no exception. Over the years, as I was involved in research on bilinguals or writing about them, I would earmark questions that I needed to come back to at some point. Among these were: Who is bilingual given that there is such a discrepancy in definitions? How many bilinguals are there? How do infant bilinguals who acquire both languages simultaneously manage to separate them? Why do some bilinguals have an accent in one of their languages whereas others do not? Can you lose a language completely, and this at any age? Is language processing selective or non-selective? Do you really change your personality when you change language? What does it mean to be both bilingual and bicultural?, and so on. Of course, answers to these questions have been proposed by scholars over the years but never totally satisfactorily. This is because the evidence is either absent or unclear, new studies have contradicted earlier ones, the underlying theories diverge, and so on.

In this book, we will examine eleven unresolved issues and, based on past and recent research, we will give the best explanation we have for them. There will be four parts, each part containing two or three chapters. In Part I, Bilingual Adults and Children, the first chapter concerns who is bilingual. We will examine how bilinguals and bilingualism have been characterized and how this has changed over time. To help us do so, we will call on surveys, dictionary entries, as well as definitions proposed by language scientists. We will also discuss important characteristics of bilingual people and see how self-report questionnaires deal with them. The second chapter will address the question of how many bilinguals there are. We will examine why it is so difficult to obtain exact figures and will concentrate on a few national censuses that offer sufficient data from which numbers of bilinguals can be estimated. Finally, the third chapter concerns one of the most intriguing phenomena in bilingualism: how do infants who acquire two or more languages simultaneously manage to separate them? Even though their task seems daunting, a number of studies indicate how they start doing so perceptually as well as pragmatically.

In Part II, Linguistics and Neurolinguistics, we will start with the issue of having an accent in a language. After examining the phonetic and prosodic characteristics of accents, we will present the main factors that account for having an accent – from traditional ones such as maturational aspects to more recent ones such as type and amount of language input. We will also address having an accent in a third language. This will be followed by a chapter on language loss, in adults and in children. As concerns adults, we

The Mysteries of Bilingualism, First Edition. François Grosjean.

will cover characteristics of attrition, and go in search of factors that account for language loss. For children, we will describe experimental studies that attempt to see if there are remnants of a language forgotten in very early childhood. We will end with two studies, already quite old, that appear to show that a lost language may be recovered under hypnosis. Finally, the third chapter in this part concerns bilinguals with aphasia, that is those bilinguals who suffer language and speech impairment due to brain damage. We will discuss patterns of language recovery and the factors that account for them. We will also examine language mixing in the speech of aphasic bilinguals and show that it is not always a sign of pathology.

Part III, Language Use and Language Processing, examines first how bilinguals call on their languages, separately or together, when interacting with others. How is the language of interaction – the base language – chosen, and what factors govern whether the other language is brought in in the form of code-switches and borrowings? This will be followed by a chapter on what a bilingual's languages are used for. Bilinguals usually acquire and use their languages for different purposes, in different domains of life, with different people. This has a very real impact, not yet fully recognized, on language production and perception, language acquisition, memory, mental calculation, and so on. Finally, the third chapter in this part will deal with the question of whether language processing is selective or non-selective when only one language is being use. In other words, when bilinguals perceive and produce just one language, is only that language involved, or do(es) the other(s) intervene? Experimental research these last 20 years has brought answers to these questions.

The last part, Part IV, deals with Biculturalism and Personality. In the first chapter, we describe bilinguals who are also bicultural: how they can be defined, how they become bicultural, how they adapt their behaviors to different cultural situations, and how they identify with their cultures. And in the second chapter, we attempt to answer a question often asked: do bilinguals change personalities when they change language? We will review opinions and beliefs, examine the results of past and present studies, and look at variables that are involved in feeling different when using different languages. We will end with an explanation that finally solves this enigma.

Two points need to be made here. First, the book has been written so that each chapter is self-contained: it raises an issue and then discusses the research that has been done to help solve it. When information that is required is given in another chapter, it is evoked succinctly in the chapter being read and then a reference is given to the other chapter. The second point is that bilingual adults and children are discussed together in every chapter unless there is a reason to separate them. This is the case, for example, in Chapter 5 on language loss where the larger of the two parts concerns children. And, of course, Chapter 3 on language separation is wholly dedicated to them.

This book can be used for courses in psycholinguistics, linguistics, neurolinguistics, cognitive sciences, speech and language pathology, bilingualism, applied linguistics, and first and second language acquisition. It is suitable for upper level BA and BS courses, first- and second-year graduate studies, as well as for laypersons who wish to find out about unresolved issues in bilingualism research.

I would like to thank those at Wiley Blackwell who helped me with the book: Tanya McMullin, Commissioning Editor, who believed in the project and gave me a contract; Rachel Greenberg, Commissioning Editor, who accompanied it through to its completion and production; Clelia Petracca and Anya Fielding, Editorial Assistants; Hannah Lee and Mandy Collison, Managing Editors; John Bowdler, Copy Editor; Kanimozhi Ramamurthy, Content Refinement Specialist; and Gopu Rasuvel, Designer.

Finally, preparing and writing a book such as this one could not have been possible without the kind help of numerous colleagues – experts in their respective domains – who shared with me their publications, answered my questions, and even read and commented on segments of my manuscript, or even on whole chapters. They are: Roman Abel, Dylan Antovich, Mariem Boukadi, Jeffrey Bowers, Mirjam Broersma, Krysta Byers-Heinlein, Jiyoun Choi, Deborah Cobb-Clark, Anne Cutler, Jean-Marc Dewaele, Jennifer Fayard, James Flege, Rosalie Footnick, Mira Goral, David Green, Jason Gullifer, Michael Gurven, Joanne Hans, Ying-yi Hong, Keerthana Kapiley, Michele Koven, Jan Kuipers, Ekaterina Kuzmina, Marjorite Lorch, Ping Li, Sven Matthys, Elke Montanari, Alene Moyer, Elena Nicoladis, Bertrand Ouellet-Léveillé, Christophe Pallier, Ken Paap, Johanne Paradis, Michel Paradis, Silke Paulmann, Lara Pierce, Nairan Ramirez-Esparza, Oliver Robinson, Jenny Saffran, Monika Schmid, Mark Sebba, Wing Chee So, Ágnes Szabó, Debra Titone, Mehrgol Tiv, Janet Werker, and Magdalena Wrembel.

As a sign of my gratitude, I dedicate this book to them.

Part I

Bilingual Adults and Children

1

Who Is Bilingual?

One of the most complex questions when studying bilingualism is quite simply: Who is bilingual? If you ask bilinguals themselves whether they are bilingual or not, you may come away with affirmative answers but also negative ones, accompanied by remarks such as, "I'm not bilingual (as) I'm not fluent in all my languages," "I don't consider myself bilingual since I don't know how to write my other language," "I didn't grow up with two languages, so I'm not bilingual," and even, "I have an accent in Spanish so I can't be considered bilingual." Then, if you look up the word "bilingual" in dictionaries, you will find a variety of definitions, going from, "Having the ability to speak two languages" (Wiktionary), all the way to, "Able to speak two languages equally well" (Longman). And, finally, if you ask linguists their definitions, you also find an assortment of responses, with a preponderance pulling towards the regular use of two or more languages.

Are things a bit more straightforward when you look at the questions in self-report questionnaires given to bilinguals in an attempt to describe their bilingualism? The answer leans towards the affirmative but there is still a lot of variety. Some ask about language dominance, whereas others do not; some include questions about the biculturalism of bilinguals, but others do not; some ask about the bilingual's accent, whereas other refrain from doing so, and so on. In sum, diversity is found in both how we define bilinguals and how we describe them. This may be due, in large part at least, to the fact that the study of bilingualism is still a rather young science as compared to that of monolingualism.

In the first part of this chapter, we will spend time on how bilinguals and bilingualism have been characterized and how this has changed over time. We will begin by looking at responses from three surveys done with lay people, both monolinguals and bilinguals. Then we will examine the definitions given by dictionaries for the words "bilingual" and "bilingualism." The entries were written by lexicographers many of whom have linguistics training, so it will be interesting to see if there are any differences with what lay people say. Finally, we will look at the definitions given by language scientists over a span of about one hundred years and examine their evolution.

In the second part, we will present important characteristics of bilingual people (language proficiency, language use, functions of languages, language mode, etc.) and will also examine how they evolve over time. We will end with a quick overview of three well known self-report questionnaires given to bilinguals and see what they have in common and where they differ.

The Mysteries of Bilingualism, First Edition. François Grosjean.

Definitions and Their Evolution

What Lay People Say

When I wrote my first book on bilingualism some 40 years ago (Grosjean 1982), I conducted a short survey in order to uncover the lay person's understanding of the term "bilingual." I asked a number of monolingual college students to answer this question: "If someone told you that X was bilingual in English and French, what would you understand by that?" The most frequent response I found (36% of the answers) was that X speaks both languages *fluently*. This was followed by X *speaks* English and French (21%), and by X *understands and speaks* English and French (18%)? Note that the summed percentages of the two latter answers, which basically say the same thing, add up to 39%. The same question asked of a group of bilinguals gave very similar results: X speaks the two languages *fluently* (31%), and *speaks* the two languages (46%). Thus, just speaking both languages (which includes both production and perception), gets a bit less than half of the responses in the two groups, and speaking both languages *fluently* is only just behind, with 36% and 31% respectively. This shows the importance of fluency[1] in the participants' mind, be they monolingual or bilingual.

Both groups were then asked to rate the importance of a number of factors that had been mentioned in definitions of bilingualism, such as being fluent in two languages, having both speaking and writing fluency in them, using two languages regularly, etc. The scale used went from 1 "not important" to 5 "very important." The monolinguals gave a mean rating of 4.7 for being fluent in two languages, and the bilinguals gave it a rating of 4.4. Speaking and writing fluency in two languages was given a rating of 4.0 by the monolinguals and 3.6 by bilinguals, and equal fluency in two languages was rated 3.7 and 4.1 by the two groups, respectively. Thus, once again both monolinguals and bilinguals felt that fluency in two languages is an important factor in describing the bilingual person.

It is interesting to note that monolinguals differed most from bilinguals on the question of language use, a factor that we will evoke often in this chapter. For monolinguals, the factor labeled "regular use of two languages" received a mean rating of 3 (that is, it was not considered a very important factor), but the bilinguals gave it a mean rating of 4.1, just below "fluency in two languages" (4.4). So here, on language use, monolinguals and bilinguals diverged a bit, probably because bilinguals are more aware of the communicative aspect of being bilingual, that is, using two languages irrespective of your fluency in them.

Where do things stand now? Two surveys were conducted this century, one by Zubrzycki (2019) and one some 13 years before by Sia and Dewaele (2006). Zubrzycki wanted to replicate the Sia and Dewaele study, which asked speakers of at least two languages: "Are you bilingual?" According to the answer they gave, they were placed in the "bilingual" or "non-bilingual" group, and it was shown, among other things, that the self-assessment of second language (L2) proficiency was higher in the "bilingual" group than in the "non-bilingual" group. This was true overall, but also for the four basic skills: Speaking, listening, reading and writing. Zubrzycki conducted the same kind of study

[1] In this chapter, the reader will see a shift from the use of "fluency" in earlier research to "proficiency" in later research. The two are used synonymously here. In chapters that follow, though, we will report on the work of some researchers, as in Chapter 5, who use "fluency/fluent" to mean that a person speaks easily, clearly, and with few hesitations.

but with a slightly different question, "Do you consider yourself bilingual?" He found practically identical percentages to Sia and Dewaele for those who labeled themselves as bilingual or not, and very similar assessment results.

Interestingly, Zubrzycki (2019) added an open-ended question to his study: "How would you define the term bilingual?" It was very similar to Grosjean's (1982) first question, and it is worth examining the answers more closely. As concerns those who self defined as "non-bilinguals," nearly 80% formulated a restrictive definition of bilingualism. Zubrzycki does not give percentages but he reports that the main criterion put forward was equal proficiency in two languages, implying thereby a native-like command of the L2 with no traces of one language when using the other and, in particular, no traces of a foreign accent. Other elements which appeared in the definitions were items such as "native level," "native speaker," "mother tongue," and "native language." And some also said that the bilingual is required to have been raised in a bilingual family or to have had a long-term stay in the L2 environment.

Of those who self defined as "bilinguals," however, over 70% were less restrictive in their answers. Among the criteria expressed, we find feeling comfortable when using the L2, and reaching a level at which communication becomes natural and effortless. There was also the ability to communicate effectively in all domains of language use and in a wide range of social contexts. Finally, a number of definitions underlined everyday use of two languages.

Thus, over a span of some 40 years, quite similar results have been obtained from lay people, with a slight difference between those who are, or who self define as, bilingual, and the others. Zubrzycki concludes that a monolingual view of bilingualism – the bilingual should be two monolinguals in one person (criticized by Grosjean 1985) – is still deeply entrenched in the lay person's perception of what it means to be bilingual. Will a similar tendency be found in dictionary definitions? They reflect the meaning of words based on current usage but they are also the work of lexicographers many of whom have some linguistic training. We now turn to this.

What Dictionaries Say

We looked up the words "bilingual" and "bilingualism" in a number of dictionaries that can be found on the internet. Many of them are well established, such as Longman, Oxford Advanced Learner's, Cambridge English, American Heritage, Collins COBUILD, Chambers, Merriam-Webster, etc. Others are newer, such as Dictionary.com and Wiktionary. For the word "bilingual," we restricted ourselves to the meaning pertaining to the bilingual person, and did not include those pertaining to a bilingual activity, event, or item, as in bilingual education, bilingual conference, bilingual book, etc. Out of a total of 11 definitions we examined, ten underlined the ability to speak two languages *fluently*. Of these, seven indicated speaking two languages equally well (e.g., Cambridge English: "able to use two languages equally well") or with nearly equal fluency (e.g., American Heritage: "using or able to use two languages, especially with equal or nearly equal fluency"), and three stressed speaking two languages fluently or extremely well (e.g., Macmillan: "able to speak two languages extremely well"). Only one definition of the 11 did not have fluency as a criterion. It was that of Wiktionary, a more recent dictionary, which stated: "having the ability to speak two languages." We should note that no definition indicated using two languages on a regular basis, nor did any include more than two languages. In addition, none mentioned dialects in their definitions. Thus, dictionaries seem to reflect closely what lay people state, at least those who do not consider themselves to be bilingual (see the previous section).

We also looked up "bilingualism" in the same 11 dictionaries. Surprisingly, three of them (Oxford Advanced Learner's, American Heritage, and Longman) did not have an entry for the word. Three of the eight that did underlined the ability to speak two languages, two of them adding equally well (e.g., Cambridge English: "the fact of being able to use two languages equally well"). This is proportionally less than for the meaning of "bilingual." And five definitions mentioned language use. Two of these mentioned use by itself (e.g., Macmillan: "the use of two languages by a person or a group"); two mentioned ability and use (e.g., Merriam-Webster: "the ability to speak two languages," as well as, "the frequent use... of two languages"); and one, Google dictionary, indicated the one or the other possibility: "fluency in or use of two languages." Again, none indicated two or more languages, and none added dialects to languages. In sum, the definitions of "bilingualism" put much less emphasis on language fluency and made more room for language use. But overall, dictionary definitions follow the lay persons' view of what "bilingual" and "bilingualism" mean. We can now turn to experts who study bilingualism.

What Language Scientists Say

Do language scientists have a different view of what it means to be bilingual? Some have indeed put the emphasis on language fluency (which they also term language proficiency or language knowledge), but over the years we have seen a gradual movement away from the very restrictive definition proposed by Bloomfield (1933) who stated that bilingualism is the "native-like control of two languages." This stance was still present with Thiery (1978) who wrote that "a true bilingual is someone who is taken to be one of themselves by the members of two different linguistic communities, at roughly the same social and cultural level." Movement away from this position can already be seen with Hakuta (1992) who simply talks of control of languages: "a bilingual individual is someone who controls two or more languages." At the time, Haugen (1969) was one of the rare exceptions who stated that fluency did not need to be that high. He stated that bilingualism begins "at the point where the speaker of one language can produce complete, meaningful utterances in the other language."

Since the turn of the century, those who use fluency or proficiency as the main criterion have been much less demanding of bilinguals. They are aware that the majority of bilinguals do not have equal proficiency in their languages, many have an accent in at least one of their languages, and many acquired their other language(s) at different points in life, and not just as children. They use their languages for different purposes, in different domains of life, to accomplish different things and so their level of proficiency in a language depends on their need for that language (Grosjean 2013).

This is starting to be reflected in the definitions proposed. For example, Luna, Ringberg, and Peracchio (2008) state that bilingualism is the "ability to communicate relatively well – including the ability to speak, understand, read, and write – in two different languages." And De Houwer (2019) actually goes all the way to simply accepting an ability to comprehend two languages. She defines a bilingual interlocutor as "a person who is in principle able to understand two (or more) language varieties at levels that are minimally appropriate for a given life stage." Finally, some researchers have decided to remain neutral on the topic of fluency. Thus, Li Wei (2007), states that a bilingual is "someone with the possession of two languages," and similarly Dewaele, Housen and Li Wei (2003) write that bilingualism is "the presence of two or more languages."

Various theoretical positions on bilingualism, such as Grosjean's holistic view (Grosjean 1985, 1989) as well as Cook's (1991) multi-competence of speakers of two or more languages, have left greater room for *language use* as a definitional factor. It had started appearing in the last century with Weinreich (1953) who stated that bilingualism is "the practice of alternately using two languages," and Mackey (1962) who proposed that it is "the alternate use of two or more languages by the same individual." The language use definition took on more importance over the years, included more than two languages (already mentioned by Mackey (1962)), and became the standard academic definition. Thus, Appel and Muysken (1987) wrote that a bilingual is "somebody who regularly uses two or more languages in alternation," Romaine (2013) stated that bilingualism is "the routine use of two or more languages in a community," and de Bot (2019) proposed that multilingualism is "the daily use of two or more languages."

For the last 40 years or so, I have defined bilinguals as *those who use two or more languages (or dialects) in their everyday lives.* Putting the emphasis on language use does not do away with language proficiency though, since you cannot use a language if you do not know it to some extent. But the range of who can be considered bilingual increases considerably with this definition. As I wrote in *Bilingual: Life and Reality* (Grosjean 2010), at one end of the range we find the migrant worker who may speak with some difficulty the host country's language and who does not read and write it. At the other end, we have the professional interpreter who is fully fluent in two languages. In between, we find the scientist who reads and writes articles in a second language but who rarely speaks it, the foreign-born spouse who interacts with friends in his first language, the member of a linguistic minority who uses the minority language only at home and the majority language in all other domains of life, the Deaf person who uses sign language with her friends but a spoken language (often in its written form) with a hearing person, and so on. Despite the great diversity among these people, they all share a common feature: They lead their lives with two or more languages.

I insist on *two or more* languages in my definition as some people use more than two languages regularly. If one wants to be specific regarding a particular person, one can specify exactly how many languages they use on a regular basis by using words like "trilingual," "quadrilingual," "quintilingual," etc. As for the word, "multilingual," many prefer to use "bilingual," as "multilingual" is mainly used to characterize societies or countries (e.g., Switzerland is a multilingual country). In addition, at least in Western societies, the majority of bilinguals only use two languages regularly, reinforcing the *bi-* in bilingual even though they may know several others. For example, I know some Italian, Spanish, American Sign Language, and even Latin, but I only use English and French on a regular basis. Thus, in terms of language use, I am only bilingual. Finally, dialects is in the definition I propose, and it is starting to appear in others too, as in some parts of the world (e.g., Italy, Switzerland, Arabic-speaking countries, etc.), dialects are a linguistic reality and people can be bilingual in a majority language and a dialect. They can also be trilingual in a national language, and in two dialects, for example. A final point should be made regarding emphasizing language use in definitions. I have found that it allows many people who live with two or more languages to accept their bilingualism and be proud of who they are. This they could not do when fluency – often equal fluency – in two or more languages was the main criterion for identifying oneself as bilingual.

Describing Bilinguals

Definitions have never replaced a good description of a phenomenon, and this also true for what it means to be bilingual. In what follows, I will present some important characteristics of bilingual people, first at a particular point in time in their lives, and then over the years, as is revealed in their language history.

At a Particular Point in Time

Language proficiency and language use are probably the two foremost factors (variables) when describing bilinguals at a particular point in time. A third one, when they actually started to become bilingual, will be dealt with in their language history below. A grid approach proposed by Grosjean (2010) can help us visualize proficiency and use together (see Figure 1.1).

Language use is presented along the vertical axis (from Never used at the bottom all the way to Daily use at the top) and language proficiency is on the horizontal axis (from Low proficiency on the left to High proficiency on the right). These labels can be replaced with numerical values if necessary. An example allows us to see the three languages of Lucia, a bilingual, and where they stand in relation to one another. Her most used and most proficient language is La (French). Her other language, Lb (English), is used slightly less frequently and she is slightly less proficient in it, although the level is still very high. This explains why its position is just below and to the left of La in the figure. She also knows a third language, Lc (German), but not very well, and she uses it rarely. Hence its position in the lower left of the grid. Lucia is clearly bilingual in English and French, on both factors, and like many others, she also has some knowledge of another language but rarely uses it. Note that in this type of presentation, the position of each language can be based either on self-assessment ratings, as in this case, or on the results of more objective tests.

Separate grids can be used for each of the bilingual's four language skills (speaking, listening, writing, and reading) since it is often the case that amount of use and degree of proficiency can be quite different in these skills in the different languages. Thus, some bilinguals may have very good oral comprehension of a language but may not speak it very well; others may know how to read and write one of their languages but not the other(s), and so on. A few years after the grid approach was proposed, two other researchers, Luk and Bialystok (2013), provided statistical evidence that bilingual experience does indeed involve at least two dimensions, language use (they call it bilingual usage) and language proficiency, and that these dimensions are not mutually exclusive. These variables are the first building blocks of the description of the bilingual to which others need to be added, as we will now see.

If one is interested in a bilingual's language use, one will invariably be confronted with the functions of the person's languages, that is which language is used, when, for what and with whom. More than half a century ago, Weinreich (1953) had already stated that

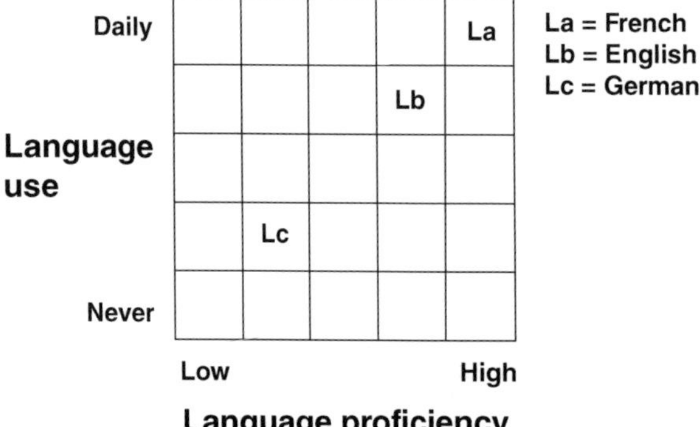

Figure 1.1 A visual representation of a bilingual's language proficiency and language use.

many bilinguals are accustomed to discuss some topics in only one of their languages. Several years later, Mackey (1962) divided language functions into external functions (language use in various situations and domains) and internal functions (the non-communicative uses of language such as counting, praying, dreaming, etc.). Clearly not all facets of life in bilinguals require the same language, nor do they demand both languages. Based on this, Grosjean (1997, 2016) proposed the Complementarity Principle, which he defined as follows:

> Bilinguals usually acquire and use their languages for different purposes, in different domains of life, with different people. Different aspects of life require different languages.

The principle is discussed and illustrated in Chapter 8, so it suffices to say here that it has an impact on a number of variables, notably language proficiency. If a language is spoken in a reduced number of domains and with a limited number of people, then it will not be developed as much as a language used in more domains and with more people. In the latter case, there will be an increase in specific vocabularies, stylistic varieties, discursive and pragmatic rules, etc. It is precisely because the need and use of the languages are usually quite different that bilinguals do not develop equal and total proficiency in all their languages. This is also true for the different language skills, such as reading and writing.

Language proficiency, language use, and functions of languages influence two other variables that are proposed when describing bilinguals. The first is language mode (Grosjean 2001), and the second is language dominance. Concerning language mode, which will be treated in more depth in Chapter 7, bilinguals have to ask themselves two questions when communicating with others: "Which language should be used?" and "Should the other language be brought in?" The answer to the first question leads to language choice, that is, choosing a base language for the exchange. As concerns the second question, bringing in or not the other language, if the answer is "no," then the bilingual is in a monolingual mode. This is the mode when speaking to monolinguals, reading in a particular language, listening to just one language, etc. If, on the other hand, the answer is "yes," as when the bilingual is speaking to another bilingual who shares his/her languages and who accepts to change base language from time to time and intermingle them (e.g., code-switch and borrow), then the bilingual is in a bilingual mode. Here, both languages are activated but the base language more so than the other language. Other examples of when the bilingual mode is required are listening to two bilinguals who are mixing languages, interpreting from one language to another, doing a study that requires the two languages, either overtly or covertly, and so on. In between these two endpoints of the continuum, bilinguals can find themselves in various intermediary modes, depending on the situation, the topic, the interlocutors, etc.

The other variable that is influenced by language proficiency, language use, and functions of languages, is language dominance. For a long time, researchers asked themselves whether dominance was based on just proficiency, or use, or both, or whether it depended on basic skills such as reading and writing a language, or even whether it concerned when the languages were acquired. Silva-Corvalán and Treffers-Daller (2016) studied dominance extensively and came to the conclusion that a dominant language is that in which a bilingual has attained an overall higher level of proficiency at a given age, and/or the language which s/he uses more frequently, and across a wider range of domains. As we see, all three factors are mentioned in their definition.

A final factor that needs to be included when describing bilinguals at a particular point in time concerns biculturalism. Are the bilinguals being described also bicultural and, if so, what impact does it have on their bilingualism (Grosjean 2015). Chapter 10 is dedicated to biculturalism but it worth mentioning here that bilingualism and biculturalism are not automatically coextensive. You can find bilinguals who are not bicultural (e.g., those bilinguals who have lived in just one culture, such as many Dutch people), biculturals who are not bilingual (e.g., British people who have migrated to the United States), as well as people who are both bicultural and bilingual. Biculturals can be characterized in the following way: They take part, to varying degrees, in the life of two or more cultures; they adapt, in part at least, their attitudes, behaviors, values, languages, etc., to these cultures; and they combine and blend aspects of the cultures involved. Being bicultural has a real impact on language knowledge and language use in bilinguals. One example that comes to mind concerns concepts in the bilingual lexicon. So called translation equivalents, such as French "pain" and English "bread" may share the same concept in bilinguals who are not bicultural, but certainly not if they are bicultural. The same is true of French "café" and English "coffee."

Language History

One can describe a bilingual at a particular point in time, as we have just seen, but one also needs to describe that person's bilingualism over time. We need to know which languages were acquired and when, whether the cultural context was the same or different, what the pattern of proficiency and use was over the years, how much language separation or language intermingling took place, which language(s) went through restructuring under the influence of another language, and whether some languages became dormant or even entered attrition. In addition, we need to find out about the bilingual's moments of language stability and moments of language change where a language may suddenly acquire new importance, as when a person immigrates. These transition periods, which can last several years, are important in order to understand the evolution of a person's bilingualism.

A crucial factor in language history is the age of acquisition of each language. We need to know whether the person acquired both languages simultaneously as an infant (something that is relatively rare; see Chapter 3), or whether one language was acquired first followed by another a few years later, or in adolescence, or even in adulthood. We also want to know about the context in which each language was acquired, such in the family, outside the home, in the classroom, etc. Information is also needed as to the age at which individual skills started to be acquired in each language (speaking, reading, etc.), how many years were spent in formal learning of a language, etc.

The question of language dominance is also something to examine in a person's language history. One should be careful not to assume that a first language or "mother tongue" is automatically the dominant language. People's personal language history may show quite different bilingual configurations at different moments in time. Thus, Grosjean (2010) describes how his dominance has changed four times over a stretch of some fifty years, with two periods, both some ten years long, where the second language was his dominant language.

Finally, information is needed on how people became bicultural, if that is the case. Did it happen in the family when they were young children, or when they came into contact with a second culture in school, or when, as adolescents, already anchored in a culture, they pursued their studies in another culture, or even when they emigrated as adults? And information on the evolution of their biculturalism over their lifespan will also be required.

Self-report Questionnaires

As the preceding section has shown, describing a bilingual fully, at a particular point in time, and over a life time, is particularly demanding. One approach that has been used is to ask bilinguals to fill in self-report questionnaires that aim at obtaining the kind of information we described. If used along with various verbal tasks, such as picture naming, word and sentence perception and production, etc., they allow us to have a good description of those who interest us (see de Bruin 2019, for a critical review). Three major self-report questionnaires are now available in the field for adults, while other, smaller ones, examine specific behaviors (e.g., language choice and code-switching), or are aimed at describing the bilingualism of children (these are filled in by parents or caretakers).

The three self-report questionnaires are the Language Experience and Proficiency Questionnaire (LEAP-Q) proposed by Marian, Blumenfeld, and Kaushanskaya (2007), the Language and Social Background Questionnaire (LSBQ) proposed by the York University Lifespan Cognition and Development Laboratory (Anderson et al. 2018), and the Language History Questionnaire (LHQ3) proposed by Li, Zhang, Yu, and Zhao (2020). Since they have very similar acronyms, and to facilitate reading, I will use Q-A for the LEAP-Q, Q-B for the LSBQ, and Q-C for the LHQ3. I examined each questionnaire keeping in mind the factors I discussed above, those pertaining to bilinguals at a particular point in time, and those that concern their language history, and will briefly summarize what I found. This is not meant to be a critical review but simply a way of illustrating how one goes about obtaining extensive biographical language data from bilinguals, and the diversity one can find among the tools available.

Concerning the first aspect – bilinguals at a particular point in time – all three questionnaires request some biographical information, and they all ask questions regarding the first three factors I outlined: Language proficiency, language use, and functions of languages. It should be noted though that Q-A does not ask about writing proficiency, nor does it ask many questions about the languages used in domains such as work, school, shopping, religion, etc. As concerns different language behaviors in different language modes (e.g., language switching or mixing in certain situations), both Q-B and Q-C ask at least one question whereas Q-A does not. The latter, however, is the only one to ask about language dominance. As for biculturalism, Q-B does not ask any questions, and both Q-A and Q-C ask about cultural identity but nothing on bicultural conduct, such as adapting ones behavior, attitudes, and even personality to different cultural situations. It should be noted that two of the three questionnaires (Q-A and Q-C) ask about the bilingual's degree of foreign accent whereas Q-B does not. Finally, Q-C is the only one to ask questions regarding the person's language learning skills, their results on standardized proficiency tests, as well as their use of dialects.

As for language history, all three questionnaires ask about the order of acquisition of each language, when they were acquired, and their manner of acquisition. Q-C also asks at which age each language started being used at home, with friends, at school, etc. Q-B is the only one to ask if there were periods when a language was not used, and if so, for how long. Finally, none ask about when the person became bicultural.

The three questionnaires reflect, in their own ways, where things stand concerning the description of bilinguals. They are strong on reported proficiency and use, age and manner of acquisition, and also do well, with one exception, on language functions. They may need to do more, though, on change of language behavior when in monolingual and in bilingual situations, on the evolution of the bilingual's languages over the years, and on biculturalism. Specific questionnaires already exist for language switching and mixing (e.g., Rodriguez-Fornells et al. 2012) so this may the route they could take in the future for the elements that need to be investigated further.

References

Anderson, John A. E., Lorinda Mak, Aram Keyvani Chahi, and Ellen Bialystok. 2018. "The language and social background questionnaire: Assessing degree of bilingualism in a diverse population." *Behavioral Research Methods*, 50: 250–263.

Appel, René, and Peter Muysken. 1987. *Language Contact and Bilingualism*. London: Edward Arnold.

Bloomfield, Leonard. 1933. *Language*. New York: Holt.

Cook, Vivian. 1991. "The poverty-of-the-stimulus argument and multi-competence." *Second Language Research*, 7: 103–117.

de Bot, Kees. 2019. "Defining and assessing multilingualism." In *The Handbook of the Neuroscience of Multilingualism*, edited by John W. Schweiter, 3–18. Hoboken, NJ: John Wiley.

de Bruin, Angela. 2019. "Not all bilinguals are the same: A call for more detailed assessments and descriptions of bilingual experiences." *Behavioral Sciences*, 9 (3): 33. DOI: 10.3390/bs9030033.

De Houwer, Annick. 2019. "Language choice in bilingual interaction." In *The Cambridge Handbook of Bilingualism*, edited by De Houwer Annick and Lourdes Ortega, 324–348. Cambridge, UK: Cambridge University Press.

Dewaele, Jean-Marc, Alex Housen, and Li Wei. 2003. *Bilingualism: Beyond Basic Principles*. Clevedon, UK: Multilingual Matters.

Grosjean, François. 1982. *Life with Two Languages: An Introduction to Bilingualism*. Cambridge, MA: Harvard University Press.

Grosjean, François. 1985. "The bilingual as a competent but specific speaker-hearer." *Journal of Multilingual and Multicultural Development*, 6: 467–477.

Grosjean, François. 1989. "Neurolinguists, beware! The bilingual is not two monolinguals in one person." *Brain and Language*, 36: 3–15.

Grosjean, François. 1997. "The bilingual individual." *Interpreting*, 2 (1/2): 163–187.

Grosjean, François. 2001. "The bilingual's language modes." In *One Mind, Two Languages: Bilingual Language Processing*, edited by Janet Nicol, 1–22. Oxford: Blackwell.

Grosjean, François. 2010. *Bilingual: Life and Reality*. Cambridge, MA: Harvard University Press.

Grosjean, François. 2013. "Bilingualism: A short introduction." In *The Psycholinguistics of Bilingualism*, edited by François Grosjean and Ping Li, 5–25. Malden, MA and Oxford: Wiley-Blackwell.

Grosjean, François. 2015. "Bicultural bilinguals." *International Journal of Bilingualism*, 19 (5): 572–586.

Grosjean, François. 2016. "The Complementarity Principle and its impact on processing, acquisition, and dominance." In *Language Dominance in Bilinguals: Issues of Measurement and Operationalization*, edited by Carmen Silva-Corvalán and Jeanine Treffers-Daller, 66–84. Cambridge: Cambridge University Press.

Hakuta, Kenji. 1992. "Bilingualism." In *International Encyclopedia of Linguistics*, edited by William Bright, 175–178. Oxford: Oxford University Press.

Haugen, Einar. 1969. *The Norwegian Language in America: A Study in Bilingual Behavior*. Bloomington, IN: Indiana University Press.

Li, Ping, Fan Zhang, Anya Yu, and Xiaowei Zhao. 2020. "Language History Questionnaire (LHQ3): An enhanced tool for assessing multilingual experience." *Bilingualism: Language and Cognition*, 23 (5): 938–944. DOI: 10.1017/S1366728918001153.

Luk, Gigi, and Ellen Bialystok. 2013. "Bilingualism is not a categorical variable: Interaction between language proficiency and usage." *Journal of Cognitive Psychology*, 25 (5): 605–621.

Luna, David, Torsten Ringberg, and Laura A. Peracchio. 2008. "One individual, two identities: Frame switching among biculturals." *Journal of Consumer Research*, 35 (2): 279–293.

Mackey, William. 1962. "The description of bilingualism." *Canadian Journal of Linguistics*, 7: 51–85.

Marian, Viorica, Henrike K. Blumenfeld, and Margarita Kaushanskaya. 2007. "The language experience and proficiency questionnaire (LEAP-Q): Assessing language profiles in bilinguals and multilinguals." *Journal of Speech, Language, and Hearing Research*, 50 (4): 940–967.

Rodriguez-Fornells, Antoni, Ulrike M. Kramer, Urbano Lorenzo-Seva, Julia Festman, and Thomas F. Münte. 2012. "Self-assessment of individual differences in language switching." *Frontiers in Psychology*, 2: 388. DOI: org/10.3389/fpsyg.2011.00388.

Romaine, Suzanne. 2013. "The bilingual and multilingual community." In *The Handbook of Bilingualism and Multilingualism*, edited by Tej K. Bhatia and William C. Ritchie, 445–465. Oxford: Blackwell.

Sia, Jennifer, and Jean-Marc Dewaele. 2006. "Are you bilingual?" *Birkbeck Studies in Applied Linguistics (BISAL)*, 1: 1–19.

Silva-Corvalán, Carmen, and Jeanine Treffers-Daller. 2016. Language Dominance in Bilinguals: *Issues of Measurement and Operationalization*. Cambridge: Cambridge University Press.

Thiery, Christopher. 1978. "True bilingualism and second-language learning." In *Language Interpretation and Communication*, edited by David Gerver and H. Wallace Sinaiko, 145–153. New York: Plenum.

Wei, Li. 2007. "Dimensions of bilingualism." In *The Bilingualism Reader*, edited by Li Wei, 3–22. London and New York: Routledge.

Weinreich, Uriel. 1953. *Languages in Contact: Findings and Problems*. New York: Publications of the Linguistic Circle of New York 1.

Zubrzycki, Kamil. 2019. "Am I perfect enough to be a true bilingual? Monolingual bias in the lay perception and self-perception of bi- and multilinguals." *International Review of Applied Linguistics (IRAL)*, 57 (4): 447–495.

2

How Many Bilinguals Are There?

Bilingualism is widespread and can be found in practically every country of the world, in all classes of society, and in all age groups. It has been estimated that probably more than half of the world's population is bilingual; that is, it uses two or more languages (or dialects) in everyday life. But this is just an estimation and, unfortunately, we are still a long way away from knowing exactly how many people are indeed bilingual. Are things easier if we try to assess the number of bilinguals country by country? Not really as there are huge gaps in what we know. And when some data does exist, it is far from satisfactory.

In the first part of this chapter, we discuss why it is that bilingualism is so widespread and why, wherever one goes in the world, one meets people who know and use two or more languages (or dialects) in their everyday lives.

The second part discusses why it is so difficult to obtain exact figures on the extent of bilingualism. Some national censuses simply do not have language questions. Others have a few but for very specific reasons which do not have to do with bilingualism. Countries that have appropriate questions do exist but they often focus on specific types of bilinguals and not on all bilinguals.

In the third part, we choose a few of countries and report on the state of bilingualism of their inhabitants. Their national censuses, or large language surveys, give us sufficient data from which estimates of bilingualism based either on language use, language knowledge, or both, can be worked out. These include the United States, Canada, and a number of countries in Europe.

Finally, in the last part, we move up to the level of the world and track down how a percentage of the bi- and multilinguals in the world was estimated by two recognized experts, and the many problems that were encountered when doing so.

The Extent of Bilingualism

It has long been recognized that bilingualism is extremely widespread and that it can be found in practically every country of the world, in all classes of society, and in all age groups. There are many reasons for this. A very straightforward one is that there are some 7,117 languages in the world according to *Ethnologue: Languages of the World* and they are housed in 195 countries (Eberhard, Simons, and Fennig 2020). Even if not all

The Mysteries of Bilingualism, First Edition. François Grosjean.

countries have 36 or so languages (an average based on these numbers), it does mean that countries house many languages and there will be language contact within them. In addition, some countries have many more languages such as 719 in Indonesia,[1] 461 in India,[2] 390 in Australia[3] and so on. Contact between language groups means learning and using other languages or, at the very least, acquiring a common language of communication and hence often becoming bi- or multilingual.

In addition, some countries have a language policy that recognizes and fosters several languages such as India, Canada, Belgium and Switzerland among others. Children in these countries often learn their group's language and one or two others. Many countries have only one national language and members of other linguistic groups are expected to become bilingual in their own language and the national language (for example, the Kabyles in Algeria, the Kurds in Turkey, the Finns in Sweden, and so on).

Trade and business are a major cause of language contact and hence bilingualism. For example, Greek was the language of buyers and sellers in the Mediterranean during the third, fourth and fifth centuries BCE and, of course, English has become a major language of trade and business today. It is well known that some business people in countries such as The Netherlands, Sweden, Switzerland and Singapore, among many others, will speak English all day at work and return home to speak their native language.

Another important cause of bilingualism is the movement of peoples. The reasons are many – political, religious, social, economic, educational – and go back to the beginning to time. People have always moved to other regions or countries in search of work and better living conditions. For example, in the United States, Batalova and Alperi (2018) report that the foreign-born share of the population is at its highest level since 1910, with approximately 44 million immigrants representing 13.5% of the overall population. In the United Kingdom, in 2018, people born outside country made up a similar percentage (14%),[4] and in Switzerland, in 2019, as many as 25% of the population was made up of foreigners.[5] All this leads to substantial bilingualism.

People also travel, within a country or between countries, to be schooled or to go to college in a different language. The United States, Russia, the United Kingdom and many others welcome foreign students for their studies who often stay for several years. Even shorter stays are enough to anchor a new language. The world's most successful mobility program is the European Erasmus program. Since it began in 1987–1988, it has provided over three million European students with the opportunity to go abroad and study at higher education institutions or train in a company.[6]

There are many other reasons for the extent of bilingualism one of which is intermarriage. This often results in households being bilingual where at least one spouse has learned the language of the other and uses it at home, and where children often learn different languages. Another reason is simply that many professions require people to

---

[1] https://www.ethnologue.com/country/17-93.

[2] https://www.ethnologue.com/country/17-92.

[3] https://www.ethnologue.com/country/17-10.

[4] Migrants in the UK: An overview. 4 October 2019. The Migration Observatory. https://migrationobservatory.ox.ac.uk/resources/briefings/migrants-in-the-uk-an-overview.

[5] SWI Swissinfo.ch. Immigration to Switzerland continues to rise. Feb 15, 2019. https://www.swissinfo.ch/eng/foreigners-_immigration-to-switzerland-continues-to-rise/44758558.

[6] Erasmus: Facts, figures and trends https://ec.europa.eu/assets/eac/education/library/statistics/erasmus-plus-facts-figures_en.pdf.

know and use two or more languages: language teaching, interpretation and translation, the hospitality, travel and leisure industries, diplomacy, media, research, and so on.

In sum, bi- and multilingualism is extensive, and wherever one goes in the world, one meets people who know and use two or more languages or dialects. Is this reflected in the national statistics of countries that house these people?

On the Difficulties of Counting People Who Are Bilingual

One could expect, perhaps naively, that countries would be interested in those who know and use several languages, and would make available statistics that reflect the bi- or multilingualism of their population. As we will see below, this is far from the case. In fact, finding out how many bilinguals there are in countries such as Canada, the United Kingdom, France, Switzerland and the United States, among many others, is a very real challenge.

Some nations simply do not have language questions in their censuses. Belgium and France are two examples of this. In Belgium, the last census that contained such questions was in 1947. Up to that date, the results had been used to either attend to inhabitants in their own language (if 30% of the population declared speaking a language other than the official language in the area in question) or to change the official language of the municipalities (if 50% of the population declared speaking it). But under the pressure of certain groups who did not want to accept language shifts in areas around Brussels, language censuses were abolished in Belgium in 1961. No official information about language knowledge and use has been obtained since then via the census. It is only by going to other information sources, such as European surveys of languages, that one can get an idea of the level of bilingualism in Belgium, as we will see in the next part.

France does not have language questions in their census either. The word "langue" (language) does not appear in the 2020 census form, nor in the preceding ones. When I wrote in 2013 to the French National Institute of Statistics and Economic Studies (INSEE) which is in charge of the census, the curt reply I received was that the information I requested did not fall within what it offers. This is due to the fact that, officially, the French Republic wants to give equal treatment to everyone by interacting directly with the individual, without going through minorities, communities, or groups, be they religious, regional, linguistic, etc. A less official reason is that it also prefers not to put too strong a light on the fact that France contains many minority languages, including immigrant languages, spoken by literally millions of people. This said, regional languages were finally recognized as belonging to the French national heritage in an amendment to the French Constitution in 2008, and various language surveys do exist, some sponsored or cosponsored by the state. It will be one of these surveys that we will refer to in the next part.

There are many other countries that do not have questions on languages in their censuses, and even less on bilingualism. Thus, Christopher (2011) states that in the Commonwealth, only 37 of the 71 census authorities included language questions in recent censuses, leaving many without such questions.

Other national censuses do have language questions but for very specific reasons which do not really have to do with bilingualism. The examples we will mention here are those of England and the United States. In England, before 2011, no question about language had been asked in its censuses, unlike in Wales, Scotland and Northern Ireland where one question had been asked. The Office of National Statistics finally decided to ask two questions in 2011 for a number of reasons, according to Sebba (2017). Among these we find: enabling the government bodies to meet their duties under legislation governing race relations and disability discrimination; allowing local and central government to allocate resources for teaching English as a second language, and for translation services within public services; and supporting regional or minority languages like Cornish and British Sign Language.

Question 18 of the 2011 Census was, "What is your main language?" and Question 19 (asked only of those who had indicated a language other than English to the previous question), "How well can you speak English?" The four possible answers for the latter were: "Very well," "Well," "Not well" and "Not at all." The results obtained only allow us to get an idea of the degree of bilingualism, based on language knowledge and not language use, for a very small proportion of the population for whom English is not their main language, a mere 7.7%. As Sebba (2017) writes, bilingualism is statistically visible only for those who have a "main language" other than English. We know nothing about the bilingualism status of 92.3% of the population! Once again, only European surveys can help us get at the state of bilingualism in England and, more generally, in the United Kingdom, as we will see below.

Another country that has language questions, but with very specific reasons, is the United States. The three questions that were developed in 1980, and that have been used since 2000 in the yearly American Community Survey (ACS), came about in an effort to respond to the necessity to know more about those with limited English language proficiency (Siegel, Martin, and Bruno 2001). So as to implement the Civil Rights Act, The Bilingual Education Act, and the Voting Rights Act, there was a need to accommodate people who had difficulties communicating in English. The questions are: "Does this person speak a language other than English at home?," "What is this language?," "How well does this person speak English? Very well, Well, Not well, and Not at all." There are definite limits to how far this assessment goes. Thus, children under five are not covered, people who use a second or third language in their everyday lives, but only English at home, are not counted, English proficiency is self assessed and may be influenced by a person's original culture, and so on. However, as we will see in the next part, the results to these questions do allow us to get a far better picture of the status of bilingualism in the United States than in England.

Finally, there are those countries that have the appropriate language questions in their censuses to work out the proportion of bilinguals but that put the emphasis on specific classes of bilinguals. Here we will consider Canada and Switzerland. The questions and answers of the census that Canada conducts every five years are a dream for anyone interested in languages and bi-/multilingualism in a country. The 2016 version contains five language questions, the last two in the long form of the questionnaire only:

- 7. Can this person speak English or French well enough to conduct a conversation?
- 8a. What language does this person speak most often at home, and 8b. Does this person speak any other languages on a regular basis at home?
- 9. What is the language that this person first learned at home in childhood and still understands?
- 16. What language(s), other than English or French, can this person speak well enough to conduct a conversation?
- 45a. In this job, what language did this person use most often? and 45b. Did this person use any other languages on a regular basis in this job?

A quick glance at these questions, and at past censuses, shows that the census agency is primarily interested in the country's two official languages, English and French. Statistics Canada states this clearly in its documentation as well as on its many web pages dedicated to the results. Thus there is a page, "Statistics on official languages in Canada,"[7] where the two languages are lauded with statements such as, "French and English are the languages of inclusion," and "Official languages and bilingualism are at the heart of Canadian identity." This said, non-official languages (immigrant languages and aboriginal languages) are increasingly being analyzed and reported.

With the tables made available by Statistics Canada, and with a bit of help from agency statisticians, one can get a good overview of bilingualism in Canada based on language knowledge (see Questions 7 and 16 above) and on language use (Questions 8a and 8b, as well as Questions 45a and 45b). The one result that is not easily available is the proportion of the population that uses two or more languages in daily life whatever the activity (work, home, social activities, etc.) and without counting a person twice.

Switzerland also has a national census that asks the right sort of questions, although fewer than Canada, and that allows one to get at the proportion of bilinguals in the country if done correctly. But here problems occur with how Swiss Statistics define bilingualism. I will concentrate on the first language question as it is the data obtained with this question that was used by the agency in 2012 to estimate the number of bi- or multilinguals in the country.[8] Here is a translation of the question: "What is your main language, i.e. the language in which you think and that you know the best? If you think in several languages and know them very well, then name these languages." This was followed by a number of language categories which often grouped together a national language and a dialect such as "German or Swiss German."

As I stated in an article at the time (Grosjean 2012), the people who thought of the question clearly had a very restrictive view of bilingualism. It was assumed that people have one main language and that if they have another main language, then they must know it very well. In addition, it was stipulated that one must think in each of one's languages to be able to list them. The fact that thinking can take place independently of language and can be visual-spatial, or involve non-linguistic concepts, was not taken into account. Also, speakers of both Swiss German and German, among others, were given just one language category to check and hence could not list their two languages. And yet, the majority of Swiss Germans (close to two-thirds of Swiss people) use both Swiss German and German in their everyday lives and are de facto bilingual.

The outcome was that Swiss Statistics stated that a mere 15.8% of the Swiss population was bi- or multilingual. This was less than the percentages found in largely monolingual countries such as the United States and France (around 20% of bilinguals at the time). And yet, any visitor to Switzerland will have noticed how extensive bi- and multilingualism is in the country with people often using two or more languages in their everyday lives, and knowing at least one other learned in school. In the next part, we will see how the other questions in the Swiss Census allowed us to estimate a truer percentage of bilinguals.

In sum, finding out how many bilinguals there are in a country is particularly difficult. Some countries do not have language questions, others do but they are few in

---

[7] https://www.canada.ca/en/canadian-heritage/services/official-languages-bilingualism/publications/statistics.html.

[8] Swiss Statistics Press Release of June 19, 2012. No. 0351-1206-30.

number and the results have little to say about bilingualism, and others still have enough questions but the data is not analyzed adequately so as to get at the extent of bilingualism in the country.

The Proportion of Bilinguals in a Number of Countries

In this part, we report on the state of bilingualism of the inhabitants of a number of countries. National censuses, or large language surveys, offer data from which estimates of bilingualism can be worked out based either on language use, or language knowledge (potential bilinguals are also included here), or both.

The United States

I have always been fascinated by the state of bilingualism in the United States maybe because I lived there for many years and one of its eminent scholars, Einar Haugen, himself a Norwegian-English bilingual, became a close colleague and friend. As stated above, the US Census Bureau does not keep track of bilingualism as such, but ever since 1980, and annually since 2000 with the American Community Survey (ACS), three language questions are asked (see the preceding part), and they allow us to work out, to a large extent, who is bilingual and where bilinguals are situated.

The 2018 ACS found that 67.3 million inhabitants (native-born, legal immigrants, and illegal immigrants) spoke a language other than English at home (Zeigler and Camarota 2019). Among those people, some 63 million also knew and used English and hence were bilingual. This represents 20.55% of the population. If we add to this number bilingual children under 5 (not covered by the survey) as well as people who use a second or third language in their everyday lives but only English at home, then probably close to 23% of the population can be considered bilingual.

The percentage of bilinguals is definitely on the rise. Researcher Jeffrey Bloem at the University of Minnesota helped me extract the appropriate numbers from the census and ACS databases. For each year, we tabulated those who spoke a language other than English, as well as English to varying degrees, and we worked out a percentage based on the total population. The results are plotted in Figure 2.1.

As can be seen in the graph (dark grey function), there is a steady increase of the percentage of bilinguals between 1980 and 2018. Back in 1980, the percentage of bilinguals was 10.68% whereas in 2018, the last ACS survey for which we have data, it was 20.55%. Thus the percentage has practically doubled in 38 years. One will want to study the reasons for this constant rise since 1980. There is, of course, the arrival of new immigrants who learn English and hence become bilingual. Some maintain their languages from generation to generation and hence bilingualism continues. Other reasons may be the (re)learning of some older immigration languages, as well as of Native American languages, and of American Sign language. To these should be added the effort that is being made to allow children and adolescents to acquire and use a second language in the home, as well as more natural language learning opportunities in some schools with immersion and dual language programs.

Some might say that the increasing number of bilinguals goes hand in hand with an increase of inhabitants who know no English. The results of those who report that they do not know any English is plotted in the same graph (Figure 2.1; light grey function) and, as can be seen, the percentages remain very low throughout all these years. English

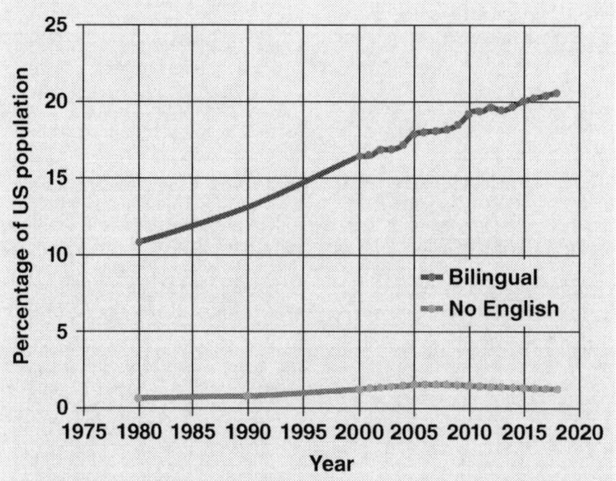

Figure 2.1 The percentage of bilinguals, and of inhabitants who know no English, since 1980 in the United States.

is so important in the United States that close to 98.7% of the population know it, and use it in everyday life, according to the ACS results. The position of prominence that English has in the US is in no danger, but some room is now being made for other languages.

Bilingualism in the US is very diverse. English-Spanish bilinguals represent 61% of all bilinguals and hence Spanish is definitely America's second language (41,460,427 speakers in 2018). Other important languages, but to a far lesser extent, are Chinese (3,471,604), Tagalog (1,760,468), Vietnamese (1,542,473), Arabic (1,259,118), French (1,232,173) and Korean (1,086,335). Bilinguals are not equally distributed across the nation. Some states contain proportionally very few (e.g., West Virginia, Mississippi, Montana, Kentucky) whereas others have a far greater proportion (e.g., California, Texas, New Mexico, New Jersey, New York, etc.). As for cities, the ones with the most bilinguals are Los Angeles, Houston, New York, Phoenix and Chicago.

Bilingualism in the United States has traditionally been transitional – a passage, over one or two generations, from monolingualism in a minority language to monolingualism in English. However, there is an increasing awareness that the country's knowledge of the languages of the world is a natural resource that should not be wasted. Hence a growing number of families are fostering bilingualism either by making sure the home's minority language and culture are kept alive or by encouraging their children to acquire and use a second language.

Canada

As we saw in the preceding part, Canada obtains data both on language knowledge and language use in its censuses. Concerning language knowledge, it is a person's ability to speak the language(s) well enough to conduct a conversation. For a child who has not yet learned to speak, this includes languages that the child is learning to speak at home.[9]

[9] This information was given to me by Joanne Hans, a consulting-analyst with Statistics Canada (September 15, 2020).

Two questions in the 2016 census get at language knowledge, and the combined results show that 39% of the population report being able to conduct a conversation in more than one language, of which 17.9% report that the languages involved are English and French. It is important to note that these percentages concern actual bilinguals but also potential bilinguals as some do not actually use two languages in their everyday life, even though they know a second language well enough to do so.

To get at actual bilingualism, that is, the regular use of two or more languages in everyday life, one has to look at the results of the languages spoken at home, on the one hand, and at work, on the other. Concerning the home,[10] 19.4% of the population report speaking more than one language at home (this is a rise from 17.5% in 2011). The languages involved can concern the two official languages, English and French, or one of these languages along with a non-official language (aboriginal language or immigrant language). People with a non-official mother tongue who use a language other than their mother tongue at home usually adopt English or French as their main language or as a secondary language. Only 28.0% of people with a mother tongue other than English or French speak only their mother tongue at home. By comparison, 94.3% of people with English as their mother tongue and 83.1% of people with French as their mother tongue speak only their mother tongue at home.

Researchers Schott, Kremin, and Byers-Heinlein (2019) examined child bilingualism in the home based on the 2016 census. They found that 15.7% of children aged 0 to 4 grow up with two or more languages at home. The percentage varies, of course, according to the region or province in question, with the highest percentage in Northern Canada (29%), and the lowest in Newfoundland and Labrador (4%). Quebec and Ontario are close to the mean with 17%.

The 2016 census also examined the state of bilingualism at work.[11] The proportion of workers who use more than one language at work was 15.4% in 2016, up from 13.9% in 2011. Were we to add the percentage of bilingualism at home and at work, we would obtain close to 35% of people who use two or more languages in their daily lives, without counting other activities though. But this percentage includes some people who are counted twice, once in the home and once at work, and so one needs to estimate a reduced combined percentage. For the 2016 census, collaborators at Statistics Canada could not help me with this, but for the 2011 census, Ms. Camille Bouchard-Colombe from the same bureau gave me an estimate of 26%. Since the level of bilingualism is higher both at home and in the work place in 2016, a fair estimate could be 28%. Thus, slightly more than a quarter of inhabitants in Canada are actual bilinguals.

It is interesting that there is a 11% difference between potential bilinguals (39%) and actual bilinguals (some 28%). This percentage, which can vary in size as we will see below, reflects the fact that some people can master two or more languages sufficiently to conduct a conversation in them but do not actually use them all on a regular basis. This is true in Canada but also in all other nations in the world.

European Countries

In 2012, a survey conducted for the European Commission interviewed some 26,751 respondents in 27 member states of the European Union. The results appeared in a

[10] https://www12.statcan.gc.ca/census-recensement/2016/as-sa/98-200-x/2016010/98-200-x2016010-eng.cfm.

[11] https://www12.statcan.gc.ca/census-recensement/2016/as-sa/98-200-x/2016031/98-200-x2016031-eng.cfm.

report that same year, *Europeans and their languages* (TNS Opinion & Social 2012). Even though not as a complete as a census with good language questions (but see above for the problems many have), it is a fine base to get a feel for the status of bi- and multilingualism in Europe. The report contains several sections and we will concentrate once again on language knowledge, and on language use, so as to be able to compare, when possible, the results with those from North America.

To the language knowledge question, "... which other languages, if any, do you speak well enough in order to be able to have a conversation?," 54% of the respondents are able to hold a conversation in at least one additional language, 25% are able to speak at least two additional languages, and 10% are conversant in at least three languages. This confirms what everyone knows: many Europeans know other languages! Of course, there is a great deal of variability with countries like Luxemburg, Latvia, The Netherlands, Malta, Slovenia and Sweden having percentages of "at least one other language" above 90%, and countries like Hungary, Italy, the United Kingdom, and Portugal having less than 40%. English dominates as the most common language that Europeans are most likely to be able to speak (38%), followed by French (12%), German (11%), Spanish (7%) and Russian (5%).

Four years after the 2012 survey, Eurostat published *Foreign language skills statistics*[12] in which levels of second language skills were examined. The results were equally varied for those who know their best-known foreign language at a proficient level (this means understanding a wide range of demanding texts, using a language flexibly, and mastering the language almost completely). Thus, more than half of respondents in Luxemburg, Sweden and Malta reached this proficiency level, whereas less than a quarter of the British, French, Polish, Romanians, Czechs and Italians did so.

With regard to language use, *Europeans and their languages* gives some interesting results. As we saw above, 54% of Europeans mentioned one other language when asked the question about the additional languages they speak well enough in order to be able to have a conversation. But when asked, "How often to do you use your first additional language?," the mean percentage dropped down to 24% for everyday or almost everyday use. Thus, one in four Europeans are bilingual. Of course, once again there is a lot of variation, with percentages as high as 67% for Luxemburg, 49% for Malta, 44% for Latvia, 41% for Denmark, and so on, and as low as 7% for Portugal, 9% for Italy (but keep in mind that many Italians are bilingual in a regional dialect and Italian), and 11% for Poland. Two of the countries we discussed in the first part of this chapter, Belgium and the United Kingdom, have 29% and 28% respectively.

France and Switzerland are worth discussing separately. For France, the percentage given for daily or almost daily use is 19%, a figure that is very close to that of a large survey, "Etude de l'histoire familiale," conducted in France itself in 1999 by the French Institute for Demographic Studies (INED). Three language questions were asked, and the third one gets at what we are interested in: "... do you find yourself talking with people close to you (partner, parents, friends, colleagues, store keepers...) in a language other than French? If so, which is it/are they?." The first thing to note was that some 400 different languages were mentioned, a number that clearly shows that France is multilingual even though officially it is monolingual. There are regional languages, but most with far fewer speakers than before, and many immigrant languages such as Arabic, Berber, Turkish, Portuguese, Spanish, Chinese, and so on. And to the question asked,

[12] https://ec.europa.eu/eurostat/statistics-explained/index.php/Foreign_language_skills_statistics.

21% of the respondents stated that they speak a language other than French in their everyday life. We should note that many more inhabitants in France's overseas territories use two languages regularly: 57% in Mayotte, 41% in New Caledonia, 38%, on Reunion Island, and so on.

As for Switzerland, we saw above that in 2012, Swiss Statistics had stated that the 2010 census had shown that a mere 15.8% of the Swiss population was bi- or multilingual. This was because Swiss German and German had been collapsed into one language category, and the criterium for writing down two languages in the "What is your main language?" question was extremely restrictive. In the article I wrote for *Le Temps* criticizing this approach (Grosjean 2012), I suggested that Swiss Statistics look at the data obtained for the second and third questions: "Which language(s) do you speak normally at home/with family members?" and "Which language(s) do you speak normally at work/at school?." The reaction I received was at first quite chilly (it isn't done to criticize your census bureau!) but a few months later one of the collaborators there sent me the results obtained for these questions. The percentage was now 41.9%! To this percentage, one can add a few percentage points to take into account those who use a language that does not appear in the set list of 11 languages (they were put into the monolingual category!) as well as those not counted such as international diplomats and their families. Thus, close to half of the inhabitants of Switzerland use at least two languages in their everyday life.

Other fascinating results accompanied this new finding. First, the majority of these respondents were bilingual (26.1%), others were trilingual (10.4%) and still others quadrilingual (3.7%). As for the languages concerned, the greater number of bilinguals were Swiss German/German speakers, as expected, and the greater number of trilinguals concerned speakers of these two languages along with English. These new results were published in Grosjean (2013).

Estimating the Percentage of Bilinguals in the World

To end this chapter, it is worth moving up to the level of the world and trying to find out what could be the global percentage of people who are bi- or multilingual. I am reproducing below the post I wrote for my *Psychology Today* "Life as a bilingual" blog (Grosjean 2014).

When asked how many bilinguals there are in the world, I usually state that there are no precise figures but that probably half or slightly more than half of the world's population is bilingual, that is uses two or more languages (or dialects) in everyday life.[13] When asked to be more precise, I usually stay around the 50% mark. I immediately add that we are still a long way away from knowing exactly how many people are indeed bilingual. Rare are the national censuses that have a question pertaining to bi- or multilingualism, and when they do, the meaning they give to this notion can be very restrictive. In addition, those countries that only ask about languages, not bilingualism, can reflect a certain partiality concerning what it means to know a language, and then there are those countries that do not even ask language questions in their censuses.[14]

[13] Dr. Krista Byers-Heinlein has reminded me that we exchanged emails on this topic several years before writing this chapter and that, at that time, I had mentioned that my estimate had been influenced by Professor William Mackey of Laval University. He had written in his *Bilingualism as a World problem* (1967, 11) that bilingualism affects the majority of the world's population.

[14] These various points were discussed in the preceding parts.

One day, as I was watching Dr. Kim Potowski, Associate Professor of Hispanic linguistics at the University of Illinois at Chicago, give her TEDx talk, "No child left monolingual" (Potowski 2013), I heard her say, "Now the fact is that 65% of the world today is bilingual or multilingual…." I was intrigued by this sudden jump in numbers and so I wrote to Dr. Potowski to ask her what the source was for her figure. She kindly replied that she had found it in a book published in 2002 which I immediately consulted, but I had no success finding the figure. I left it at that although her number seemed really high to me.

More than a year later, it was a pleasant surprise to hear from Dr. Potowski again who told me that she had finally found the source. The figure had been given by Colin Baker and his colleague, Sylvia Prys Jones, both of Bangor University in Wales, in the Preface to their monumental *The Encyclopedia of Bilingualism and Bilingual Education* (1998). In it, they state, "… around two-thirds of the world's population are bilingual."

So the next stage in my quest was to write to Colin Baker to ask him where they had obtained that figure, or how they had worked it out. Over several exchanges of emails, he explained to me how they had guesstimated the figure. They put together a rough spreadsheet with estimates of each country's bilingual population. They used *Ethnologue*, THE source about languages in the world today, to which they added several other sources. At the time, the language sources were incomplete (e.g., on the bilingual language minorities in China and in other large countries) or, quite simply, the data was inaccurate.

Colin Baker continued, "My memory is that we estimated that the 'true' value was probably between 50% and 70% if we were rather generous in our definition of a 'bilingual'. Under 50% seemed too small and above 70% rather unlikely. While 60% would have been a midpoint, it would have been spurious and dishonest to suggest we could be that accurate. Hence 'two thirds' became a less spurious way of giving our generous guess."

I asked Colin Baker if they had taken the mean of percentages worked out for each country, in essence giving each country the same weight even if the populations are of different sizes, or if they had taken the total estimated number of bilinguals, across all countries, divided by the world's population at the time. He replied that they had used the latter approach but that they had to exclude some countries from the total for sheer lack of data.

Colin Baker added an important remark to this. They had included those learning a second language, particularly English, which adds literally millions of people to the numerator. Based on this, and on the fact that at the time the numerical bilingual data was so poor, he now thinks that it would have been wiser to give upper and lower boundaries for the guesstimate, that is, between 50% and 70%, "… as this would have better expressed what is not definable, measurable or likely to be agreed upon."

So where do we stand on this question today? Colin Baker summarized his answers to my emails with, "I suppose the real answer is: we do not know …." In addition, because his figure included language learners, it overestimated active bilinguals by including potential bilinguals. Given all of this, I think that I will continue to state that probably more than half of the world's population is bilingual, and hope that one day we will be able to have a more precise figure.

But will that hope ever materialize? Let's give Colin Baker the last word and imagine a British gleam in his eyes as he says it: "And to add to the fun – perhaps the question about the percentage of the world's population who are more than bilingual (multilingual) could be posed. I'd not even offer a guess on that one!"

References

Baker, Colin, and Sylvia Prys Jones. 1998. *Encyclopedia of Bilingualism and Bilingual Education*. Clevedon, UK: Multilingual Matters.

Batalova, Jeanne, and Elijah Alperi. 2018. "Immigrants in the U.S. states with the fastest-growing foreign-born populations." Migration Policy Institute. https://www.migrationpolicy.org.

Christopher, Anthony J. 2011. "Questions of languages in the Commonwealth censuses." *Population, Space and Place*, 17: 534–549.

Eberhard, David M., Gary F. Simons, and Charles D. Fennig, eds. 2020. *Ethnologue: Languages of the World*, 23rd edn. Dallas, TX: SIL International. Online version: http://www.ethnologue.com.

Grosjean, François. 2012. "Langues: la statistique se fourvoie." *Le Temps*, September 11. https://www.letemps.ch/opinions/langues-statistique-se-fourvoie.

Grosjean, François. 2013. "L'OFS rectifie: près de la moitié des Suisses sont bilingues." *Le Temps*, June 3. https://www.letemps.ch/opinions/lofs-rectifie-pres-moitie-suisses-bilingues.

Grosjean, François. 2014. "Chasing down those 65%." *Life as bilingual* blog. Psychology Today. https://www.psychologytoday.com/intl/blog/life-bilingual/201411/chasing-down-those-65.

Mackey, Wiliam F. 1967. *Bilingualism as a World Problem*. Montreal, Canada: Harvest House.

Potowski, Kim. 2013. "No child left monolingual." TEDx talk. https://www.youtube.com/watch?v=pSs1uCnLbaQ.

Schott, Esther, Lena V. Kremin, and Krista Byers-Heinlein. 2019. "Child bi- and multilingualism in the home in Canada: Rates and language pairs." *Poster presented at the International Symposium on Bilingualism, Edmonton, Canada*, June 23–28, 2019.

Sebba, Mark. 2017. "Awkward questions: Language issues in the 2011 census in England." *Journal of Multilingual and Multicultural Development*, 181–193. DOI: 10.1080/01434632.2017.1342651.

Siegel, Paul, Elizabeth Martin, and Rosalind Bruno. 2001. *Language Use and Linguistic Isolation: Historical Data and Methodological Issues*. Washington, DC: U.S. Census Bureau.

TNS Opinion & Social. 2012. "Europeans and their languages." Special Eurobarometer 386. European Commission. https://ec.europa.eu/commfrontoffice/publicopinion/archives/ebs/ebs_386_en.pdf.

Zeigler, Karen, and Steven A. Camarota. 2019. "67.3 million in the United States spoke a foreign language at home in 2018." Center for Immigration Studies, October 2019.

3

Bilingual Infants' Journey to Language Separation

One of the most intriguing phenomena in bilingualism is how infants who acquire two or more languages simultaneously manage to separate their languages. These future little bilinguals, who represent less than 20% of all bilingual children, have to differentiate the spoken input they perceive into distinct languages. How do they do it, we keep asking ourselves.

Bilingual infants are raised in a bilingual environment from birth and hence hear, and later produce, two or more languages regularly. The linguistic challenge they meet is considerable. As Byers-Heinlein (2020) writes, they have to detect and track two language systems, learn two sets of sounds, words, and grammatical structures, process speech in language-specific ways, and separate their languages – all this while hearing them one at a time (when only one language is spoken to them) or together (when they hear mixed speech).

At first sight, the task seems daunting, especially as they receive less exposure to each language than do monolingual infants, who only hear one language; and sometimes the exposure is not balanced – one language is used more in their life than the other. In addition, some of their caretakers may have an accent in one of their languages and/or use mixed language.

There are three parts to this chapter. In the first, the longest, we will describe a number of important studies done over the last 20 years or so, all of which have increased our understanding of how bilingual infants start to separate their languages perceptually. We will show how these infants are sensitive to phonetic, prosodic, phonotactic, visual, and statistical regularity information. Their perceptual sensitivities help them discriminate their two languages and start the process of building the structural knowledge of each.

In the second part, we will examine how these infants are helped by taking into account pragmatic aspects of communication such as specific contexts and situations, particular people, and so on. This will be very useful in the ongoing process of language differentiation. In these two parts, the studies will be organized based on the age of the infants tested – from newborns to toddlers – and we will use the terminology and concepts presented in each. There will be, therefore, some diversity in the theoretical underpinnings, but we will make sure that the main findings of each study is clear.

Finally, in the third part, we will step back from these studies and offer a brief overview of how language separation may take place based on the writings of Krista Byers-Heinlein.

The Mysteries of Bilingualism, First Edition. François Grosjean.

The question of how and when young bilinguals achieve language separation is one of the oldest and thorniest questions in the field, writes Byers-Heinlein (2020), and she addresses it with her Gradual Language Separation Hypothesis.

Perception Studies

In this part, we will describe a number of studies that help us understand how bilingual infants start to separate their languages perceptually. When we delve into the literature,[1] we discover innovative studies using complex methodology, as well as astute experimental procedures – both behavioral and with brain imaging. This is because, as Byers-Heinlein (2018) reports, "... newborns cannot do much – they cannot answer an experimenter's questions, press a button, or even move their heads very well." In addition, testing them is demanding. Sessions are often stopped because of excessive fussiness, failure to do what is required (e.g., look at a screen), falling asleep, etc. not to mention equipment problems and experimenter errors.

Born with a Preference for Two Languages

It has been known for some time that newborn infants with monolingual mothers have become sensitive *in utero* to some characteristics of the spoken language they are exposed to. Thus, when tested just after birth, they show a preference for their mother's voice as well as their mother's native language over another language that is rhythmically different. But what about infants who have bilingual mothers? Do they show a preference for their mothers' TWO languages? Byers-Heinlein, Burns, and Werker (2010) were the first to study language preference in bilingual neonates.

They took newborn infants (0 to 5 days old) and presented them with speech, alternating each minute between English and Tagalog, a language spoken as a native language or a second language by nearly all Filipinos, and which is rhythmically quite different from English. Half the infants had mothers with a monolingual English background (they had only spoken English during pregnancy) and half with a bilingual, Tagalog-English, background. The researchers employed a testing technique – called high-amplitude sucking – that makes use of newborns' sucking reflex. The babies were given a rubber nipple to suck on and the researchers recorded how often they did so. The greater the frequency of sucking, the more interested the infants were. The question asked was the following: Would both groups of infants produce a greater frequency of high-amplitude sucking when listening to English and to Tagalog sentences, or would it only be those infants with bilingual mothers?

What they found was that infants with monolingual mothers marked a clear preference for English over Tagalog – their sucking rate was greater for the former. The infants with bilingual mothers, on the other hand, were interested in both languages – they did not favor one over the other. They sucked similarly during English and Tagalog minutes, suggesting that they recognized both of their mother's native languages. They had been in contact with them prenatally and hence they responded positively to both. The results of this study demonstrated that prenatal bilingual exposure affects infants' preferences.

---

[1] I wish to thank Professor Krista Byers-Heinlein, of Concordia University, and Professor Janet Werker, of the University of British Columbia, who have guided me in the literature, and have answered my numerous questions. I am most grateful to them.

Other newborn infants, this time with mothers who spoke both Chinese and English, were tested by the researchers on the same stimuli. As compared to the previous two groups, they showed an intermediary pattern. They were less interested in Tagalog than were the infants with bilingual mothers, but they were more interested in it than were the infants with English monolingual mothers. Based on the fact that Tagalog shares some characteristics with Chinese but also differs on some others, the researchers took this to mean that the newborns with mothers bilingual in Tagalog and English had indeed been sensitive *in utero* to characteristics of the two languages.

The other follow-up study the researchers undertook was to check that the Tagalog-English newborns had not regrouped their two languages into one broad category of familiar language sounds. They wanted to ascertain that the bilingual newborns could tell the difference between their two languages, even though they didn't have a preference for one over the other. Hence, they ran a discrimination study of English and Tagalog. They used a sucking habituation procedure in which the infants were habituated to sentences from one of the languages, either English or Tagalog. Habituation was observed when, having heard a language for a period of time, the infants started to slow down their sucking rate (basically, the language wasn't interesting them anymore). When a preset point was reached, the other language was played to them and the researchers observed whether the infant's interest was revived, as shown by a sudden increase in sucking.

What they found was that newborns who heard the language switch increased their sucking, suggesting that they noticed the switch and had therefore discriminated the languages. Thus the infants with bilingual mothers did react to the other language; they had not "lumped" the two into one broad language category.

According to Byers-Heinlein (2018), this research provided two important insights. First, both monolingual and bilingual infants are born ready to pay special attention to their native language(s). And second, at birth, bilingual newborns are able to discriminate their two native languages based on the different rhythm of each language. Curtin, Byers-Heinlein, and Werker (2011) concluded that perceptual biases and learning work together to lay the foundation of either monolingual or bilingual acquisition, depending on the input encountered.

Visual Language Information

The auditory signal is not the only source of information available to bilingual infants. Some of the differences that distinguish one language from another are present on talking faces by means of mouth and facial movements. Weikum et al. (2007) wanted to find out if young bilingual infants – 6 and 8 months old – could discriminate their two languages visually, in this case French and English. Once again, an habituation procedure was used. During the habituation phase, infants sat on their caretaker's lap and were shown video clips of women producing sentences in one of the languages until they habituated. And during the test phase, the language was switched for half the infants and kept the same for the other half. The bilingual infants looked significantly longer at the language switch trials compared to the same trials, showing discrimination, and this at both 6 and 8 months. Monolingual infants could discriminate the languages at 6 months but no longer at 8 months. Thus, bilingual infants maintain their perceptual sensitivity to language differences – something they need in order to separate and learn their two languages – whereas monolingual infants lose it by the age of 8 months since they no longer need it.

But what is it that bilingual infants look at on someone's face? Lewkowicz and Hansen-Tift (2012) first tracked what happened to the eye gaze of monolingual infants of various ages while they watched and listened to a person reciting a prepared monologue in English. They monitored where they looked by using an eye tracker. They were interested in two main areas on the face: one around the eyes and one around the mouth. At four months old, infants looked longer at the eyes, but then a shift took place so that by eight months old they looked longer at the mouth. Then, during the next few months, a second shift occurred so that infants who were 12 months old looked for an equal amount of time at both mouth and eyes. The researchers explained the first shift towards the mouth by the fact that as they are learning to process speech, infants are attracted by the auditory AND visual speech signals that are produced by the speaker and that are perceptually salient and redundant. As for the second shift, back to the eyes, the infants' emerging speech output reduces their need to have direct access to both visual and auditory speech cues, and they can now concentrate on various social cues available in the speaker's eyes.

What about bilingual infants who are brought up with two languages? Pons, Bosch, and Lewkowicz (2015) hypothesized that because bilingual infants need to process two languages, and keep them apart, they may well use audiovisual speech cues more than monolingual infants. After having confirmed the earlier American study with monolingual infants being brought up in Catalan or Spanish, they tested bilingual infants who were being brought up with a native (dominant) language – it could be either Spanish or Catalan – and who were also exposed to another language for at least 25% of the time. For the Spanish native language group, the other language was Catalan, and for the Catalan native language group, the other language was Spanish. Of course, these bilingual infants watched two videos, one in each of their languages.

In both their languages, the four-month-old bilingual infants looked equally at the eyes and the mouth (recall that the monolingual infants of that age group looked more at the eyes), the eight-month-olds looked longer at the mouth (as did the monolinguals), and the 12-month-olds again looked longer at the mouth (whereas the monolinguals looked equally at the mouth and the eyes). How is this explained? The greater perceptual salience of audiovisual speech cues help bilingual infants identify distinct language-specific features that keep the languages apart. Four-month-old infants become aware of this, hence their earlier attentional shift to the mouth, even though they also look at the eyes a lot. Attention to the talker's mouth increases from then on and continues throughout their first year since redundant audiovisual speech cues are of primary importance for these children. In a word, they exploit the perceptual information of these cues earlier and for a longer period of time than do monolingual infants.[2]

Prosodic Information

Prosody is concerned with variables such as intonation, duration, speaking rate, stress and tone, loudness and rhythm. Gervain and Werker (2013) wished to see if bilingual infants exploit prosodic cues in conjunction with word frequency to discriminate the typical word order of two languages. They created long speech streams with alternating frequent and infrequent words concatenated without pauses. For example:

fira**ge**ro**fi**du**ge**ka**fi**to**ge**riy

[2] For a more recent study on the same topic with different results, see Morin-Lessard et al. (2019).

where **fi** and **ge** are frequent words (you can see them being repeated in the string above), whereas ra, ro, ka, du, to, etc. are infrequent. Frequent words were nine times more frequent than infrequent words. They then constructed two familiarization streams based on the prosodic patterns of Object-Verb (OV) languages such as Japanese and Basque, and on Verb-Object (VO) languages such as English and Italian. The first, the OV prosody condition, had a high pitch on the prominent infrequent words and low pitch on the non-prominent frequent words. In the other condition, VO, the prominent infrequent words were long and the non-prominent frequent words were short.

Bilingual infants with a mean age of 7.5 months, who were learning both a VO and an OV language, were seated on a parent's lap in a sound-attenuated room. During the familiarization phase, each speech stream was played symmetrically from both sides of the room and the lights blinked contingently on the infant's looking behavior, but independently of the sound. One group of infants heard the VO prosody condition and the other group the OV condition. Then the test phase began. The infants heard eight four-syllabic chunks from each stream but with flat prosody and equal syllable durations. Four had a FI (frequent word initial) order (for example, **fi**fo**ge**bi) as in VO prosody, and the other four had an IF (frequent word final) order (for example, ka**fi**pa**ge**), as in OV prosody.

The results the researchers obtained were clear: when the infants familiarized with the OV prosody heard the stream that corresponded to the OV prosody, they parsed the speech stream in the OV way; that is, they looked longer (were surprised) when they heard the other stream (frequent word final). Infants familiarized with the VO prosody showed the opposite pattern. As Byers-Heinlein (2018) writes, the results suggest that bilingual infants separate their languages based on prosody and use this information to form expectations about the word order they are hearing. This perceptual ability could help them acquire languages with different word orders.

Phonotactics

Another variable bilingual infants are sensitive to very early on is the phonotactics of their languages, that is the allowable sequences of syllables and phonemes in each: the number and type of syllables that are allowed in a word, the combinations of consonants and vowels that can occur, the type of consonant clusters allowed, etc. Languages have their own rules and infants learn them in their first year. Are bilingual infants also sensitive to phonotactics? Sebastián-Gallés and Bosch (2002) tested Catalan-Spanish 10-month-old bilingual infants whom they grouped into those dominant in Spanish and those dominant in Catalan. The infants heard lists of one-syllable non-words with a consonant-vowel-consonant-consonant (CVCC) structure. Half the lists contained non-words that were legal in Catalan, such as "dost, tusk, sost, kurn, pirt," and half contained illegal non-words also in Catalan, such as "depf, petr, sitr, rapf, lok." Note that all these were illegal in Spanish.

The infants were seated on their mother's lap while the mother listened to music through headphones. A trial started by the blinking of a green light in front of the infant. As soon as he/she looked in that direction, the light was turned off, and one of the lateral lights began to blink. When the infant's gaze was directed to it, the auditory material was played. The light continued blinking until completion of the trial, or until the infant ceased to look in that direction for more than two consecutive seconds. The experimenters calculated the average length of looking times for legal and illegal lists.

For the bilingual Spanish-dominant infants, the mean looking times were 7.8 seconds for the legal lists, and 7.1 seconds for the illegal lists, thereby showing that they paid more attention to legal sequences. Bilingual Catalan-dominant infants behaved in a similar way. Their looking times were also longer for the legal lists than for the illegal lists (8.1 seconds and 6.7 seconds respectively). An analysis of variance showed no difference between the two groups. The experimenters concluded that bilingual infants are sensitive to possible and impossible phonotactic patterns of one of their two languages regardless of their dominant language and despite the fact that they had had less exposure to each language compared to monolingual infants.

Sound Contrasts

An important step in bilingual infants' separation of languages is discovering the phonemes of each language. They must learn which sound contrasts are meaningful (phonemic) within and between their languages. This will assist them in the building of the two language systems.

Burns et al. (2007) used a visual fixation procedure to study the development of phonetic representations in English monolingual infants, and English-French bilingual infants. They studied their ability to discriminate different points along a voice onset time continuum, with the clear voiceless consonant [p] preceding the vowel [a] at one end, and the clear voiced consonant [b] followed by [a] at the other. The infants were tested individually. They sat on their caretaker's lap and watched a checkerboard on a monitor. While doing so they heard an intermediate syllable which was perceived as "pa" by adult French speakers and as "ba" by adult English speakers. In what follows, we'll refer to it as intermediate "ba."

The syllable was repeated a number of times through a loudspeaker positioned above the checkerboard until there was habituation. At that point, one of two new syllables was presented. One, [ba], was perceived as a clear "ba" by both English and French adult speakers, and the other, [p^ha], was perceived as a clear "pa" by both groups. If infants could discriminate the new sound then their interest would be revived and they would start looking at the checkerboard again. Researchers talk of dishabituation when this happens.

The results showed that monolingual and bilingual infants behaved in exactly the same way when they were 6 to 8 months old. They dishabituated to the clear "ba" syllable [ba] but not to the clear "pa" [p^ha] syllable. However, when ten to 12-month-old infants were tested, the results from the two groups were quite different. The English monolingual infants looked significantly longer at the board when they heard the clear "pa" syllable (this syllable was now heard as different from the intermediate syllable) but not when they heard the clear "ba" syllable. Both the intermediate syllable, and the clear syllable [ba], were now a "ba" for them, hence no dishabituation. Thus, they still had two categories although the boundary between the two had shifted.

What about the bilingual infants? Unlike their monolingual peers, they showed dishabituation to BOTH the clear "ba" and "pa" syllables. The intermediate "ba" was perceived as different from the clear "pa" [p^ha]. There is an English phonetic boundary between the two, hence the dishabituation. And the intermediate "ba" was also heard as different from the clear "ba" [ba] as there is a French phonetic boundary between the two. Thus the infants showed the existence of two phonetic boundaries, one for English and one for French. The authors concluded that infants exposed to two languages from birth are equipped to process each language in a native manner, at least at the phonetic level. As Byers-Heinlein (2018) states, "While monolinguals become specialized to perceive sound contrasts in their native language, bilinguals continue to perceive sound contrasts in both of their languages."

One question we can ask is whether any type of exposure to two languages, through human interaction but also through audio input, television, DVDs, etc., will encourage infants to develop the phonetic categories of their languages. Kuhl, Tsao, and Liu (2003) replied negatively based on a study they undertook. They exposed nine-month-old English-learning American infants to 12 sessions with Chinese native speakers who read and played with them in Mandarin. A second group of similar infants received the same amount of Mandarin language exposure but only through DVDs and audio input.

The infants were then tested using a computer-synthesized version of a Mandarin Chinese phonetic contrast that does not occur in English. A head-turn conditioning procedure was used to test their Mandarin speech discrimination. The results were clear. Whereas the live human exposure infants showed they had acquired the Mandarin phonetic contrast, the second group had not. This shows that phonetic learning doesn't rely only on raw auditory sensory information. The presence of a live person interacting with an infant generates interpersonal social cues that attract the infant's attention and motivate learning.

What are the lessons to be learned from the discrimination of sound contrasts research? If bilingual infants are exposed to two languages through human interaction, they will acquire the phonetic categories of the languages by the end of their first year, approximately. If the two languages have many similar sounds, then they make take a bit more time. Of course, we should keep in mind that phonetic categories are just one of the building blocks of language. There are many others at all linguistic levels (morphology, syntax, semantics, discourse, etc.) and these will be acquired over several years.

Statistical Regularities

We have known for some time that monolingual infants are sensitive to statistical regularities in the speech stream (Saffran 2020; Saffran, Newport, and Aslin 1996). For example, they are able to differentiate patterns of syllables within a word that co-occur with high probabilities from patterns of syllables spanning word boundaries that co-occur with lower probabilities. To understand the notion of syllable co-occurrence, let us take an example from Saffran, Newport, and Aslin (1996). The first syllable of "baby," is a frequent syllable and can be followed by other word internal syllables to produce "basic," "baker," "basil," etc. The syllable can also occur at the ends of words – its pronunciation is the same but its spelling may be different – and it is then followed by the first syllable of the next word, such as "obey me." In this case it forms a word external pair with the syllable that follows. It has been shown that word-internal pairs of syllables, such as in "baby," will tend to occur more frequently than word-external pairs. This means that the transitional probability of word internal syllables is higher than the transitional probability of word-external syllable pairs. It is this statistical cue that infants are sensitive to as it will help them find word boundaries in the stream of speech that they are immersed in.

What about bilingual infants? Are they also sensitive to statistical regularities? And if so, in one language only, or in both of their languages? This is what Antovich and Graf Estes (2020) set out to discover.[3] They wanted to know whether infants growing up with

[3] My thanks go to these authors, who kindly helped me understand their study and who shared with me extracts of the material they used.

two languages could acquire statistical regularities when listening to a dual speech stream. They didn't actually get infants to listen to two languages but they simulated this by using two voices and having different words in each speech stream. In one, which they labeled L1, a man's voice was heard uttering a continuous stream of four made-up words (also known as non-words): timay, dobu, kuga, pimo. These were repeated numerous times, in a pseudorandom order, and there were no pauses between them. The subjective impression the stream gives is that of an array of bisyllabic items, some coming through more clearly than others. Here is a very short extract of the stream (spaces have been inserted to help with reading):

.... pimo kuga timay dobu kuga timay pimo kuga timay dobu pimo timay ....

The other speech stream, L2, used different items – mayta, pudo, riku, mola – and were articulated by a woman's voice. Here is a short extract:

.... mayta pudo riku mayta mola riku mayta pudo mola mayta riku mayta ....

A quick examination of the words used, and the syllables they contained, shows that half the syllables that appeared in L1 also occurred in L2, but in different locations. Thus, "timay" in L1 and "mayta" in L2 share the syllable "may," just as "pimo" and "mola" share "mo," though they are in different locations. They are the first syllable of a word in one language, with a transitional probability of one, and the last syllable of a word in the other, with a transitional probability of 0.33. If the infants can track this in the two streams of speech their task will be made easier.

The monolingual and bilingual infants, all 16 months old, were tested individually. First, in the exposure period they listened to the two streams of speech, interleaved in blocks (first L1, then L2, then again L1, etc.) for approximately 8.5 minutes while they played with a caregiver in a small booth. They then changed booths and sat on their caregiver's lap, looking at a screen, as they did a listening preference task. Once their attention was captured with a video of an orange petal rotating in a circle in the center, auditory single word test items were played to them. They were either words they had heard during the exposure phase (e.g., "timay" and "dobu") or part-words they had never heard before. The latter were syllable sequences that occurred in the speech stream but crossed word boundaries rather than forming words. Thus, for example, a part-word for L1 was "moti" which combined the last syllable of "pimo" and the first syllable of "timay." An example for L2 was "tamo" which combined the last syllable of the word "mayta" and the first syllable of the word "mola."

The authors predicted that if bilingual infants segmented the words during the exposure period, they should listen longer (i.e., not turn away from the screen) to part-words than to words. This is exactly what they found. The infants reliably discriminated between words and part-words by listening longer to the latter, whereas the monolingual infants did not. This shows that bilingual infants were able to use syllable-level co-occurrence patterns to detect individual words in fluent speech. Another way of putting this is that they were able to track statistical regularities for each language.

The authors also found that those infants who had a larger proportion of bilingual caregivers, i.e., adults who interacted with the infants in two languages, did better in the task. As they state, having a larger proportion of these caregivers may confer on bilingual infants early metalinguistic knowledge about the existence of multiple language systems, and may help them parse the input to find unique speech streams.

Some ten years before this study, Curtin, Byers-Heinlein, and Werker (2011) had ventured that bilingual infants should be able to track the statistical patterns of their two languages. This could help them discriminate and separate their languages. They added though that "results are not yet available." We know now that this is indeed the case and bilingual infants have one more tool to help them do so.

Taking Pragmatics into Account

So far, we have emphasized the spoken signal that bilingual infants perceive and the wealth of information it carries in terms of phonotactics, prosody, types of sounds, statistical regularities, etc., not to mention the visual cues obtained from the talking face. As we have seen, bilingual infants use all this to start differentiating the languages spoken to them. But we should not forget that communication with and around the infant takes place in specific contexts and situations, with particular people, and at different times, and this will also help the child separate one language from the other.

At the turn of the century, researchers examined bilingual infants' ability to use their developing languages appropriately with interlocutors who spoke different languages. Nicoladis and Genesee (1996), for example, observed four little English-French bilingual boys between the ages of 1;7 and 3;0 years when in free play with each of their parents. They were being brought up with the one person–one language approach and the researchers examined when it was that they started controlling their language output – one language with the mother, the other with the father – a sure sign of language differentiation. They also examined the infants' use of translation equivalents, that is, words that have the same referential meaning in each language (e.g., "dog" and "chien"; "glass" and "verre," etc.). Evidence that they had these types of words, and that they increased in proportion over time, would attest to language separation as normally very young children resist assigning two labels to the same referential category within one language.[4]

What Nicoladis and Genesee found was that none of the children differentiated English and French appropriately during the initial sessions. However, by the sixth session, three of the children showed pragmatic differentiation with both parents, and the only child who did not had shown differentiation in two earlier sessions. There were individual differences in the age of the first appearance of differentiation which the researchers estimated to be between 1;9 and 2;4 years. As for the use of translation equivalents, they found that before the children used English-only and French-only utterances differentially, they used fewer than half of their translation equivalents in the appropriate context. The shift to generally appropriate use of translation equivalents coincided with the emergence of differential language use with both parents.

Genesee, Boivin, and Nicoladis (1996) observed another four children at one point in time, when their average age was 2 years and 2 months. This was during play sessions: once with their mother alone; once with their father; and what was new, once with a monolingual stranger. They found that each child used more of the mother's language with the mother than with the father, and more of the father's language with the father than with the mother. Use of the wrong language ranged from 19% in one instance to 0% in another, so basically the children were differentiating their languages. What is particularly interesting

[4] Krista Byers-Heinlein has pointed out to me that some researchers no longer see translation equivalents as being good evidence for language separation.

is that all the children made some accommodations to the stranger. They were sensitive to the relative language proficiency of their unfamiliar interlocutors and could adjust their language accordingly.

It is at about this age – between two and three – that some bilingual children manifest a clear wish to have interlocutors keep to just one language, by means of what has been called the person–language bond (Grosjean 1982, 2010). In the eyes of some children, a person is tagged with a particular language, and if that person addresses the child in the other language, it may cause some distress. For example, Juliette, a two-and-a-half-year-old French-English bilingual, was playing with Marc, a five-year-old English-speaking boy. Their usual language of communication was English, but to please and surprise her, Marc decided to speak to her in French. He asked his mother for the equivalent of "come" in French and then returned to Juliette and said, "Viens, viens." Much to his surprise, Juliette was far from pleased; instead of smiling, she said angrily, "Don't do that, Marc," and repeated this several times.

De Houwer (2009) gives another example, this one relating to her Dutch-English bilingual daughter Susan, with whom she always spoke Dutch. The mother had just got off the phone where she had spoken English and without realizing it she asked Susan a question in English and not in Dutch. Susan started to cry and said, in Dutch: "Nee mama, nee! Niet Engels mama!' (No mommy, no! No English, mommy!).

Psycholinguists over the years have reported on this person–language bond. Volterra and Taeschner (1978) give several examples such as the time when an Italian friend started to talk to little Lisa in German, even though their usual language of interaction was Italian. Lisa became upset and started to cry. Her mother tried to calm her down and told her that the friend also spoke German, but this only made the situation worse, and Lisa slapped her mother. Reactions such as these led the two psycholinguists to propose that this behavior may result from the fact that bilingual children of that age are still in the process of differentiating their two languages. This makes the choice of words and rules simpler for them and reduces the effort needed. They determine which language is spoken with whom, and they do everything they can keep to that language and make sure that the interlocutor does so also.

Fantini (1978) reports that his Spanish-English bilingual children, Mario and Carla, became "guardians of the appropriate language use" and often reminded their parents to speak Spanish when they were speaking English to one another. And Redlinger and Park (1980) write that little Henrik, a French-German bilingual child, showed a reluctance to speak French in the presence of the investigator, whom he considered to be a monolingual German speaker. When his French-speaking mother was with them, he would translate into German his mother's comments made in French, and then proceed to respond to his mother in German – all for the sake of the investigator.

Is the person–language bond found in all societies among bilingual children? For a long time, it was believed that this was so, to a greater or lesser extent. But Bentahila and Davies (1995) argued that it really depends on the language environment children are brought up in, and the parental strategies used with them. They reported that in Morocco, children from the middle and upper class hear both Arabic and French at home from birth, and are addressed in both languages by their parents and caretakers. Later, they are placed in nursery schools where the two languages are present. These young bilinguals are accustomed to hearing their parents and other adults use the two languages – sometimes the one, sometimes the other, and also often an intermingling of the two. As a result, children do not "tag" adults with a particular language and do not develop the strong person–language bond that other children do.

In sum, whether such a bond develops or not depends on the way bilingual children are brought up. If the languages are clearly separated during childhood, by person (e.g., with the one person–one language approach) or by environment (one language at home, one outside the home), then a bond might develop. If the use of the one or the other language by individuals is freer, and the languages are interchangeable, then it probably will not.

A Brief Account of Language Separation

To end this chapter, we offer a brief account of how language separation may take place based on the writings of Krista Byers-Heinlein (2014, 2020; see also Curtin, Byers-Heinlein, and Werker 2011; Werker and Byers-Heinlein 2008).

In her Gradual Language Separation Hypothesis, Byers-Heinlein posits that infants are born equipped with the necessary perceptual sensitivities to separate the languages to which they are exposed. Language separation occurs gradually during the first years of life, at multiple levels (phonetic, lexical, syntactic, etc.), as infants become increasingly able to apply their perceptual sensitivities to different aspects of language processing and representation.

A central aspect of the hypothesis is that differentiation corresponds to the ability to treat elements of different languages (sounds, words, utterances, etc.) as belonging to different categories. We know from the pragmatic studies mentioned in the second part that slightly older children can do so: they vary the proportion of words from each language spoken to different interlocutors all the way to speaking monolingually with them; and some later insist on respecting the person–language bond when they are with them. In addition, their way of processing code-switches at this age seems to be similar to that of adults. For example, they process "Find the *chien*" with more difficulty than "Find the dog" (Byers-Heinlein 2020; Byers-Heinlein, Morin-Lessard, and Lew-Williams 2017). If words from different languages were completely equivalent (i.e., they were not from different categories), there would be no basis for a language switching cost.

There are two types of categorization according to Byers-Heinlein: perceptual and conceptual. Perceptual categorization leads to perceptual categories; it is based on sensitivities to observable differences between languages (e.g., prosody, phonotactics, statistical patterns, etc.) and emerges very early in development. As for conceptual categorization, it leads to conceptual categories. It is based on more abstract language knowledge and emerges later in development. Both of these are likely different from explicit metalinguistic awareness that there are two languages. And language categories themselves, corresponding to different linguistic levels, will probably emerge at different points in the development.

According to Byers-Heinlein, most of the studies conducted in the first year of a bilingual infant show perceptual categorization, and not conceptual categorization. They show the infant's perceptual sensitivities to various aspects of speech – prosody, visual cues, phonotactics, etc. – which will be foundational for the later development of conceptual language categories. Language clusters will emerge as infants' perceptual sensitivities and learning mechanisms detect, process, and represent regularities in the input that covary with language categories. Thus, the perception studies conducted in the first year show that young bilingual infants can form perceptual language categories but they do not necessarily reveal the operation of conceptual language categories (as was illustrated in the second part of this chapter).

A final point relates to individual differences among bilingual infants. There are many that will impact the building of conceptual categories: language pairs involved, the amount of exposure the infants have to each language, whether the input comes from monolingual or bilingual speakers, the prevalence of language mixing in the environment, and so on. In sum, as Byers-Heinlein (2014) writes, the ultimate answer to the question of when and how bilinguals develop the ability to categorize their languages is almost certain to be complex – *and truly fascinating*, we could add.

References

Antovich, Dylan M., and Katharine Graf Estes. 2020. "One language or two? Navigating cross-language conflict in statistical word segmentation." *Developmental Science*, 23 (6): November. desc 12960.

Bentahila, Abdelali, and Eirlys E. Davies. 1995. "Patterns of code-switching and patterns of language contact." *Lingua*, 96: 75–93.

Burns, Tracey C., Katherine A. Yoshida, Karen Hill, and Janet F. Werker. 2007. "The development of phonetic representation in bilingual and monolingual infants." *Applied Psycholinguistics*, 28 (2): 455–474.

Byers-Heinlein, Krista. 2014. "Languages as categories: Reframing the 'one language or two' question in early bilingual development." *Language Learning*, 64 (Suppl. 2): 184–201.

Byers-Heinlein, Krista. 2018. "Speech perception." In *The Listening Bilingual: Speech Perception, Comprehension and Bilingualism*, edited by François Grosjean and Krista Byers-Heinlein, 153-175. Oxford, UK: Wiley Blackwell.

Byers-Heinlein, Krista. 2020. "Challenges of infant language acquisition in bilingual environments." Unpublished manuscript, Concordia University.

Byers-Heinlein, Krista, Tracey C. Burns, and Janet F. Werker. 2010. "The roots of bilingualism in newborns." *Psychological Science*, 21 (3): 343–348.

Byers-Heinlein, Krista, Elizabeth Morin-Lessard, and Casey Lew-Williams. 2017. "Bilingual infants control their languages as they listen." *Proceedings of the National Academy of Sciences*, 114 (34): 9032–9037.

Curtin, Suzanne, Krista Byers-Heinlein, and Janet F. Werker. 2011. "Bilingual beginnings as a lens for theory development: PRIMIR in focus." *Journal of Phonetics*, 39: 492–504. DOI: 10.1016/j.wocn.2010.12.002.

De Houwer, Annick. 2009. *Bilingual First Language Acquisition*. Bristol, UK: Multilingual Matters.

Fantini, Alvino. 1978. "Bilingual behavior and social cues: Case studies of two bilingual children." In *Aspects of Bilingualism*, edited by Michel Paradis, 283–301. Columbia, SC: Hornbeam Press.

Genesee, Fred, Isabelle Boivin, and Elena Nicoladis. 1996. "Talking with strangers: A study of bilingual children's communicative competence." *Applied Psycholinguistics*, 17: 427–442.

Gervain, Judit, and Janet F. Werker. 2013. "Prosody cues word order in 7-month-old bilingual infants." *Nature Communications*, 4: 1490. DOI: 10.1038/ncomms2430.

Grosjean, François. 1982. *Life with Two Languages: An Introduction to Bilingualism*. Cambridge, MA: Harvard University Press.

Grosjean, François. 2010. *Bilingual: Life and Reality*. Cambridge, MA: Harvard University Press.

Kuhl, Patricia K., Feng-Minh Tsao, and Huei-Mei Liu. 2003. "Foreign-language experience in infancy: Effects of short-term exposure and social interaction on phonetic learning." *Proceedings of the National Academy of Sciences*, 100 (15): 9096–9101.

Lewkowicz, David J., and Amy M. Hansen-Tift. 2012. "Infants deploy selective attention to the mouth of a talking face when learning speech." *Proceedings of the National Academy of Sciences*, 109 (5): 1431–1436.

Morin-Lessard, Elizabeth, Diane Poulin-Dubois, Norman Segalowitz, and Krista Byers-Heinlein. 2019. "Selective attention to the mouth of talking faces in monolinguals and bilinguals aged 5 months to 5 years." *Developmental Psychology*, 55 (8): 1640–1655.

Nicoladis, Elena, and Fred Genesee. 1996. "A longitudinal study of pragmatic differentiation in young bilingual children." *Language Learning*, 46 (3): 439–464.

Pons, Ferran, Laura Bosch, and David J. Lewkowicz. 2015. "Bilingualism modulates infants' selective attention to the mouth of a talking face." *Psychological Science*, 26 (4): 490–498.

Redlinger, Wendy E., and Tschang-Zin Park. 1980. "Language mixing in young bilinguals." *Journal of Child Language*, 7 (2): 337–352.

Saffran, Jenny R. 2020. "Statistical language learning in infancy." *Child Development Perspectives*, 14 (1): 49–54.

Saffran, Jenny R., Elissa L. Newport, and Richard N. Aslin. 1996. "Word segmentation: The role of distributional cues." *Journal of Memory and Language*, 35: 606–621.

Sebastián-Gallés, Nuria, and Laura Bosch. 2002. "Building phonotactic knowledge in bilinguals: Role of early exposure." *Journal of Experimental Psychology: Human Perception and Performance*, 28 (4): 974–989. DOI: 10.1037/0096-1523.28.4.974.

Volterra, Virginia, and Traute Taeschner. 1978. "The acquisition and development of language by bilingual children." *Journal of Child Language*, 5: 311–326.

Weikum, Whitney M., Athena Vouloumanos, Jordi Navarra, Salvador Soto-Faraco, Núria Sebastián-Gallés, and Janet F. Werker. 2007. "Visual language discrimination in infancy." *Science*, 316 (5828): 1159.

Werker, Janet F., and Krista Byers-Heinlein. 2008. "Bilingualism in infancy: First steps in perception and comprehension." *Trends in Cognitive Sciences*, 12 (4): 144–151.

Part II

Linguistics and Neurolinguistics

4

Having an Accent in One of Your Languages

Having an accent in one of your languages is the norm for bilinguals; not having one is the exception. One could think that this is due to how well you know a language, but there is no clear relationship between knowledge of a language and whether one has an accent in it.

In what follows, we will first discuss the definitions that are given to having a accent, the myth that is attached to it, and the disadvantages and advantages of having an accent. We will also show that we are acutely sensitive to accents and can detect one with very little input. This will be followed by a discussion of the phonetic characteristics of accents, at the level of individual segments (sounds and syllables) and in terms of prosody. An empirical study that shows the link between pronunciation measures and accentedness will then be described.

Next, we will turn to how understandable accented speech is and will review a few studies that have examined both comprehensibility and intelligibility. We will also examine at what age children start showing adult-like behavior when asked to understand speech spoken with an unfamiliar accent.

We will then concentrate on an unresolved issue in the field: What are the main factors that account for the presence of an accent and the variations in its strength? Maturational aspects which have been operationalized as age of onset, or age of learning the second language, immediately come to mind. Some have proposed that a language can be "accentless" – in the sense of not being influenced by another language – if acquired before age six; others extend the window to age 12 or even 15. But things are not that clear, as we will see. We will also discuss the importance of other explanatory variables such as language input, motivation, and attitudes.

We will end with a few words on having an accent in a third language. Does it depend, for example, on the first language learned, or the second language acquired, or how much a language is used? We will see that things are much more complex than we could have thought at first.

General Aspects

There exist a number of definitions of what it means to have an accent. Baker and Prys Jones (1998) have an all-englobing definition stating that it corresponds to people's pronunciation and intonation which may reveal, for example, which region, country, or

The Mysteries of Bilingualism, First Edition. François Grosjean.

social class they come from. Moyer (2013) concurs and writes that it is a set of dynamic segmental and suprasegmental habits that convey linguistic meaning along with social and situational affiliation. She states that defining accent is not an easy task and that it is much more than a phonetic phenomenon. It is a reflection of our past experiences, the languages we know, our upbringing, our affiliations with various communities and social networks. As for Wrembel et al. (2018), they concentrate on a foreign accent and write that it refers to a range of segmental and prosodic deviations from the native norms of pronunciation in a given language. In what follows, we will mainly discuss having an accent in a *second* language in bilinguals – the aspect by far the most studied in the literature – but will not forget that one can have an accent in other languages such as your first language, your third language, etc.

There is a myth that real bilinguals have no accent in their different languages, but the reality is quite different. Having an accent in a language is the norm in bilinguals, not having one is the exception. But this does not make one any less bilingual. In fact one can be an outstanding speaker or writer of a second or third language and have an accent. The famous author Joseph Conrad, whose English prose was superlative and required almost no editing, retained a strong accent in English – his first language was Polish – which prevented him from lecturing publicly.

Among the disadvantages that bilingual express about having an accent, the one mentioned most often is that it makes people stand out. In societies that are less open to linguistic differences, having a foreign accent can have a negative effect on the way you are perceived. It may also give the impression that you have not tried hard enough to learn the language of the country or the region. Having an accent can also impede communication (we will come back to this a bit later on) although this is rather rare once the person has lived in the country or region a number of years. Those bilinguals who have an accent in one of their languages are often quite aware of it and some regret it. The famous bilingual writer, Nancy Huston, wrote in her book with Leila Sebbar (Huston and Sebbar 1986) that she knows she will never get rid of hers in French. It becomes stronger when she is nervous, when she speaks to strangers, when she has to leave a message on the phone, and when she speaks in public.

But there are also many advantages to having an accent. In some societies, having a particular accent is looked upon favorably, such as having a French accent in Germany, or a British accent in France. In addition, having an accent marks you as a member of a group and some people find that this is important. The Russian–French author, Elsa Triolet, kept her Russian accent in French as it was a way of showing that she had remained loyal to her first language, Russian. As Beaujour (1989) writes, "... her accent was a hostage, a sacrifice to Russian, a constant proof that she had not really betrayed her first linguistic loyalty." Having an accent can also protect you culturally. It signals that you may not know all the social rules of the people you interact with and that they should take this into account when interacting with you.

The Phonetic Characteristics of Accents

We need to listen to very little accented speech to clearly hear that it is indeed accented. Nancy Huston (2002) had noted this in her book *Losing North* when she wrote: "No matter how lengthy and arduous (the) effort (of foreigners) ... a little something almost always gives them away. The faintest trace, just a soupçon ... of an accent." In fact, we have known this experimentally since Flege's (1984) innovative study on the topic. His aim was to examine the ability of listeners to detect a foreign accent. He presented increasingly short excerpts of the English spoken by native speakers of French, and native speakers of English, and he asked his participants (native English-speaking listeners) to identify whether the speakers were native or non-native.

In his first experiment, he presented the short phrases, "two little dogs" and "two little birds," produced in isolation and also in story speaking tasks. The listeners were very good at identifying the non-natives: 89% of the phrases produced by the French native speakers were correctly identified as "non-native" as against only 0.5% of the phrases produced by the English native speakers. In the second experiment, he extracted the "two" from these phrases and listeners were asked once again to identify whether the speakers were native or non-native. This time, the "non-native" percentage correct for the non-native speaker productions was 95%. He pursued his study with other experimental conditions and the last one involved just the first 30 milliseconds of the "two" which basically corresponded to the burst of the consonant /t/. The results showed how little information one needs to identify a foreign accent: 69% of the segments produced by the native speakers of French were correctly chosen as "non-native." Thus, detection remained reliable as the speech samples were progressively reduced from phrase to syllable to segment size. Flege concluded his study by stating that human listeners are acutely sensitive to divergences from the phonetic norms of their native languages, such as those of a foreign accent.

A careful phonetic analysis of a person's accented speech will reveal a number of traits which depend in large part on the speech characteristics of both the first and second language. Thus, if the latter has a sound that isn't found in the first language, the speaker may use a replacement that is phonetically close. For example, there is no "ch" sound in Portuguese (as in "church") and so a Portuguese person speaking English may say "shicken" instead of "chicken." The same is true for the English "th" sound replaced by "s" or "z" or "f" or "v" by French speakers, who may say "sanks" instead of "thanks." And if the second language has two rather similar sounds where the first language has only one, the speaker may fail to distinguish the two sounds and use only one, based in part on the first language. A well-known example is that of Japanese speakers who have only one liquid consonant and hence have difficulties distinguishing English /r/ and /l/ in their production. The French have similar difficulties with the two "ee" sounds in English (/ɪ/ and /iː/), and sometimes pronounce "hit" and "heat," and "rim" and "ream," in the same way.

Subtle aspects of vowel and consonant production can also be involved such as vowel quality, aspiration, and so on. Wrembel et al. (2018) give a list of speech errors produced by Polish–English bilinguals in Polish. These involve vowel quality distortion, vowel reduction, the misarticulation of nasal vowels, the lack of consonant palatalization in certain contexts, among others. And at the level of syllables, one may find the reduction or substitution of consonant clusters, and the insertion of vowels into clusters.

At the level of prosody, variables such as intonation, stress, speech rate, rhythm, pause, etc. are also impacted when a person has a foreign accent. Thus, a French speaker with an accent in English may put the word stress on the wrong syllable as in "e-DIN-burgh" instead of "E-dinburgh." Kang (2010) showed that the international teaching assistants that she analyzed placed stress on many function words also which is very rare in English (e.g., be, the, that…). In addition, they had restricted pitch range, and their pausing pattern was irregular with long pauses within sentences, not just at sentence breaks.

Crowther et al. (2018) were interested in seeing how strongly pronunciation and fluency measures were correlated with the "accentedness" of speakers of English as a second language. They described accentedness as the listener's perception of how strongly speech in a second language is influenced by the speaker's native language or is colored by other non-native features. They obtained speech productions from speakers of four distinct language groups (Farsi, Hindi/Urdu, Mandarin, and Romance languages) and asked native English listeners to evaluate the recordings. The latter were asked to give scale ratings for accentedness, frequency of segmental errors (these concerned individual consonants and vowels within a word), frequency of word stress errors (placement of stress), appropriateness of intonation (pitch movement such as rising tones in yes/no questions), naturalness of rhythm (stress differences between content and function words), and appropriateness of speech rate (overall pacing and speed of utterance delivery).

In the speech productions that corresponded to picture narratives, the researchers found the highest correlation between the frequency of segmental errors and degree of accentedness ($r = 0.95$). Basically, the higher the number of consonant and vowel errors, the more a person's production was considered accented. The second highest correlation ($r = 0.82$) was between frequency of word stress errors and accentedness. Rhythm was also highly correlated with accentedness ($r = 0.78$) as was intonation ($r = 0.72$). Speech rate arrived last but the correlation was still quite high ($r = 0.56$). These results clearly show the importance of both segmental and prosodic errors in the perception of accented speech by non-native speakers.

How Well Is Accented Speech Understood?

Listening to someone with an accent does not normally impede communication, but from time to time this can happen when we meet a person who has a very strong accent in the language being spoken. The person may be quite fluent but the accent is so strong that it almost seems as if the person is speaking their other language. When this happens, one looks for strategies to understand what is being said. Here is one of these developed by an English–Spanish bilingual listening to her mother, originally from Guatemala, who is speaking English to her:

> My mother and father had accents in their English all their lives, yet they spoke fluently. My mother always struggled with the letter "z" though, since that doesn't exist in her native language. She also struggled with differentiating "b" and "v." In Spanish they sound alike, unlike English. So whenever she was writing, and she asked me for the spelling of an unfamiliar English word that began with one of those letters, I would say, "It starts with V, like *vaca* or B, like *bebé?*"

Sometimes someone's accent is so strong that one may have to shorten the interaction but such instances are relatively rare.

Research has examined how well speakers with a foreign accent are understood. For example, Munro and Derwing (1999) examined both the comprehensibility of accented speech, that is the listeners' *perception* of how easily they understand the speech, and the intelligibility of accented speech, that is, the extent to which it is *actually understood* by the listeners. The first measure uses a rating scale in which, for example, participants circle a number from 1 to 9 where 1 corresponds to "easy to understand" and 9 to "impossible to understand." The second measure, intelligibility, is more complex as the speech uttered by the accented speaker is transcribed by the participants and an intelligibility score is assigned based on the number of words correctly written down.

Munro and Derwing asked ten native speakers of Mandarin, proficient speakers of English, who had learned English after puberty, to take part in their study. They had all spent a minimum of one year in Canada and spoke English with a moderate to heavy accent. They described a story from a page of cartoons over a two to three minute period. Excerpts from the recording were then used in the study. Listeners who were native speakers of English were asked to assign a comprehensibility rating as indicated above. In addition, they had to transcribe the excerpts in standard orthography. The two authors then coded the transcriptions and assigned intelligibility percentages on the basis of the number of words that exactly matched an errorless version.

The distribution of the comprehensibility ratings was right skewed, indicating that most ratings were in the easy to understand end of the scale. It should be noted that when the same listeners were asked to give an accentedness judgment, they were much harsher. Here the distribution was flatter, with almost as many judgments occupying the 2 to 8 ratings (1 corresponded to no foreign accent and 9 to very strong accent). Of more interest to us, though, are the intelligibility scores, that is whether the non-native speakers were understandable. The distribution was highly right skewed with almost two thirds of the intelligibility scores situated in the 91% to 100% range. Basically, the non-native speech samples used in the study were highly intelligible. One of the authors' conclusions is that the presence of a strong foreign accent, as indicated by an accentedness task, does not necessarily result in reduced comprehensibility or intelligibility.

In a later study, Isaacs and Trofimovich (2012) investigated which linguistic variables most strongly influence one's comprehensibility judgment of foreign accent. Francophones from a predominantly French-speaking area of Quebec were recorded telling a picture story in English, a language they used on average 20% of the time, and native English-speaking listeners assigned comprehensibility scores. The productions were also transcribed and analyzed for errors. In what follows we will concentrate on those from two categories – "phonology" and "fluency" – as they are the ones most closely tied to pronunciation.

The variable that showed the highest correlation with the comprehensibility ratings ($r = -0.76$) concerned word stress errors which concerned misplaced or missing primary stress in polysyllabic words (e.g., "BUIL-ding" spoken as "buil-DING"). This was followed by vowel reduction (e.g., the last syllable in "people" should be reduced; if not, it is an error). Here the correlation was $r = 0.74$. Then we have the mean length of runs (i.e., the number of syllables between two adjacent filled or unfilled pauses): $r = 0.71$. Other variables with correlations in the 0.51 to 0.58 range were pause errors (inappropriately produced filled and unfilled pauses, inside clauses for example), pitch contour (patterns at the end of phrases), repetition/self-correction, and segmental errors (number of phonemic substitutions such as "fan" for "fun").

To end this section, it is worth describing a study by Bent (2018) which examined at what age children start showing adult-like behavior when asked to understand speech spoken with an unfamiliar accent. English speaking children ranging from 5 to 15 years old, grouped into different age groups, were asked to listen and repeat short sentences of the type, "The lady packed her bag" and "The little boy left home." They were read by a monolingual speaker of English and a non-native speaker whose first language was Japanese. The latter's pronunciation deviated on a number of variables such as consonant and vowel substitution, distortion, deletion, and addition. Although the sentences were presented in noise and in quiet, we will concentrate on the results in the quiet condition.

Concerning the speech spoken by the native speaker, the 5- and 6-year-old children's word identification accuracy was significantly lower than the adults, but the other three age groups (8–9, 11–12, 14–15) did not differ from the adults. Thus, the children reached mature performance by eight to nine years of age. However, for speech produced with a foreign accent, all age groups except the 14- and 15-year-old children were significantly less accurate than the adults. Thus, the ability to comprehend words by talkers whose production patterns deviate from the child's home dialect appears to take well over a decade to reach maturity.

Factors that Affect the Degree of a Foreign Accent

Even though accent research is now quite advanced, there is one area that remains enigmatic. It concerns the factors that account for the fact that some people have a foreign accent in their second language (L2) whereas others do not. The extensive literature on the topic has come up with many factors, some being preferred to others, but in the end, a consensus has not been reached by researchers. In what follows, we will review a few of them.

Maturational Aspects

Flege and MacKay (2011) help us set the stage. They write, "The prevailing view of L2 speech learning, especially that of non-academics and non-specialists, can be summarized as follows. Everyone (or nearly everyone) who begins to learn an L2 after puberty is destined to forever speak it with a foreign accent whereas anyone lucky enough to begin learning an L2 before the end of a "critical period" will learn the L2 effortlessly, rapidly, and perfectly."

The notion of a critical period, later called a sensitive period, is linked to the seminal book by Eric Lenneberg (1967), *Biological Foundations of Language.* He concentrated on first language (L1) acquisition and stated, among other things, that there is a critical period for language acquisition. He wrote that the beginning of the period is limited by lack of maturation, and its termination seems to be related to a loss of adaptability and an inability for reorganization in the brain. Lenneberg devoted a few pages to second language (L2) acquisition and stated that most individuals are able to learn a second language after the beginning of their second decade although the incidence of "language-learning blocks" rapidly increases after puberty. He did admit that a person *can* learn to communicate in a foreign language later on (he cites the age of 40) but, and these are his exact words, "foreign accents cannot be overcome easily after puberty" (p. 176). In a summary table (p. 181), he wrote that foreign accents emerge between the ages of 11 and 14.

Lenneberg's few words on foreign accent have had an amazing impact on researchers who sometimes repeat what he said and sometimes adapt or extend his statements. One example of the latter is Long (1988) who wrote that learners starting later than age six often become communicatively fluent, but typically finish with measurable accents. Another example is Moyer (2013) who wrote that Lenneberg predicted that accent in foreign language would be especially difficult to acquire beyond age 9 or 10 years, although she does continue by saying that the brain is surprisingly plastic, well into adulthood, and that phonological processes may therefore be less constrained by specific neural substrates than previously assumed.

Even though the exact age by which a foreign accent becomes inevitable differs according to researchers, the explanations they have given have been quite similar to what Lenneberg stated. Moyer (2013) proposes that muscular constraints restrict the ability to form new articulatory patterns past a certain age. Hopp and Schmid (2013) mention constraints in neurological and fine motor skills as well as reduction in cerebral plasticity. And Flege, Munro, and MacKay (1995) mention an age-related decline in the second-learner's recognition that certain auditorily detectable differences between L1 and L2 sounds are phonetically relevant.

Studies examining maturational aspects, which were operationalized in different ways for a second language – age of acquisition, age of learning, age of onset, even age of arrival in the country of that language – started very soon after Lenneberg's book came out. Some results confirmed what he said whilst other raised doubts. One study which was to mark its time was done by Flege, Munro, and MacKay (1995) and is worth being described in detail. In Ottawa, Canada, they tested 240 native Italian participants, all born in Italy, who had lived there a mean of 32 years (the range extended from 15 to 44 years). They had begun learning English between the ages of 2 and 23, and used both languages on a daily basis. They were asked to repeat a number of short sentences such as "I can read this for you," "The red book was good," and "He turned to the right." Each sentence was preceded and followed by a context sentence. For example, "In which direction did he turn?/*He turned to the right*/In which direction did he turn?."

Twenty-four native English-speaking judges, all born in Canada and not exposed to Italian in their childhood, were asked to rate the accent of the participants by positioning a lever on a response box at some point along a range whose extremities were "native speaker of English – no foreign accent" and "native speaker of Italian – strongest foreign accent." The midpoint of the range was labeled, "medium foreign accent."

The results obtained were presented in their 1995 paper in the form of graphs but have been redrawn in a more explicit manner by Flege in later publications. Figure 4.1 (below) was presented by him (Flege 2012) at a conference he gave in Łódź, Poland. He has kindly accepted that I reproduce it here.

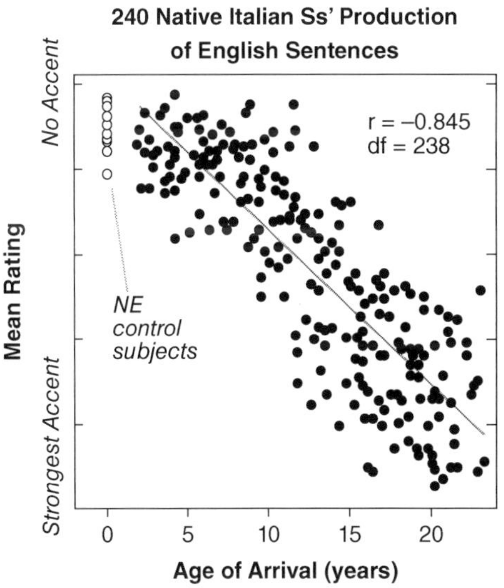

Figure 4.1 Degree of foreign accent in English as a function of age of arrival for 240 native Italian speakers and for control participants. (Reprinted from Flege 2012, with permission).

The linear relation the authors found between degree of accent and age of arrival is quite striking. The earlier the participants arrived in Canada, the weaker their accent, with many having no accent at all in the very early ages. The later they arrived, the stronger the accent. The correlation is amazingly high (r = –0.85) which means that age of arrival or, if one prefers, age of onset of the second language, accounts for 72% of the variance. All other things being equal, there seems to be some truth, at first sight at least, to the layperson's opinion, "the earlier, the better," concerning a foreign accent. The longer you wait to learn a second language, the stronger will be your accent, it would appear, and the lower the probability of not having an accent at all. The authors report that very few of those who began learning English after the age of 15 received ratings that fell within the native English range.

Two other aspects of the results are of interest. First, there is no marked boundary between not having an accent and having an accent, as a hard version of the critical period would have us believe. As age of learning increases, so does the accentedness of the speech. Second, there is quite a bit of variability among those who arrived very early on. Many do not have traces of an accent, but some do, thus countering the fact that if you learn a second language at a very young age, you will not have an accent in it.

Flege and MacKay (2011) pursued this line of work and extended the age of learning range. They tested 54 native Italians which they broke down into three groups: "AOA-10," i.e., those who arrived between ages seven and 13 years, "AOA-18," those who arrived between ages 17 and 19 years, and a new age group, "AOA-26," those who arrived between 23 and 35 years. There was also a group of English native speakers. Once again, they used a delayed repetition technique to elicit the production of English sentences word for word. The degree of foreign accent was assessed by native English speakers by means of a scale ranging from 1 ("very strong foreign accent") to 9 ("no foreign accent").

The results they obtained confirmed those of the 1995 study. The native English group achieved the best results, as was expected. More interestingly, the "AOA-18" group was perceived to have a stronger accent than the "AOA-10" group, and the new group, "AOA-26" group had a stronger accent than the "AOA-18" group. All three results were significantly different from the other. The authors used these findings to criticize the critical period hypothesis even though it comes through in part as the "AOA-10" and "AOA-18" groups are in the right order. However, it does not explain why the native English group did better than the "AOA-10" group. Another problem is that beyond the critical period, and with a group much older than the maximum age of the 1995 study, the degree of accent grew even stronger.

As the years went by, James Flege and his associates started having doubts about the variable they had used – age of arrival/age of acquisition (AOA) – as the explanatory variable of accented speech. Flege (2009) wrote that the effect of AOA is often assessed because it is easy to measure and is related to a wide range of variables that have been hypothesized to affect L2 learning directly. Among these we find: the state of neurological development, the state of cognitive development, and the state of development of L1 phonetic category representations, all three when L2 learning begins; L1 proficiency; language dominance; the frequency of L2 (and L1) use; and the kind of L2 input that is experienced (e.g., native speaker speech vs. foreign accented speech). Thus AOA is a complex variable associated with underlying variables.

As Flege (2018) stated, the primary problem is not that the maturational hypothesis, symbolized in part by the critical/sensitive period proposal, is wrong but that its widespread appeal has discouraged the search for better, falsifiable explanations of age-related effects on L2 speech learning. Moyer (2018) went in the same direction and wrote that it is important to challenge the simplistic notion that our capacity to become fluent strictly depends on age of onset with a new language, that is, the age of first exposure, either through immersion or instruction. This said, the results presented in Figure 4.1 remain extremely appealing for a maturational account – without having to call on a critical/ sensitive period explanation – and the linear decrease of a native-like accent, extended up to 35 years old in a later study, will have to be explained adequately in the years to come.

Language Input

Over the last years, researchers have moved on to other explanatory variables to account for degree of accent. The primary one is language input in the first and the second language. For example, Moyer (2013) states that the aspect of language experience most significant for accent is apparently the degree to which one engages meaningfully with native speakers of the target language. And Flege (2019), who has studied this question for numerous years, proposes that the immigrants' success in learning the second language may be the result of differences in the input they receive. Concerning his 1995 study, he mentions that those who arrived in Canada before the age of 15 obtained a substantial amount of formal education in English-speaking schools which was likely to have impacted on the quantity and quality of the English language input they received. They learned English from their native English teachers and classmates with whom they often developed lifelong friendships and sometimes married.

Input in the second language is crucial therefore to render the accent less foreign-like, it would seem. But the *amount* of input in the first language is also important and may also have an effect on accent, according to Flege (2019). He reports re-examining sentences spoken by 40 early learners from the 1995 study; they had arrived in Canada at a mean age of 5.8 years and had lived there for an average of 34 years. The strength of their foreign accents depended on language use. The accents were weaker for the early learners who used English often and Italian seldom, and stronger for the early learners who used English seldom and Italian often. Flege, Yeni-Komshian, and Liu (1999) also report on another study examining the accent of Korean immigrants. Native Korean participants who used English relatively often, and Korean seldom, were found to have a significantly better pronunciation of English than native Korean participants, matched on age of arrival, who used English relatively seldom and Korean often.

The amount of first and second language input over a bilingual's life would seem to have an impact, therefore, although this still needs to be confirmed precisely. The quality of the input is also just as crucial. Flege (2019) states that in the 1995 study, the Italian immigrants who arrived after the age of 15, and in particular the Italian males, worked outside the home and learned English from native speakers but also from fellow Italian immigrants who spoke foreign-accented English and who matched their own foreign accent. They also heard English spoken by other non-natives of English, whose first language was not Italian. This would explain in part their accent in English. Early arrivals, on the contrary, usually received more native English L2 input, mainly in school as we saw, which would account for their better accent.

Motivation and Attitudes

We will end this section with two factors that are difficult to separate from one another. For a long time, motivation was broken down into integrative motivation, that is the wish to adapt and integrate into the new culture – language being one of the means to do so – and instrumental motivation, that is the wish to learn the language for practical reasons. Moyer (2018) writes that nowadays, motivation is understood in more complex terms, namely as a function of self-concepts or beliefs about oneself, including beliefs about one's competence as a language learner. She adds that pronunciation learning beyond early childhood relies not just on cognitive variables, but also on motivational as well as attitudinal variables, including the need to build a new identity of sorts and a willingness to project that identity through new sound patterns. Moyer (2013) states that attitudes – towards language learning, towards the target language, and towards its culture and community of speakers – are in fact closely related to motivation. In her later writings, she covers both notions under the term "sociopsychological factors."

It is worth mentioning three studies that examined motivation and attitudes, along with other factors, and that showed their impact on degree of accentedness in a second language. Bongaerts, Planken, and Schils (1995) wanted to examine whether there are cases of late learners who have acquired such a good pronunciation of their second language that they can pass themselves off as native speakers of the language. They asked a group of native speakers of Dutch, who were highly successful learners of written and spoken English, and who either studied it or taught it, to do several tasks in English: talk spontaneously as well as read aloud short sentences and words. Two other groups did the same thing: native speakers of English, and native speakers of Dutch who had an accent in English. They then asked native speakers of British English to rate each speech sample on a 5-point scale, 1 indicating a very strong foreign accent and 5 no foreign accent at all.

They found that the highly successful learners did as well as the group of native speakers of English. The two groups were indistinguishable with respect to their pronunciation. Of course, both groups were significantly different from the group of accented English speakers. When the successful learners were questioned, a number of aspects came through: they were taught almost exclusively in English at university; they were schooled in phonetics and attended pronunciation tutorials; they had intensive contacts with native speakers of English; and for most of them, it was very important to be able to speak English without a noticeable accent. In sum, these were highly motivated learners of English who had also received a great amount of English input. Piske, MacKay, and Flege (2001) ask themselves if differences in the amount of L2 experience and age of learning may not have been responsible for their success. They do admit though that motivation may be a potent factor for people who are required by their profession to speak a second language without a foreign accent. This would not be the case for ordinary immigrants.

Nikolov (2000) undertook a very similar study but this time with exceptional adult learners of Hungarian as a second language. She found a number of participants who were considered native speakers by exterior judges. When she examined their language history and their motivations, she found they were avid readers of Hungarian, they listened to the media and tried to feel at home in the culture as well as in the language. They sought out moments to improve their second language proficiency, and shared a real motivation to speak the language well. They were outgoing characters who liked to socialize and they appeared to be proud and conscious of their achievement. In addition, they had a very strong integrative motivation to become residents of Hungary.

Finally, on attitudes specifically, Moyer (2007) undertook a study to examine whether learner attitudes are relevant to phonological attainment once more traditional measures of language exposure such as age of onset are take into account. She also wished to see if there were any apparent differences between attitudes towards the language itself and attitudes towards the culture when it comes to accent in a second language. Forty-two non-native students who had lived in the United States for a mean of 5 years, representing 15 different languages, were asked about their language background as well as their sociopsychological orientation concerning English and the United States. They also did a series of speech production tasks: reading words, sentences, and paragraphs, describing a picture and speaking freely. Raters were asked to evaluate each individual's accent on a 5-point scale, with 1 corresponding to "no foreign accent" and 5 to "strong foreign accent."

Among the language-directed attitudes, the desire to improve one's accent was correlated r = 0.52 with degree of accent. Wanting a better accent had an impact of the accent itself through various kinds of linguistic behaviors aimed at improving it. Another factor concerned reasons for learning English. 71% of the participants reported both personal and professional reasons for learning English and here the correlation was r = 0.37. Among the culture-related attitudes, 95% felt they could easily assimilate, and as a consequence comfort with the idea of cultural assimilation and degree of accent was correlated r = 0.37. 60% planned to stay in the USA permanently or for at least five years, and hence, intention to reside in the US long-term and accentedness were correlated r = 0.34. In general, the author found that attitudes towards the target language were more powerfully linked to accent than were culture-directed attitudes, though both played a role. She concluded that a combination of experience and a positive orientation appeared to be particularly important for attaining greater authenticity in accent.

We will end this section by mentioning other factors that have been put forward to explain degree of accent but which are either disputed or not studied sufficiently (Flege 2019; Moyer 2013; Piske, MacKay, and Flege 2001; Wrembel et al. 2018). Among the variables that are disputed, we find length of residence in the L2 country (results have been both in favor and against, but it may play a role in the first months of stay) and gender (there has been contradictory evidence here). Among the factors that have not been studied sufficiently are formal instruction (there is little evidence to date of the role it plays), language learning aptitude (it is often mentioned but the studies have not followed), and typological distance of the bilingual's languages.

Accent in a Third Language

In an earlier publication (Grosjean 2010), I asked the question: Where does an accent in a third language come from? I answered with the statement that it really depends on a number of factors and I gave as an example my own English-accented Italian in my teens. English was my stronger language at the time, although not my first language and so, I reasoned, it explained why I had an English accent in Italian. Had I acquired Italian earlier, during my years in France, I might have had a French accent or no accent at all.

Finding the source of an accent in a third language is much more complex than one might think at first. Wrembel (2012a, 2015) lists a number of factors that play a role. There is the first language acquired, the L1, which brings with it the phonetic production motor routines acquired as a child. There is also the first foreign language acquired, the L2, which has been termed the "foreign language effect." In addition, there are such factors as the chronology of the L2 and L3 acquisition, and the intensity of language use of each language. If the L2 was acquired much before the L3, and used more intensely, then it will have more influence. Before continuing with other aspects, let me describe briefly a study which shows the importance of these factors.

Wrembel (2012a) asked a number of judges, native, or near-native speakers of English, to identify the first language of a group of participants. The latter were all native speakers of Polish with very good command of French as their L2 and limited competence of English as their L3. The judges only heard speech samples of their L3, that is, English, and had to choose their native tongue (L1) from a list which included English, French, German, Polish, Spanish, and Other. The judges correctly identified the first language as Polish in 63% of the cases and French in 16% of the case. This is in line with the first factor given above, the first language acquired. The second factor, the first foreign language, gets some support, but maybe not as much as it could have. The reason is that English had in fact been the speakers' second language chronologically (their first contact with it had been in primary school) whereas French had been their third language chronologically (they started acquiring it in secondary school). But then, French had take over as their stronger foreign language.

In another study that same year, Wrembel (2012b) did the same experiment with speakers whose L2 was English this time and whose L3 was French. Thus English was the L2 both in terms of chronology of acquisition and intensity of language use. The judges heard them speak French, their L3. The results gave the same L1-L2 order, but the percentage was closer between the L1, Polish (47%) and the L2, English (30%), showing thereby the importance of the first language (Polish) and the first foreign language acquired (English).

Among additional factors which play a role in the accent of an L3, we find the level of proficiency of the L2. A strong L2 will influence the L3 more than a weak L2. And another factor is the typological distance between the languages. If there is a close proximity between either the L1 or the L2, and the L3, then the L3 will take on characteristics of the language concerned. Of course, several of the factors listed in this section will be at work simultaneously which will lead L3 accents to sometimes be influenced by both the L1 and the L2. Finally, one can also find cases where the L1 is being impacted by the L2 and/or L3. This can happen, for example when the L1 is used much less than the other two due language loss.

References

Baker, Colin, and Sylvia Prys Jones. 1998. *Encyclopedia of Bilingualism and Bilingual Education*. Clevedon, UK: Multilingual Matters.

Beaujour, Elizabeth. 1989. *Alien Tongues: Bilingual Russian Writers of the "First" Emigration*. Ithaca, NY: Cornell University Press.

Bent, Tessa. 2018. "Development of unfamiliar accent comprehension continues through adolescence." *Journal of Child Language*, 45: 1400–1411.

Bongaerts, Theo, Brigitte Planken, and Erik Schils. 1995. "Can late starters attain a native accent in a foreign language? A test of the critical period." In *The Age Factor in Second Language Acquisition*, edited by David Singleton and Zsolt Lengyel, 30-50. Clevedon: Multilingual Matters 30–50.

Crowther, Dustin, Pavel Trofimovich, Kazuya Saito, and Talia Isaacs. 2018. "Linguistic dimensions of l2 accentedness and comprehensibility vary across speaking tasks." *Studies in Second Language Acquisition*, 40: 443–457.

Flege, James E. 1984. "The detection of French accent by American listeners." *Journal of the Acoustical Society of America*, 76 (3): 692–707.

Flege, James E. 2009. "Give input a chance!" In *Input Matters in SLA*, edited by Thorsten Piske and Martha Young-Scholten, 175–190. Bristol: Multilingual Matters.

Flege, James E. 2012. "The role of input in second language (L2) speech learning." *VIth International Conference on Native and Non-native Accents of English*. Łódź, Poland, December 6–8.

Flege, James E. 2018. "L2 speech learning: Time to change the paradigm." *Conference given at the Center for Research on Bilingualism*, Stockholm University, June 11, 2018.

Flege, James E. 2019. "A non-critical period for second-language learning." In *A Sound Approach to Language Matters – In Honor of Ocke-Schwen Bohn*, edited by Anne Mette Nyvad, Michaela Hejná, Anders Højen, Anna Bothe Jespersen and Mette Hjortshøj Sørensen, 501–541. Denmark: Department of English, School of Communication & Culture, Aarhus University.

Flege, James E, and Ian R. A. MacKay. 2011. "What accounts for 'age' effects on overall degree of foreign accent?" In *Achievements and Perspectives in SLA of Speech: New Sounds 2010*, vol. II, edited by Magdalena Wrembel, Malgorzata Kul and Katarzyna Dziubalska-Kolaczyk, 65–82. Bern: Peter Lang.

Flege, James E., Murray J. Munro, and Ian R. A. MacKay. 1995. "Factors affecting strength of perceived foreign accent in a second language." *Journal of the Acoustical Society of America*, 97 (5): 3125–3134.

Flege, James E., Grace Yeni-Komshian, and Serena Liu. 1999. "Age constraints on second-language acquisition." *Journal of Memory and Language*, 41: 78–104.

Grosjean, François. 2010. *Bilingual: Life and Reality*. Cambridge, MA: Harvard University Press.

Hopp, Holger, and Monika S. Schmid. 2013. "Perceived foreign accent in first language attrition and second language acquisition: The impact of age of acquisition and bilingualism." *Applied Psycholinguistics*, 34: 361–394.

Huston, Nancy. 2002. *Losing North: Musings on Land, Tongue and Self*. Toronto: McArthur.

Huston, Nancy, and Leila Sebbar. 1986. *Lettres parisiennes: Histoires d'exil*. Paris: Editions J'ai lu.

Isaacs, Talia, and Pavel Trofimovich. 2012. "Deconstructing comprehensibility: Identifying the linguistic influences on listeners' L2 comprehensibility ratings." *Studies in Second Language Acquisition*, 34: 475–505.

Kang, Okim. 2010. "Relative salience of suprasegmental features on judgments of L2 comprehensibility and accentedness." *System*, 38: 301–305.

Lenneberg, Eric H. 1967. *Biological Foundations of Language*. New York: John Wiley & Sons.

Long, Michael H. 1988. "Maturational constraints on language development." *University of Hawai'i Working Papers in ESL*, 7 (1): 1–53.

Moyer, Alene. 2007. "Do language attitudes determine accent? A study of bilinguals in the USA." *Journal of Multilingual and Multicultural Development*, 28 (6): 502–518.

Moyer, Alene. 2013. *Foreign Accent: The Phenomenon of Non-native Speech*. Cambridge: Cambridge University Press.

Moyer, Alene. 2018. "An advantage for age? Self-concept and self-regulation as teachable foundations in second language accent." *The CATESOL Journal*, 30 (1): 95–112.

Munro, Murray, J., and Tracey M. Derwing. 1999. "Foreign accent, comprehensibility, and intelligibility in the speech of second language learners." In *Phonological Issues in Language Learning*, edited by Jonathan Leather, 285–310. Oxford, UK: Blackwell.

Nikolov, Marianne. 2000. "The Critical Period Hypothesis reconsidered: Successful adult learners of Hungarian and English." *International Review of Applied Linguistics*, 38: 109–124.

Piske, Thorsten, Ian R. A. MacKay, and James E. Flege. 2001. "Factors affecting degree of foreign accent in an L2: A review." *Journal of Phonetics*, 29: 191–215.

Wrembel, Magdalena. 2012a. "Foreign accentedness in third language acquisition: The case of L3 English." In *Third Language Acquisition in Adulthood*, edited by Jennifer Cabrelli Amaro, Suzanne Flynn and Jason Rothman, 281–309. Amsterdam: John Benjamins.

Wrembel, Magdalena. 2012b. "Foreign accent ratings in third language acquisition: The case of L3 French." In *Teaching and Researching English Accents in Native and Non-Native Speakers*, edited by Ewa Waniek-Klimczak and Linda R. Shockey, 31–47. Berlin: Springer Verlag.

Wrembel, Magdalena. 2015. "Cross-linguistic influence in second vs. third language acquisition of phonology." In *Universal or Diverse Paths to English Phonology*, edited by Ulriche Gut, Robert Fuchs and Eva-Maria Wunder, 41–70. Berlin: De Gruyter Mouton.

Wrembel, Magdalena, Marta Marecka, Jakub Szewczyk, and Agnieszka Otwinowska. 2018. "The predictors of foreign-accentedness in the home language of Polish–English bilingual children." *Bilingualism: Language and Cognition*, 22 (2): 383–400.

5

Language Loss in Adults and Children

When we speak to others about languages we knew well but no longer use, we often hear statements such as: "I really should have kept up my Spanish," "I wish I could speak Chinese the way I used to as a child," or "My German is going to pot." They are often said with regret and sometimes a hint of sadness or even guilt.

Events such as changing school or employment, moving to another region or country, or losing a close family member with whom a language was used exclusively, may lead to a change in the relative importance of the languages that are used, and the greater influence of one language on the other. They may even lead to a person's bilingualism becoming dormant all the way to actual language loss. This chapter will concentrate on the latter.

One should keep in mind that language loss is simply the flip side of language acquisition and that it is just as interesting linguistically. But the attitudes towards it are very different. Whereas language acquisition is seen positively ("Isn't it wonderful that you're learning Russian!"), language loss is not talked about in such terms. Nancy Huston (2002), a Canadian writer who now lives in France, gives a short description of the way she is received back home when she visits: "You go 'home' and people can't believe their ears. *What*? You call that your *mother tongue*? Have you seen the state it's in? I don't believe it! *You've got an accent*! You keep slipping French words into your speech! ... Come on, talk normally!"

This chapter will have two parts. The first concerns language loss in adults, and the second longer part, language loss in very young children. Concerning adults, we will examine how language behavior is affected by attrition, and the search for factors that account for it. As for children, we will concentrate on those who stopped using a language, either their first or their second language, at a very young age. The question we will ask is whether remnants of the lost language can re-emerge through behavioral experiments and brain imaging. We will end with an approach, not used very often in the last 50 years, which seems to give rather startling results in this area.

Language Loss in Adults

The field that examines language loss is called language attrition and the bilinguals undergoing such changes, language attriters. When I asked one of the leading researchers in this field, Monika Schmid (2019), whether attrition involves the loss of language

The Mysteries of Bilingualism, First Edition. François Grosjean.

knowledge, or language use, however labored and hesitant, or both, her answer was quite clear: "If you define 'knowledge' to be the deeply rooted fundamental structure of the language which allows you to produce and understand it in the first place, and 'use' as any concrete instance of it, such as an individual utterance, language attrition tends to affect mainly 'use.'" This, she said, concerns people who are older than 12 years.

To illustrate language loss in adults, we will start by reporting on a case study of an elderly German–American who stopped using her mother tongue in her 20s. We will then report on some experimental studies that have examined the variables involved in language loss, and will mention the difficult search for factors that may underlie loss.

A Case Study

This is the story of BJ as reported on by Stolberg and Münch (2009). She was born in Lower Silesia – at the time part of Germany – in the mid-1920s. She lived there until she was 28 and then emigrated to the United States where she had been living for almost 50 years at the time the researchers met her. She had married an American and they spoke English together almost exclusively. She had only loose ties to a relative living in Germany and her exposure to German in daily life was practically non-existent.

The two researchers, both German–English bilinguals, recorded her speaking German in free, informal conversations, over a span of four years. The topics included the informant's childhood in Germany, her life during World War II, her work experience in Germany and the USA, the reasons for her emigration to the USA, her life there, and her art work. The interlocutors were in a German bilingual mode during the interviews, 15 in all, that is, they spoke German but would code-switch and borrow from English from time to time.

Stolberg and Münch found that despite the fact that BJ rarely used her German in everyday life, she was able to keep up a rather fluent conversation in the language, conveying a wide range of concepts, ideas, and thoughts. Of course, her fluency was less good than in English: she produced more self-interruptions in German (in the order of 3–5% per 100 words) and far less in English (0.3–3%). She also produced deviations of various types. At the lexical level, she had word-finding problems, and made errors on expressions and idioms. Her morphology was sometimes problematic (she would use the wrong case, gender, and plural markings), and her syntax suffered with its incomplete structures, deviant verb placements, and wrong word order.

At first, BJ would switch to English with the interviewers out of need since she couldn't find the right German word or expression to fit the concept she had in mind. By the end of the four-year period, however, it was mainly for discourse reasons that she would switch as when signaling a quotation or making a comment. In general, by the time the recordings were over at the end of the four years, and because these conversations had allowed her to practice her German, she had fewer lexical retrieval problems, produced less syntactic deviations, and was noticeably more fluent than at the beginning.

The researchers concluded that BJ's problem was one of accessibility to her linguistic knowledge and not to the knowledge itself. According to them, her German language proficiency over the years seemed to have been affected surprisingly little by language loss, leaving the impression that much of her German was preserved at the level it was at when she emigrated. They concluded that a first language is preserved in bilinguals like BJ who emigrate as adults and that it can be recovered quickly as soon as the language is used once again.

What Stolberg and Münch report on with BJ is confirmed by other researchers in the field. Thus, Köpke and Genevska-Hanke (2018) state that attrition of a highly entrenched first language is a phenomenon affecting language processing only and that it is likely to regress quickly after exposure. As for Yilmaz and Schmid (2018), they state that attrition is due to the growing presence of the second language and is primarily a consequence of the slowed down mechanisms involved in speech processing. The degree of atrophy of the knowledge of the first language is minimal in adult bilinguals, they add.

Manifestations of Language Attrition

Everyday observations of people using a language they are losing reveal a number of characteristics: hesitant language production as they search for appropriate words or expressions; pronunciation (sounds, intonation) that is marked increasingly by the other language or languages; "odd" syntactic structures or expressions that are borrowed from the stronger language; frequent code-switching, borrowing, and interferences as the person calls on the dominant language for help; as well as many writing difficulties, particularly in spelling but also at other linguistic levels.

Language comprehension is less affected, although the person may not know new words and new colloquialisms in the language that is being forgotten. People who are in this extended process of forgetting a language often avoid using the language because they no longer feel sure about their knowledge of it and they do not want to make too many mistakes. If they do have to use it, they may cut short a conversation so as not to have to show openly how far the attrition has progressed (Grosjean 2010).

Over the years, researchers have undertaken a number of studies to confirm observations such as these. Thus, for example, Schmid and Yilmaz (2018) point to accentedness (changes in the segmental and prosodic features of the language leading some attriters to be perceived as non-native), fluency (attriters sometimes show a slower speech rate and have higher number of pauses, repetitions, and self corrections), lexical access (they are less productive at generating items in verbal fluency tasks), overt pronouns (they add pronouns to their sentences when natives would not do so), etc.

These characteristics have been observed in spontaneous speech but also in experimental studies. For example, Schmid (2007) studied the speech production of first language speakers of German who had lived, on the one hand, in the Greater Vancouver area for an average of 37 years and, on the other, in the Netherlands for an average of 34 years. These attriters were asked to produce in German as many items as they could that belonged to two semantic fields (animals, fruit, and vegetables) in 60 seconds. The results of both groups were lower than that of a control group of German speakers in Germany.

In a second task, they had to watch a ten-minute sequence from Modern Times, a silent Charlie Chaplin movie, and retell what had happened in their own words. Here the two groups of attriters produced more pauses than the controls, more repetitions, and made more self corrections. All of these differences were statistically significant.

In another study, Schmid and Yilmaz (2021) examined the attrition of Turkish and Moroccan long term migrants in The Netherlands, and compared them to reference groups in their country of origin, Turkey and Morocco. In a first task, they were interviewed about daily life in their countries of origin, as well as about their hobbies, holidays, language habits, experiences as migrants, and so on. The authors found their speech was lexically less diverse than the control groups, and that it was more disfluent.

In a second task, they asked their participants to do a picture naming experiment. They presented them with a set of pictures which they had to name. This task required that they lexicalize concepts into words in the same way one does so when planning and selecting lexical items when speaking. Once again, the attriters did less well. Their response times were slower than those of the controls.

In Search of Factors that Account for Language Loss

When one reads the literature on language loss, one is struck by the difficulty researchers have had to find clear factors that account for loss in adult bilinguals, with one exception though. Schmid (2002) was able to establish a link between the persecution that individual speakers have suffered and the degree of language attrition attained. In her study, German–Jewish Holocaust survivors who had managed to emigrate showed a high degree of loss of German many years later when she interviewed them.

But apart from this exceptional case, things are far less clear. As Köpke (2019) writes, for many years there was an assumption that attrition in migrants results from lack of use of the language, in conjunction with a long period since immigration as measured by the length of residence (LoR) in the new country. Rather surprisingly however, and despite repeated attempts, research did not manage to demonstrate a direct relationship between the degree of attrition and frequency of use, LoR, or even attitudes towards the languages.

Schmid and Jarvis (2014) write that there is only one language use factor which is a significant predictor of attrition. It is the use of the first language for professional purposes: the more migrants use it at work, the less they show attrition. Their reasoning is as follows: in everyday life, the migrants who use their first language informally do so with other bilinguals such as family members and friends, and hence are in a bilingual language mode (Grosjean 2001; see also Chapter 7). Thus, they do not need to deactivate, or inhibit, their other language. Schmid and Köpke (2017) explain that frequent use of the first language where code-switching is normal may trigger contact-induced changes in that language as shown, for example, by Grosjean and Py (1991). In a professional context, however, migrants are usually in a monolingual language mode (language mixing is not appropriate) and they resist the intrusion of the other language. This is a great help for the maintenance of the first language if and when it is used in this situation.

A word of caution needs to be expressed to end this first part. Both Yilmaz and Schmid (2018) and Schmid and Yilmaz (2018) remind us that attriters form extremely heterogeneous groups. Some attriters remain within the native range in their first language while others fall squarely outside it. They also differ on personal background factors such as age of acquisition, education, and length of residence in the second language (L2) country, as well as social and psychological variables linked to attitude, motivation, and affiliation. Many of these factors interact with others, leading to a complex web of interrelated factors. Hence, the fact that the impact of specific predictor variables has remained largely inconclusive.

Of course, if the shift to another language takes place in childhood, and is complete, then attrition will indeed take place, and may well be quite dramatic. As Schmid (2019) states, children under 12 years old, "can and do lose (...) languages, almost entirely, if they stop using them." We will now turn to this aspect.

Language Loss in Young Children

Children can lose a language for many different reasons. Keijzer and de Bot (2019) mention having parents who separate or remarry, having new caretakers, staying abroad for a length of time or permanently, such as in immigration, going through adoption, attending daycare or a new school, or simply as a result of a change in the family language. A well-known example of language loss in a child was reported by anthropologist Robbins Burling (Burling 1978). His family had moved to the Garo Hills district of Assam in India when their son, Stephen, was sixteen- months-old. There, Stephen quickly acquired Garo since he spent a lot of his time with a local nurse.

When the family left the Garo region a year and a half later, Stephen, was bilingual in Garo and English, maybe with a slight dominance in Garo. He translated and switched from one language to the other as bilingual children do. The family then traveled across India and Stephen tried to speak Garo with people he met, but he soon realized that they did not speak it. The last time he tried to use the language was in the plane going back to the United States. He thought that the Malayan boy sitting next to him was a Garo and, as Robbins Burling writes, "A torrent of Garo tumbled forth as if all the pent-up speech of those weeks had been suddenly let loose." Within six months of their departure from the Garo Hills, Stephen was having problems with the simplest of Garo words.

At the end of his article, Robbins Burling raised an issue that researchers are interested in currently: "I hope that some day it will be possible to take him back to the Garo Hills and to discover whether hidden deep in his unconscious he may not still retain a remnant of his former fluency in Garo that might be reawakened if he again came in contact with the language."

I wrote to Robbins Burling a few years ago and asked him if Stephen had indeed gone back to the Garo Hills. He replied that he hadn't but that he had acquired Burmese at age six in Burma. He spoke it quite fluently for a while but then forgot it. Robbins Burling finished his message by stating that in his early childhood, Stephen had learned three languages and had forgotten two!

Early Experimental Studies on Lost Languages

Some twenty-five years after Burling's fascinating case study, scientists started looking for the remnants of a language that was forgotten in very early childhood. In a first study, a group of Paris-based researchers (Pallier et al. 2003) tested adults who had been born in Korea and who had been adopted by French families in their early childhood (between the ages of 3 and 8). There were eight in all with a mean age of 26.8 years at the time of testing. All claimed that they had completely forgotten their native language, Korean, and all spoke French fluently with no perceptible foreign accent.

Along with a control group of eight French monolingual speakers, the adopted adults were asked to do three tasks. The first was a language identification task in which they had to recognize Korean sentences amid other sentences spoken in five different languages. They had to provide on a scale from 1 to 7 a degree of confidence that the sentence was in Korean and not in any of the four other languages. The second task was a word recognition task in which they chose which of two Korean words, presented orally, was the correct translation of the French word displayed on a screen. Finally, they did a fragment detection task whereby they had to ascertain whether a short speech fragment came from a sentence which could be in one of four languages, one of them being Korean. During this task, brain imaging (fMRI) was performed.

The results obtained were clear and did not favor the remnants hypothesis. The adults who had been adopted as very young children did not differ in any way from the monolingual controls. Their ratings in the language identification task were similar to those of the controls. They also behaved like them in the word recognition task and, similarly, they could not detect fragments from Korean sentences any better than the controls. As for the brain imaging results, the cortical regions that showed greater response to the known language, French, were similar in the adopted participants and in the French controls. The only difference was that the extent of the activation was larger in the controls. The authors proposed that the native French participants' greater experience with French may have resulted in this widening of the cortical maps for language processing. They concluded that the adoptees' native language, Korean, had in a large part been lost and that it had been replaced by French, the language of their new environment.

Instead of putting this question to rest, the study encouraged others to investigate further the issue but with an additional slant – making sure that there was some reexposure to the lost language in participants, at least some of them. A few years before these studies were undertaken, I had gone to interview Noam Chomsky on bilingualism and I had asked him whether a language could be totally lost. He responded that even if a person can no longer use a language, he/she can relearn the language much faster than someone who has never known that language. According to him, "There's got to be a residue of the language somewhere .... You can't really erase the system."

Ventureyra, Pallier, and Yoo (2004), from the same research group in Paris, divided the adult Korean adoptees they used into two groups: nine had not been reexposed to Korean since adoption whereas nine others had been to Korea in the past four years for stays ranging from 10 days to 6 months. Would the latter group show some evidence of the lost language? The stimuli that were used were Korean pseudowords made up of two consonant-vowel syllables. The first syllable always started with a consonant specific to Korean and was followed by one of three vowels. The second syllable was always the same, [ma]. These pseudowords were paired with a second pseudoword that was the same as the first pseudoword or that contained a different vowel or a different first consonant. The task the participants were given was a phoneme discrimination task in which they had to determine whether two stimuli were identical or not. To do so, they were asked to press a same or different button as quickly and as accurately as possible.

The results obtained were similar to the ones Pallier et al. (2003) had reported. The adoptees did not perceive the differences between the Korean phonemes any better than native French controls who had never been exposed to Korean. And the adoptees who had been reexposed to Korean behaved similarly to those who had not with one tiny exception. Faced with this largely negative evidence, the authors concluded that the Korean adoptees had become like native French speakers in their perception of Korean consonants.

Could even more reexposure to the first language manage to change the results? This is the question that a research team in Sweden asked itself a few years later (Hyltenstam et al. 2009). They compared two groups who were current or former students of Korean. One group was made up of adult Korean adoptees who had arrived in Sweden as children and who had not been exposed to Korean for an average of 22 years. They had then studied Korean for three years on average. The other group was made up of native Swedes who were also current or former students of Korean. They had spent much more time studying Korean than had the adoptees. Both groups were given a perception test involving Korean consonants that could be aspirated, unaspirated or glottalized.

They listened to pairs of words and had to decide whether they heard the same word or different words by pressing one of two keys on a computer keyboard.

Once again, there was no significant difference between the group of adoptees and the group of native Swedes. But once again, there was a glimmer of something present, as in the Ventureyra, Pallier, and Hi-Yon study: the group of adoptees showed much more variation in their results. One-third of them scored higher than all the native Swedes and this in spite of the fact that several of the native Swedish learners had had more advantageous learning conditions than the adoptees and were considerably more advanced in their general Korean proficiency. The authors' conclusion was that if reexposure to the first language takes place over a certain period of time and is intensive, then remnants of a seemingly lost language are more likely to be retrieved.

A Breakthrough in This Research

Bowers, Matthys, and Gage (2009), also convinced that reexposure could be critical, decided to see if a period of intense phonetic training could help participants regain sensitivity to a phoneme contrast in their childhood language. They worked with seven native adult English speakers, not adoptees this time, who had spoken either Hindi or Zulu as children due to their parents' work abroad. They too had no remaining knowledge of their childhood languages at the time of testing. The stimuli consisted of pairs of Hindi and Zulu consonant-vowel-consonant syllables that are difficult to distinguish. For half of them, the two syllables started with the same phoneme; for the other half, they started with a critical contrastive phoneme. The task of the participants was to listen to each pair and to decide whether the first sound of the syllables started with the same phoneme or not by pressing a same or different key. They were given feedback (correct vs. incorrect) after each response. Participants did thirty sessions approximately one per day, with 112 pairs per session. As the senior author of the paper wrote to me via email, "(it was) not the easiest experiment to run"!

The question asked was whether the participants with a Hindi or Zulu background would selectively learn to perceive the contrasts they had been exposed to and would do so more quickly than control participants. The results were quite clear. First, the controls with no previous exposure to Hindi or Zulu showed no learning over the thirty sessions. Second, and this is the breakthrough, the English individuals who had lost these languages, and who were under age 40, selectively relearned sound contrasts they once knew – the Hindi ones for those who had known Hindi, and the Zulu ones for those who had known Zulu. In fact, their improvement was so dramatic that by the end of the 30 sessions, their performance for the forgotten phonemes approached native performance. Interestingly, the individuals over 40 failed to show any learning, and were not different from the controls.

The authors concluded that their findings provided clear evidence of preserved knowledge of a forgotten childhood language. Early but time-limited exposure to a language, according to them, has a long-lasting impact on a person's ability to relearn that language, even after complete separation from the language. As for why only the participants under 40 showed the effect, they proposed that the older individuals, over the course of 40 or more years of disuse of Hindi or Zulu, may have lost the knowledge they once had of these languages. They added a final point: the knowledge of the forgotten language in the under 40 participants emerged only after 15 to 20 sessions (out of 30) – quite a long time, therefore – and this might explain why previous studies failed to show any preserved knowledge. It was only by employing a sensitive behavioral measure, namely relearning of specific contrasts over several weeks, that they were able to reveal the preserved knowledge.

At the time the study by Bowers et al. was done, in 2009, it was clearly the one that signaled most clearly that there are remnants of languages that were forgotten in childhood. A few years later, in Canada, Pierce et al. (2014) sought to find neural evidence for this by using brain imaging. They tested three groups of young people whose mean age was 13 years old. One group was made up of adoptees who had come from China to Quebec when they were one year old. Since then, they had grown up speaking French only and had no longer been exposed to Chinese. The second group was composed of Chinese/French bilinguals who had continued speaking Chinese at home and had used French everywhere else. And the third group was made up of monolingual French speakers who knew no Chinese whatsoever.

The brain activation of the participants was examined using functional magnetic resonance imaging (fMRI) while they were doing a Chinese lexical tone discrimination task. In this task, they were asked to listen to pairs of phrases containing three syllables that were either pseudowords (e.g., da-shao-fa) or non-speech hummed versions of the same syllables. Both pseudowords and their hummed versions contained tone information. The two elements of the pair were either identical, or the final syllable varied on tonal information. Participants were asked to respond with a button press indicating whether the final syllable was the same or different in the pair.

What is interesting in this study is that it used tones which are processed differently depending on whether one knows a tonal language or not. Thus, the Mandarin word "ma" can mean "mother," "hemp," "horse" or "scold" to listeners of Chinese depending on the tone used, whereas the meaning remains the same ("mine") for listeners of French despite the change in tone. In the case of these French listeners, it is the right hemisphere's frontal and temporal regions that process acoustic frequency information that are activated when listening to lexical tones. But it is the left hemisphere language regions that are activated in Chinese listeners since tones are linguistically relevant in their language. The authors reasoned that because lexical tone is not present in the adoptees' postadoption language environment, any native-like activation to this linguistic element must be due to the maintenance of early established representations.

How did the three groups of participants react to the stimuli they heard? In the monolingual French speakers, only the right hemisphere was activated, more precisely the right temporal regions which process complex, but non-linguistic, auditory signals. In the bilingual participants, who knew and used both Chinese and French, the largest peaks of activation were in the left hemisphere (left temporal regions) showing thereby that they were using their linguistic knowledge of tones to process what they heard. What about the adoptees who had functionally lost their Chinese and had no conscious recollection of it? Their neural patterns matched those of the bilinguals showing thereby that they maintained their early neural representations over time even though they had received no Chinese language for some twelve years! The authors concluded that the representations acquired early in life are indeed present and can be revealed if the right procedure is used.

The results obtained by both the Bowers et al. study, and the Pierce et al. study are very compelling and do seem to show that lost languages can be reawakened under the right conditions. Did later studies confirm these findings? Not totally. For example, Zhou and Broersma (2014) tested the discrimination of tone contrasts in Chinese and Cantonese adoptees in The Netherlands while they were still children, some five years after adoption. Given this rather short period of time since adoption, they expected to see them do better than Dutch controls. But they didn't, either before, during or after training. The authors could only conclude that it took them very little time to lose their sensitivity to their birth language tone contrasts after adoption.

Choi, Broersma, and Cutler (2017a) also tested Dutch adoptees, from Korea this time and as adults, and found mixed results. They trained them on their birth-language speech sounds and compared their initial learning trajectory to those of closely matched Dutch control participants. All were asked to identify Korean voiceless stop consonants in pseudo-words and were trained on them. They were tested before training, midway through, and after training. Overall, the adoptees and the controls did not differ from one another (there was no group effect) but an interesting thing happened: the adoptees showed a faster learning curve as shown by their results at the midway test, before the controls caught up with them at the final test. The authors concluded that the adoptees had retained phonological knowledge which was revealed in the rapidity with which learning developed.

Of course, as more research is conducted in this domain, the story will become clearer but also probably more complicated. Others factors may be found to have some importance. For example, the Pierce et al. (2014) study found that the children who were adopted at later ages showed more activation in a part of the left hemisphere, the planum temporale, than those who were adopted earlier. So, the amount of input that a language received before being forgotten will probably play a role. Other questions are what exactly was acquired linguistically before attrition occurred, how sensitive is the research task used, what type of reexposure or learning is needed to "reawaken" a language, how long should training last, and so on.

The Production of a Lost Language

The vast majority of studies trying to find remnants of a lost language have used perception tasks. What would happen if one studied the production of the language? Choi, Cutler, and Broersma (2017b) did just that. They asked whether residual knowledge of the birth language by international adoptees not only helps them relearn a perceptual discrimination but also supports more efficient speech production.

They first trained their participants, adult Dutch adoptees from Korea, to listen to voiceless stop consonants (see above). At the outset and at the end of the intensive perceptual training, over a period of 10 to 12 days, they asked them to do a rapid-repetition task. The participants heard pseudo-words one at a time and were asked to repeat each one immediately. To help them, they saw at the same time a symbol of the consonant to be produced. The participants' recording were then given to native listeners of Korean who were asked to do two things: identify the consonant by pressing on one of three keys, and rate the consonant's pronunciation on a scale of 1 (very poor) to 4 (very good).

The results were encouraging. Identification accuracy was comparable across groups (adoptees, controls) at the beginning of the training period, but it was significantly higher for the adoptees at the end. As for the ratings, the same pattern of results was found; no difference at the onset of training for the two groups, but a significant difference at the end. The adoptee's production improved significantly more across the training period than that of the controls. Basically, their sounds became more identifiable and more highly rated. The authors concluded that the residual knowledge of the birth language may be helping them to relearn a perceptual discrimination and also make production more efficient.

Speech production, of course, is much more than pronouncing consonants and vowels, and one wonders how future research will be able to tap into other processing levels leading to continuous speech. Is there a way to help speakers reawaken, or have access to, a forgotten language so that they can actually speak it? This is precisely what two truly fascinating studies that used hypnosis attempted to do in the last century. The first was done in 1962 by Arvid Ås, and the second in 1970 by Erika Fromm. There is a more recent study by Footnick (2007) but since it is not clear how much the speaker's lost language was recovered through practice, outside of hypnosis, we will not describe it further.

Ås (1962) reports on an 18-year old freshman at Stanford University who had spoken Swedish in Finland in his early years. Then, following his emigration to the United States with his mother, and her second remarriage, Swedish was no longer spoken in the home. He was about eight years old at the time and from then on, he simply didn't use Swedish since he didn't need it.

When Ås met him and had hypnotic sessions with him, the young man maintained that he had forgotten Swedish entirely except for a couple of words. And yet, when he was age-regressed to first grade, that is, mentally taken back in time to that age, he showed that he still remembered a good deal of Swedish. For example, a Swedish-speaking assistant asked in Swedish: "Where are you?," and the freshman replied in English: "In class." Before hypnosis he did not understand the Swedish question, "How old are you?," but during age-regression he answered in Swedish this time, "Five years." And when asked to count to ten in Swedish before hypnosis, he could not recall a single number. When regressed, he correctly listed six out of ten numbers.

The author of the article also gave him a language test before hypnosis and again under hypnosis when he was age-regressed to first grade. The test comprised of simple questions or commands in Swedish that a child five years of age could respond to. For example, "How old are you?," "Do you have a brother?," "Point to your mouth," "Please stand up," "What is the color of grass?," etc. There were also cards with pictures and he was asked to name what he saw. The results showed that there was a clear improvement in the test results due to being under hypnosis and regressed to an age when he knew the language. The author concluded that the results were interesting enough to use hypnosis to attempt to recover a forgotten language.

This is precisely what Professor Erika Fromm, the famous German–American psychologist and co-founder of hypnoanalysis, went about doing. In a remarkable study, Fromm (1970) relates how she met a young Japanese–American graduate student – she called him Don – at the University of Chicago in the late sixties. On her return from Japan where she had learned some Japanese, an assistant of hers asked her to watch a hypnotic training sessions she was giving him. Don had reported that he knew and spoke no Japanese except for a handful of polite words used as a very young child. When Fromm entered the office, he was already in a deep trance, age-regressed to seven years old. She asked him a few questions in Japanese but he did not seem to understand. As she wrote in her article: "None of them seemed to strike a spark."

A few months later, in front of observers, Fromm hypnotized Don herself this time. She age-regressed him to 8 years old and they spoke in English. Then, she told him to close his eyes again and to go back further in time, to age 3. Here is what happened, according to Fromm: "For a few moments there was silence. Then, suddenly, in a high-pitched child's voice, Don broke into a stream of rapid Japanese.... He talked on and on in Japanese for about 15 to 20 minutes. He seemed to want to involve me in his Japanese talk, and so again I used any Japanese words I knew.... I was more than surprised at his flood of Japanese." Afterwards, Don was astonished to hear that apparently fluent Japanese had spurted forth from his lips.

Four months later, Fromm once again age-regressed Don during a psychotherapy session, and tape recorded him this time. When he reached age three, Fromm triggered his Japanese with a homophone (English "hi" and Japanese "hai" meaning "yes") and Don switched over to Japanese and talked happily and excitedly about a puppy he had. Fromm writes, "Apparently he had just received it. He said, 'Thank you, Mother, thank you, Mother,' and asked what the puppy's name was. Over and over he happily reiterated, 'It's mine, it's my dog, it's mine.'"

When he awoke, he said: "It was like my lips all of a sudden would move into these funny shapes. And then I would want to say something and wouldn't know what I was really saying. The words just came out and I wasn't sure whether they were real or not." He listened to the tape and he said that he understood a part of the recording, but by no means all. In the weeks that followed, Don regained progressively more knowledge of his forgotten language.

After each session, Erika Fromm had asked Don about his past and this allowed her to reconstruct his childhood. He was born in San Jose, California, five days before Pearl Harbor, and in 1942 his parents and he were put into a relocation camp. At that time he had spoken Japanese as well as English to his parents. After the war, they had moved to Utah and there he had had trouble communicating with kids on the street so his parents had stopped talking Japanese to him. English became the only language he spoke as of age four, in and out of the house.

Through lack of use, Don had forgotten Japanese. But according to Fromm there was also a repression factor at work. He had had a strong desire to be considered fully American upon leaving the relocation camp. Unconsciously, he must have felt at some point that he could better attain his goal if he knew no Japanese and spoke only English. We should note that repression of a language is not always required for it to be recovered during hypnosis, as we saw with the Ås study where the freshman had simply stopped using Swedish as a child.

It would appear therefore that a lost language may indeed be recovered under hypnosis. A word of caution is needed though: studies that have produced negative results probably exist but have not been published. In addition, some people are not easily hypnotized, and age-regression may not be used in all situations. This said, when I interacted with Christophe Pallier, the researcher who restarted this line of research at the beginning of the century, he told me that he would have loved to have replicated Fromm's study and that he does not exclude doing so in the future!

References

Ås, Arvid. 1962. "The recovery of forgotten language knowledge through hypnotic age regression: A case report." *American Journal of Clinical Hypnosis*, 5 (1): 24–29.

Bowers, Jeffrey S., Sven L. Matthys, and Suzanne H. Gage. 2009. "Preserved implicit knowledge of a forgotten childhood language." *Psychological Science*, 20 (9): 1064–1069.

Burling, Robbins. 1978. "Language development of a Garo and English-speaking child." In *Second Language Acquisition*, edited by Evelyn Hatch, 54–75. Rowley, MA: Newbury House.

Choi, Jiyoun, Mirjam Broersma, and Anne Cutler. 2017a. "Early phonology revealed by international adoptees' birth language retention." *Proceedings of the National Academy of Sciences of the United States of America (PNAS)*, 114 (28): 7307–7312.

Choi, Jiyoun, Anne Cutler, and Mirjam Broersma. 2017b. "Early development of abstract language knowledge: Evidence from perception-production transfer of birth-language memory." *Royal Society Open Science*, 4: 160660.

Footnick, Rosalie. 2007. "A hidden language: Recovery of a 'lost' language is triggered by hypnosis." In *Language Attrition: Theoretical Perspectives*, edited by Barbara Köpke, Monika S. Schmid, Merel Keijzer, and Susan Dostert, 169–187. Amsterdam: John Benjamins Publishing.

Fromm, Erika. 1970. "Age regression with unexpected reappearance of a repressed childhood language." *International Journal of Clinical and Experimental Hypnosis*, 18 (2): 79–88.

Grosjean, François. 2001. "The bilingual's language modes." In *One Mind, Two Languages: Bilingual Language Processing*, edited by Janet Nicol, 1–22. Oxford: Blackwell.

Grosjean, François. 2010. *Bilingual: Life and Reality*. Cambridge, MA: Harvard University Press.

Grosjean, François, and Bernard Py. 1991. "La restructuration d'une première langue: l'intégration de variantes de contact dans la compétence de migrants bilingues." *La Linguistique*, 27: 35–60.

Huston, Nancy. 2002. *Losing North*. Toronto, Ontario: McCarthur & Co.

Hyltenstam, Kenneth, Emanuel Bylund, Niclas Abrahamsson, and Hyeon-Sook Park. 2009. "Dominant-language replacement: The case of international adoptees." *Bilingualism: Language and Cognition*, 12 (2): 121–140.

Keijzer, Merel, and Kees de Bot. 2019. "Unlearning and relearning of languages from childhood to later adulthood." In *The Cambridge Handbook of Bilingualism*, edited by Annick De Houwer and Lourdes Ortega, 267–285. Cambridge: Cambridge University Press.

Köpke, Barbara. 2019. "First language attrition: From bilingual to monolingual proficiency?" In *The Cambridge Handbook of Bilingualism*, edited by Annick de Houwer and Lourdes Ortega, 349–365. Cambridge, UK: Cambridge University Press.

Köpke, Barbara, and Dobrinka Genevska-Hanke. 2018. "First language attrition and dominance: Same same or different?" *Frontiers in Psychology*, 9: 1963.

Pallier, Christophe, Stanislas Dehaene, Jean-Baptiste Poline, Denis LeBihan, Anne-Marie Argenti, Emmanuel Dupoux, and Jacques Mehler. 2003. "Brain imaging of language plasticity in adopted adults: Can a second language replace a first?" *Cerebral Cortex*, 13: 155–161.

Pierce, Lara J., Denise Klein, Jen-Kai Chen, Audrey Delcenserie, and Fred Genesee. 2014. "Mapping the unconscious maintenance of a lost first language." *Proceedings of the National Academy of Science (PNAS)*, December 2, 2014, 111 (48): 17314–17319.

Schmid, Monika S. 2002. *First Language Attrition, Use and Maintenance: The Case of German Jews in Anglophone Countries*. Amsterdam: John Benjamins.

Schmid, Monika S. 2007. "The role of L1 use for L1 attrition." In *Language Attrition: Theoretical Perspectives*, edited by Barbara Köpke, Monika S. Schmid, Merel Keijzer, and Susan Dostert, 135–153. Amsterdam: John Benjamins.

Schmid, Monika S. 2019. Interview "Understanding language loss: Why and how do bilinguals lose a language." In François Grosjean's blog, "Life as a bilingual," *Psychology Today*, https://www.psychologytoday.com/intl/blog/life-bilingual/201908/understanding-language-loss.

Schmid, Monika S., and Scott Jarvis. 2014. "Lexical access and lexical diversity in first language attrition." *Bilingualism: Language and Cognition*, 17: 729–748.

Schmid, Monika S., and Barbara Köpke. 2017. "The relevance of first language attrition to theories of bilingual development." *Linguistic Approaches to Bilingualism*, 7 (6): 637–667.

Schmid, Monika S., and Gülsen Yilmaz. 2018. "Predictors of language dominance: An integrated analysis of first language attrition and second language acquisition in late bilinguals." *Frontiers of Psychology*, 9: article 1306.

Schmid, Monika S., and Gülsen Yilmaz. 2021. "Lexical access in L1 attrition: Competition vs. frequency. A comparison of Turkish and Moroccan attriters in the Netherlands." *Applied Linguistics*, 1–27. DOI: 10.1093/applin/amab006.

Stolberg, Doris, and Alexandra Münch. 2009. "'Die Muttersprache vergisst man nicht' – Or do you? A case study in L1 attrition and its (partial) reversal." *Bilingualism: Language and Cognition*, 13 (1): 19–31.

Ventureyra, Valérie, Christophe Pallier, and Hi-Yon Yoo. 2004. "The loss of first language phonetic perception in adopted Koreans." *Journal of Neurolinguistics*, 17: 79–91.

Yilmaz, Gülsen, and Monika S. Schmid. 2018. "First language attrition and bilingualism: Adult speakers." In *Bilingual Cognition and Language: The State of the Science across Its Subfields*, edited by David Miller, Fatih Bayram, Jason Rothman, and Ludovica Serratrice, 225–249. Amsterdam: John Benjamins.

Zhou, Wencui, and Mirjam Broersma. 2014. "Perception of birth language tone contrasts by adopted Chinese children." Fourth International Symposium on Tonal Aspects of Languages (TAL-2014), 63–66. Nijmegen, The Netherlands. ISCAA Archive, May 13–16, 2014. http://www.isca-speech.org/archive.

6

Brain Injury and Bilingualism

Communication with language(s) is so much part of our lives that we take it for granted. However, when it breaks down, we suddenly realize how crucial it is to our existence. Over the years, researchers have been intrigued by bilinguals with aphasia, that is those bilinguals or multilinguals who suffer language and speech impairment due to brain damage. They are the object of this chapter.

According to the National Aphasia Association,[1] aphasia is an impairment of language affecting the production or comprehension of speech and the ability to read or write. Aphasia is always due to injury to the brain, most commonly from a stroke, particularly in older individuals. Brain injuries resulting in aphasia may also arise from head trauma, from brain tumors, or from infections. As concerns bilinguals, Peñaloza and Kiran (2019) write that bilingual aphasia can be defined as the impairment of one or both languages in bilingual speakers that is not always followed by equal degrees of recovery across languages.

We will start this chapter with a personal testimony of aphasia. The person is quadrilingual and was an active business executive until suffering a stroke which paralyzed the right side of her body and left her unable to utter a single sound. We will relate the first two years of her efforts to recover the use of her languages.

We will then enter the domain of language impairment and recovery patterns observed in bilinguals with aphasia. The majority show parallel recovery: their languages are similarly impaired and they are restored at the same rate. But there are also other types of recovery, such as differential, blended, selective, and successive. Some are particularly intriguing such as antagonistic, and alternating antagonistic, recoveries.

This will be followed by the factors that account for the impairment bilinguals with aphasia suffer in their languages and for their patterns of recovery. Many have been proposed over the years and it is only by analyzing a large number of studies using meta-analysis that we are starting to isolate a few that appear to play major roles.

We will end with language mixing in bilinguals with aphasia. Some mix their languages when speaking and it has long been thought that this was due to their pathology. This may be true for some but to ascertain that this is so, great care needs to be taken when testing them so as to exclude communicative strategies that call upon both languages.

[1] https://www.aphasia.org/aphasia-definitions.

The Mysteries of Bilingualism, First Edition. François Grosjean.

A Personal Testimony

Back in 2019, Dr. Valerie Lim, a speech-language therapist, contacted me to tell me that one of her patients, Isabelle K., was a multilingual with aphasia who was willing to be interviewed. I was thrilled as a personal testimony can be of interest to others recovering from aphasia, their family members and friends, and the general public. It can also be motivating for the person herself who is struggling to recuperate her language(s). I conducted the interview and published it on my blog, *Life as a Bilingual.*[2] In what follows, I will summarize it as it raises interesting aspects that I will discuss later in the chapter.

Isabelle K, a business executive living and working in Singapore, is of mixed descent with a Japanese father and a Swedish mother. She was born in Sweden but lived until age 11 in Japan before moving to the United Kingdom for her secondary schooling and university studies, and then to Sweden for three years of postgraduate studies. She then lived in Paris with her French-speaking Belgian husband before moving to Singapore.

On the language front, English has been Isabelle K.'s main language. It was used in her home when she was young as well as in the international school she started attending at age 6. She then used it in the United Kingdom during her many years there, with her husband, and in her work. Her mother taught her Swedish at age 7, and she also learned Japanese when in Japan. There were Japanese classes in her school and she spoke Japanese with her grandparents and sometimes her father. A fourth language, French, was learned as a foreign language in the UK and only became a language of communication when Isabelle and her husband lived in Paris for two years. In sum, and this will be important for what follows, English was the language most used before her injury, followed by Swedish and Japanese, and lastly, and to a much lesser extent, French.

In August 2017, Isabelle K. was finishing a conference call in her office in Singapore when she suffered an ischemic stroke, that is, an artery in her brain became blocked. She was rushed to hospital where the doctors performed a decompressive craniectomy – part of her skull was removed to release the pressure – and after a few days, she regained consciousness. The right side of her body was paralyzed (hemiplegia) and she could not speak any of her languages.

Her comprehension was affected less, as is often the case. She could understand English and some French when she was still in hospital. Five weeks later, she realized she could understand her mother speaking Swedish when she skyped her, and eight weeks later, she noticed she could understand Japanese.

Her speech production took much more time. A few weeks after her operation, on the day of her birthday, and thanks to the music therapy she undertook, she managed to sing Happy Birthday in English. Her reading of English also came back early on. However, it took her about a year to be able to speak some Swedish, and 16 months for some Japanese. French was the last language to return in speech production.

Two years after her stroke, when she did the interview, she stated that she could say 70–75% of what she wanted to say in English when she was perky, but only 50% when she was tired. Her writing of English had improved greatly but it was not at pre-stroke level. She could speak Swedish, and she could read it at a 90% level, but her writing was at a 60% level. Japanese was only coming back slowly. As for French, her weakest language, she had reached a 60% level in oral comprehension after two years, but she could only say a few words in it.

[2] https://www.psychologytoday.com/intl/blog/life-bilingual/201909/multilingual-aphasia-personal-testimony.

When I contacted her again a bit more than a year after the interview, and slightly more than three years after her injury, she told me that her English had improved, "I can talk faster now and can say more complex and structured things," and her writing was slightly better. As for her spoken Japanese, it was slowly coming back.

Isabelle K.'s personal reaction to this life challenge is worth noting. She told me that it is difficult to be one day a multilingual professional, and the next day not being able to communicate properly with other people. She added that she was frustrated but not distressed: "I have been quite lucky so far to have the strength to keep fighting every day without being too depressed. I guess it is also because I am so happy to be alive and every day is a gift." Recovering her languages is a marathon, she says, but "everyday is another opportunity to make a little progress." She ended with, "Never give up – however long it takes."

Language Impairment and Recovery in Bilingual Aphasia

After the brain insult they have suffered, bilinguals with aphasia – originally called polyglot aphasics – go through three different phases. Fabbro (2001) and Cargnelutti, Tomasino, and Fabbro (2019), among others, specify what they are. First, there is the acute phase which generally lasts a few weeks after onset. During this phase, a regression of the impairment effects in unaffected brain regions occur. Several language disorders can be observed during this time, such as temporary mutism (as with Isabelle K.), severe word finding difficulties, severe impairment of language, unstable improvements in one or more languages and so on.

During the next phase, the lesion, or sub-acute, phase, which can last up to 4 to 5 months after the injury, language disorders are clearly correlated with the site and extent of the lesion. Since the disorders are more stable, it is far more convenient to carry a complete assessment of the bilinguals' residual language abilities during this phase. Aphasic disorders may or may not vary across languages in one and the same individual. As we saw, Isabelle K. did not have the same improvement in her languages. Cargnelutti, Tomasino, and Fabbro (2019) state that the regain of language functions in this phase is usually indicated as spontaneous recovery.

Finally, the late, or chronic, phase begins a few months after the brain injury. Here, different patterns of recovery can be observed in multilinguals with aphasia. Further recovery is still possible and there have been reports of rehabilitation continuing several years after the injury, something that Isabelle K. mentions in her interview.

One of the world's experts on aphasia in bilinguals and multilinguals, Michel Paradis (1977, 2001, 2004) proposed a number of language impairment and recovery patterns in bilinguals with aphasia. We will discuss them below as well as give examples taken from published cases. It is important to stress here that the terms "impairment" and "recovery" are both used in the literature concerning these patterns, even though impairment refers to brain damage, and recovery to what is recovered after brain injury. Some opt for "recovery" (e.g., Fabbro 2001; Lorch 2009; Lorenzen and Murray 2008), and some for "impairment" (e.g., Cargnelutti, Tomasino, and Fabbro 2019; Kuzmina et al. 2019). We will follow Paradis' usage in what follows keeping in mind that sometimes it is the impairment that is being talked about, sometimes the recovery, and sometimes both, as in parallel recovery below.

Parallel Recovery

The most common recovery pattern which represents 61% of the 132 cases Paradis (2001) reviewed, is parallel recovery. This occurs when both (or all of) the bilingual's languages are similarly impaired and restored at the same rate. Paradis summarizes a few case studies that have been published in the literature. In one, originally presented by Mastronardi et al. (1991), a 34-year-old woman born in Syria of Italian parents had been fluent in English, French and Italian since early childhood. She spoke English daily while she was employed at an embassy in Rome. When she became aphasic, she had the same difficulty in all three languages. After a brain operation, there was a slight recovery, to the same degree in all languages.

In another case study, originally published by Sasanuma and Park (1995) and summarized by Paradis (2001), a 29-year old man was raised in a unilingual Korean environment. At the age of 18, and for the next nine years, he was exposed to Japanese, as he attended college in Japan for 4 years and subsequently worked for a Japanese–Korean trading company in Japan before returning to Korea. There he continued to used both languages at work. Two and a half months after having become aphasic, he exhibited moderate non-fluent aphasia roughly equivalent in both languages.

There are many cases of parallel recovery and their proportion is probably greater than the 61% presented by Paradis (2001). In fact, that same year Fabbro (2001) indicated 65%, and just a few years later, Paradis (2004) went as high as 76%. As Cargnelutti, Tomasino, and Fabbro (2019) state, the published reports on this kind of impairment and recovery are simply less frequent than we would expect, probably because the authors tend to describe exceptional and unusual cases.

Differential Recovery

The second most common recovery pattern according to Paradis (2001), representing 18% of the cases he reviewed, is differential recovery. Here, according to him, impairment is of a different degree in each language relative to mastery before the brain injury. Paradis (2004) adds that it concerns cases where one language would be recovered much better than the other relative to their premorbid fluency; both languages are affected, though one more than the other. Several years later, Kuzmina et al. (2019) specify that differential patterns may manifest themselves as greater impairment in one language compared to another, or as differences in the characteristics of aphasia.

A very old case study presented by Bychowski (1919) illustrates this type of impairment and recovery. A Pole who spoke Polish (his mother tongue), German, and Russian was hit by a piece of shrapnel on the Eastern Front during World War I. He remained unconscious for three weeks and when he came to, his Russian was least impaired, his Polish was impaired but only in production (he understood it but replied in Russian), and German was the most impaired (he could only repeat phrases given to him). It is not reported how well he recovered his three languages, but we do know that his Russian was restored completely, probably because of the Russian ambience in the hospital and the language exercises given him by a Russian nurse.

Blended Recovery

The third most common recovery pattern based on Paradis' statistics (9% of the total number of cases) is blended recovery, originally known as mixed recovery. Here bilinguals with aphasia systematically mix or blend features of their languages inappropriately at any or all levels of linguistic structure. Peñaloza and Kiran (2019) specify that this is pathological involuntary switching between the two languages despite the voluntary effort of speaking only one language.

A case is reported by Fabbro, Skrap, and Aglioti (2000). They studied a Friulian–Italian bilingual with aphasia who began to speak his first language (Friulian) when addressing an Italian speaker who spoke no Friulian. He also reverted to Italian when asked to speak just Friulian. The bilingual's lesion was located in the left prefrontal cortex, part of the anterior cingulate, and the left striatum which have been proposed as sites governing the language control network.

A much older case that clearly illustrates the type of blends that can occur at the phrase and word levels, was reported by L'Hermitte et al. (1966). This concerned a 46-year-old English businessman, who had lived and worked in France for 16 years and who was very fluent in both languages. Once aphasic, his two languages interfered with one another in both writing and speaking. When asked to write in French, for example, he produced the following mixed passage that is quite incomprehensible (the interferences from English are italicized): "J'es avec une massio*dial* a et *except* dans le cissuden. *Wede* main pour la pousse tard *being*ig *maid* mouche *was* triel mal."

We will come back to language mixing and blending in bilinguals with aphasia at the end of this chapter as some reports in the literature may not in fact have been cases of involuntarily switching. Rather they depicted instances of aphasic bilinguals being in a bilingual environment and using language mixing as a conscious, deliberate, strategy to ensure communication with those interacting with them. The fact that blended recovery is the third highest type of recovery in Paradis' statistics seems to lend credence to this.

Selective Recovery

In fourth position, in terms of recovery patterns (7% of the Paradis cases), we find selective recovery. This occurs when bilinguals with aphasia do not regain the use of one or more of their languages (Paradis 2001). Peñaloza and Kiran (2019) are a bit more explicit: only one language shows clear improvement with no observable residual deficits while the other language remains impaired.

Such a case was reported by Minkowski (1927). A Swiss German, who lived the first part of his life in Zurich, spoke Swiss German as his mother tongue and learned German at school, as well as French and some Italian. At the age of 30, he moved to Neuchâtel, a French-speaking city, where he had accepted a position as professor of physics. French thus became his most-used language. At the age of 44 he had a stroke, which caused aphasia. Comprehension of his languages was restored rapidly, but he had to relearn how to speak. The first language he relearned was French. Standard German and some Italian followed, but Swiss German, his mother tongue, never returned, even though he spent the last five years of his life in Zurich.

Successive Recovery

In fifth position, representing 5% of cases according to Paradis, is successive recovery. One language does not begin to reappear until another has been maximally recovered. A case was signaled by Minkowski (1927). A Swiss German mechanic who spoke Swiss German and German and who knew some French and Italian had a motorbike accident at the age of 32. He became aphasic, and when language production was restored, he could speak only German. He spoke it to his landlady, who came to visit him frequently and who worked through German exercises with him. It was only five months after the accident, when German was almost completely restored, that the person began to speak his first language, Swiss German. As for Italian and French, there was no recuperation for at least 16 months.

Two Rarer Patterns: Antagonistic, and Alternating Antagonistic, Recoveries

We now enter far rarer recovery patterns which are nonetheless very interesting for those attempting to understand the bilingual brain. Antagonistic recovery takes place when one language regresses as the other progresses (Paradis 2001). As Peñaloza and Kiran (2019) state, one language is initially recovered but it is lost with the recovery of the other.

A case study reported by Minkowski (1928) is well known in the bilingual aphasia literature. The person's mother tongue was Swiss German and his second language was German. He had also learned a little French at school. At the age of 19, he went to France, where he lived for six years. French became his everyday means of communication and he quickly became fluent in it. When he was 25, he returned to Switzerland, worked as a railroad conductor and then as a trader. He married and settled in Zurich. The man no longer had the opportunity to speak French (his wife did not speak it) except when they went to the French part of Switzerland on vacation.

At the age of 44, nineteen years after his return from France, the man had a stroke with loss of consciousness for several hours. On recovery, it was found that he was aphasic; he recovered comprehension of his three languages within a day or two, but his speech was altered more severely. Minkowski (1928, 1963) relates that to everyone's surprise he spoke in the beginning only French, first stammering out a few words, then successively more and more correctly. His wife did not understand him, and his children with their poor school French acted as translators between their parents. His French improved quite quickly, and then he began to recover his second language, German, in which he made slow but increasing progress. As for Swiss German it did not reappear until four months after the stroke.

Six months after the injury, his best language was still French; German was improving quite rapidly, but he spoke Swiss German in a very hesitant manner still. A few weeks later, during the Christmas vacation, another change took place. His Swiss German suddenly became almost fluent, as did his German, but his French started to regress. This continued, and in time he could no longer relate in French what he had just read in a French paper; he had to resort to Swiss German and German.

As for alternating antagonistic recovery, Paradis (2001) explains that for alternating periods of time, bilinguals with aphasia have access to only one of their languages. Peñaloza and Kiran (2019) state that one language is available while the other is affected during alternating cycles of days or months. In the first report of this type of recovery, Paradis, Goldblum, and Abidi (1982) described the case of a 48-year-old nun in Morocco who was bilingual in French and dialectal Arabic. She also knew classical Arabic. She had a moped accident and became totally aphasic. Four days after her accident, she was able to utter a few words in Arabic but could not speak French, although her comprehension of the language was quite good. However, two weeks later, she spoke French quite fluently. One day later, much to the interviewer's surprise, her French was extremely poor, and her Arabic was once again quite fluent. This type of recovery pattern continued for additional days. To add to this complexity, whenever she had difficulties speaking one language, she had no problems translating into it. However, she could not do the reverse, that is translate into the language she spoke spontaneously.

Both Paradis (2004) and Green (2000) have theoretical explanations for what is happening in in this type of recovery. Paradis' theory – the Activation Threshold Hypothesis – proposes more generally that when bilingual speakers use one of their languages, the activation threshold of the other is assumed to be automatically raised so as to avoid that it intervenes. He gives the example of a Dutch–English bilingual speaking French. When that takes place, the Dutch activation threshold is raised and hence it is inhibited while French is in use. With bilinguals with aphasia, the control mechanism regulating the setting of activation thresholds is impaired. And in the case of alternating antagonistic recovery, the pattern of higher and lower activation levels alternates repeatedly.

Green (2000) takes a different perspective calling on a control mechanism that fails to generate sufficient resources to activate relevant parts of the language system when they are needed and to inhibit other parts. Since operating one language (La) consumes resources and since the rate at which resources are generated is now less than the rate at which they are consumed, the inhibitory resource available to La will cease to be adequate. Meanwhile the inhibitory resources available for use by the other language (Lb) will increase. This entails a shift from being able to use La spontaneously to a state where only Lb can be used spontaneously. But then Lb will in turn cease to dominate (resources will become insufficient) and there will be a flip back to the previous state, hence the alternating aspect.

To end this part on impairment and recovery patterns, it is important to underline a few words of caution proposed by different researchers. As Paradis (2001) states, the patterns are not mutually exclusive, either over time or between languages. Thus, two languages may be recovered in a parallel or in an antagonistic fashion, he writes, while a third remains inaccessible or is recovered only much later. Lorch (2009) states this succinctly: there may be different types and levels of severity of aphasic symptoms in the different languages, and there may be different rates of recovery of the languages.

Factors that Account for Impairment and Recovery

Ever since the beginning of scientific interest in bilingual aphasia, back in the 19th century, researchers have attempted to isolate the factors that account for the impairment bilinguals with aphasia suffer in their languages and for their patterns of recovery. We will concentrate below on language factors as well as emotional variables, before and after the injury, but we should keep in mind that the extent and location of the lesion will play a large role. Thus, Cargnelutti, Tomasino, and Fabbro (2019) write that lesion site is one of the main predictors of impairment with regard not only to the nature of the deficits but also to the language affected the most.

Peñaloza and Kiran (2019) also insist that damage can impact language capacity by impairing the cognitive control system, affecting the ability to select between the first and the second language representations for use in the appropriate linguistic context. Green and Abutalebi (2013) offer a very complete description of bilingual language control (BLC) with processes such as goal maintenance, conflict monitoring, interference suppression, selective response inhibition, and so on. They propose a neural network for these processes which includes the right prefrontal cortex, the thalamus and the left putamen and the cerebellum (Calabria et al. 2018).

First Language Acquired

One of the very first factors proposed in the literature to account for impairment and recovery is the first language acquired, also known as the native language or mother tongue. The name of Théodule Ribot is associated with this factor. His contribution in *Diseases of Memory* (1882) was to suggest that bilingual aphasia represents a specific memory impairment. His "law of regression" predicts the gradient of forgetting from the most recent to the oldest memories (Lorch 2009). Since then, Ribot's law or rule, has been understood to mean that the first learned language should be less impaired and should recover first in aphasia (Albert and Obler 1978). In the example we gave at the beginning of this chapter, it would appear that Ribot's rule is at work since Isabelle K.'s English came back first. But it was also her most used language and the language she knew best, so several factors are present. Nonetheless the first language acquired remains an important factor even though Ribot had nothing to say about those who have two first languages (simultaneous bilinguals) or who recover their languages in parallel (Lorch 2009).

Language(s) Used the Most

Another factor that was proposed very early on was the most "familiar" or most used language(s). This variable was proposed by another French scientist, Albert Pitres (1895). In his often cited paper, he wrote that the aphasic bilingual recuperates first the language (or languages) he is most familiar with. This has been termed Pitres' rule. But he immediately added that it is usually, but not always, the mother tongue, thereby giving weight to Ribot's first learned language rule. It is interesting to actually read Pitres' paper as he describes seven cases of bilinguals with aphasia and six of them recovered their mother tongue first which was also their most used language. The one exception was a person he named "Bar...," whose first language was Gascon and whose second language was French, acquired at age 12. French was used much more and came back first. The bilingual could understand Gascon after his brain injury but could no longer speak it.

Age of Acquisition (AoA) of the Second Language

Cargnelutti, Tomasino, and Fabbro (2019) are slightly critical of Pitres' rule since there are many reports of bilingual aphasics with greater impairment of their non-native language, even if used a lot. However, they mention that these people were mostly late bilinguals. This raises the interesting question of whether the age at which a language is acquired could be an important factor in recovery. The authors write that the brain representation of each language, and therefore its possible impairment, is primarily determined by age of acquisition. And Kuzmina et al. (2019), whose study we will summarize in the next part, write that it has long been argued that words acquired at an early age are the ones that are most preserved in aphasia. This said, relatively few studies explicitly address the role of age of language learning on language impairment and recovery.

Other Language Factors

A number of other language factors have been proposed over the years. For example, Cargnelutti, Tomasino, and Fabbro (2019) state that premorbid proficiency in a language is considered by many as the most relevant factor, and is useful for the prediction of rehabilitation outcomes. There is also language dominance which combines elements of the most used language (see above), language proficiency, and extent of language use. Another factor proposed over the years has been the most useful language for the bilingual. Linked to this is which language gets the most exposure. Paradis (2001) states that if one language is stimulated by the environment and/or therapy, that language may well recover better or faster, or even be the only one to improve.

To illustrate the importance of the language most used, and most useful, after the injury, we can call on the case studies we evoked above. Thus, the Polish soldier who showed a differential recovery pattern managed to relearn Russian completely, perhaps in part because of the language exercises a Russian nurse had him do. And the Swiss German mechanic who recovered German first (see the section on successive recovery) spoke it with his landlady who came to see him often and who helped him do exercises in German.

Other factors proposed are literacy (a language that a bilingual reads and writes may have a better chance of recovery than a language that is only spoken), the way a language was learned (Cargnelutti, Tomasino, and Fabbro (2019) state that formal appropriation could favor language preservation because language functions can be restored through metalinguistic knowledge), and the structural distance between the languages (Kuzmina et al. 2019 state that some have associated linguistic similarity with recovery in bilingual aphasia).

Affective Ties and Emotional Attitudes

Finally, we will evoke the importance of the affective ties and emotional attitudes bilinguals with aphasia have with their languages. Minkowski (1963) explains the non-parallel language recovery of some of his patients by resorting to affective and emotional factors. For instance, the successive restitution pattern of the young mechanic we have evoked may also have been due to his close relationship with his German-speaking landlady who visited him every day in the hospital. In addition, Minkowski explains that his slower progress in Swiss German may have been due to the fact that his relatives, who spoke Swiss German, had neglected him and that a young Swiss German woman had disappointed him in love several years previously.

Minkowski examines two other cases in the same psychological light. The case of the professor of physics, presented in the selective recovery section, who recovered French first but never recovered his mother tongue, Swiss German, is explained by the fact that French corresponded to his affectional and social needs at that time. And the railroad conductor and trader who recovered French first, a language he no longer used (see the section on antagonistic recovery), could be accounted for by the fact that his six years in France as a young man had been the most beautiful years of his life since his greatest love had been a French woman with whom he had lived for some time. Even though Minkowski and others have proposed that psychological factors play an important role in accounting for aphasic impairment and recovery, they have not been the object of more rigorous studies over the years, unfortunately.

Having reviewed several factors that may account for language impairment and recovery in bilinguals with aphasia, it is safe to say that it is probably a combination of these that can explain what is happening. In addition, Paradis (2001) reminds us that no fully satisfactory explanation has been proposed when one examines individual case studies separately. This latter issue can be resolved in part by undertaking a meta-analysis of a large corpus of case studies. This is what we will look at now.

A Recent Meta-Analysis

Kuzmina et al. (2019) observed that individual studies of bilingual speakers with aphasia – each one with their specific language background – are ipso facto unique. Analyzing a large number of published studies using meta-analysis is a way of going beyond this limitation and getting at the importance of factors that govern aphasia impairment. Kuzmina et al.'s aim was to examine what constrains language impairment following a stroke, and answer a number of questions concerning some of the factors presented above. The first pertained to the first language acquired (they called this "language status"): Do bilinguals with post-stroke aphasia show a difference in performance between the language acquired first and the later acquired language? The second question concerned the age of acquisition of the second language: Is the magnitude of the performance difference between the first and the later learned language a factor of when the latter was acquired, in other words, of when the person became bilingual (early or late)? The third, fourth, and fifth questions pertained to language proficiency, language most used, and the linguistic similarity between the languages spoken by the bilinguals. Do each of them moderate, i.e., influence, the possible performance differences between the first and the second language?

The authors took 130 cases from 65 published studies, making sure that the aphasia in each case resulted from a cerebrovascular accident, the persons were bi- or multilingual, and language performance tests after the injury were done on more than one language. They extracted a number of demographic and clinical data, as well as language background variables for each language (e.g., age of acquisition, language proficiency, language use, etc.). For those who had more than two languages, the earlier acquired second language was chosen for the analysis. The authors also obtained language performance scores from the tests conducted after injury and regrouped them into auditory comprehension scores, oral production scores, and overall performance scores.

The results obtained from the meta-analysis statistics were interesting. First, they found that the bilinguals did better in their first language compared to their later acquired language: 10% better in the overall performance, 6% better in auditory comprehension, and 10% in oral production. The authors suggested that the results supported Ribot's rule which predicts that the earlier acquired language is more resistant to brain damage. They also proposed that when past reviews such as Paradis' and Fabbro's indicate that some 60–70% of bilingual people with aphasia tend to show equivalent impairment after a stroke, this may be due to the fact that previous reviews had many more early and than late bilinguals.

Kuzmina and her coauthors went a long way to confirming this hypothesis when they examined the role of age of acquisition of the second language on the performance scores. When they divided their bilinguals into two groups – the early bilinguals who acquired their second language before age seven, and the late bilinguals who did so after – they found that the early bilinguals showed comparable performance in their two languages. On the other hand, late bilinguals showed better performance in their first language. They concluded that a language acquired early enjoys a unique status and may be differentially processed in the brain.

Two of the other three variables they examined showed some effect. First, individuals with equal proficiency in both languages before the injury showed a smaller difference between the first and the second language in oral production compared to those who were more proficient in L1. In addition, individuals with higher proficiency in their second language performed significantly better in that language overall and in oral production, but not in auditory comprehension.

As for language use, individuals who used the first language more frequently before injury showed significantly better performance in the first language than in the second language in all three performance results (overall, comprehension and production). On the other hand, those who used their second language more frequently than their first language performed comparably in both languages on all three measures. This seems to give some credence to Pitres' rule that the most familiar/most used language is well preserved. Finally, the linguistic similarity between the languages did not appear to influence the magnitude of the difference in performance between the first and the second language.

In sum, by undertaking a meta-analysis of 130 cases from 65 studies, the authors found evidence for factors that account for aphasia impairment: the first language acquired (Ribot's rule), the language most used (Pitres' rules), age of acquisition, language proficiency, and language most used.

Language Mixing and Aphasia

As we saw above, there have been published reports of blended/mixed recovery where bilinguals with aphasia systematically mix or blend features of their language inappropriately. The ones we mentioned seem to be bona fide examples of these, but is language mixing in the form of code-switching and code mixing really always inappropriate? In a review chapter on the topic, Riccardi (2012) states that the dawn of a more systematic debate on the nature of mixing in aphasia took place in the early 1980s in the pages of the journal, *Brain and Language*, between Ellen Perecman and François Grosjean. Since I am one of the two protagonists mentioned, it might be worth spending a bit of time on what took place.

Perecman (1984) wrote a short paper in which she stated that the language of some aphasic bilinguals described in case studies are strongly marked by language mixing and spontaneous translation. The mixing, especially utterance level mixing, reflects a linguistic deficit. It is "inappropriate switching," she wrote. And she added that spontaneous translation indicates a prelinguistic processing deficit. In my critical review of her paper (Grosjean 1985), I agreed with her that certain cases of language mixing in aphasic speech are undoubtedly signs of deficit. Among these we find: using a wrong base language with a monolingual interlocutor, thus leading to a breakdown in communication; code-switching with a monolingual, resulting again in non-communication; violating code-switching constraints or rules; mixing languages during oral reading in front of a monolingual, unless a communication strategy is involved; failing to switch or translate upon request, and so on.

Rare are the case studies, however, that isolate these phenomena from those that are quite acceptable in the speech of bilinguals, with or without aphasia. To do this, one needs to know more about the interaction situations in the studies: who the examiners were, what languages they knew and spoke with the bilingual, and the language mode(s) – monolingual or bilingual – they were in (see Chapter 7). From Perecman's description of some case studies, one can infer that a number of bilinguals with aphasia were probably examined by people who knew some, if not all, of the persons' languages. It that was the case, then they might well have mixed their languages voluntarily and consciously during testing.

In fact, we learn in Perecman's paper that her patient (H.B.) was indeed facing a bilingual investigator who was herself switching languages. This is confirmed when she states that HB's language mixing was particularly pronounced when the investigator shifted from one language to another within the same conversation or task; and we are actually given an extract from a dialogue in which the investigator switches languages! Why should the aphasic bilingual's switches be reflecting a deficit when those of the investigator do not? How much mixing would HB have produced had the investigator been totally monolingual?

I argued that instead of it being a reflection of a linguistic or conceptual disorder, increased switching and spontaneous translation in aphasic bilinguals may simply be reflecting a communicative strategy they were using to ensure communication with the bilingual examiners. They were aware of the production problems they were having and they therefore deliberately adopted a strategy of mixing and simultaneous translation to enhance communication.

Only good knowledge of the aphasic bilinguals' language and speech before the injury (What languages did they know and speak and with whom?, How much code-switching and borrowing did they do?, What kind of static or dynamic interferences did they produce?, etc.), as well as careful testing after the impairment (e.g., Did the examiner know some or all of the persons' languages?) will show if spontaneous translation and language mixing do indeed reflect deficits. In sum, language mixes and spontaneous translations in the speech of bilinguals with aphasia can have many causes. Some reflect the language and conceptual deficits mentioned by Perecman, but others are the result of quite conscious, deliberate communicative strategies on the part of the bilingual.

A few years later, Marty and Grosjean (1998) undertook a study to show the importance of the situation, and the varying language status of examiners, when interacting with bilinguals with aphasia. They wanted to know if the latter could take into account the type of speaker they had in front of them – monolingual or bilingual – and whether this had an impact on the amount of language mixing they produced.

They tested eight bilinguals with non-fluent aphasia who had had a stroke. They were bilingual in Swiss German and French and had used both languages regularly before their stroke. Four were slightly dominant in Swiss German and four in French. They were asked to undertake various language tasks in French: place one of several cards in a specified position on a board, describe a postcard in enough detail so that it can be found among several similar postcards, take part in a topic-constrained interaction, and, finally, talk freely about any topic which comes to mind.

The critical independent variable was the aphasic bilingual's interlocutors. There were two of them. The first was a totally monolingual French speaker who did not know any German or Swiss German whatsoever. The other was a bilingual in Swiss German and French who used both languages on a regular basis, and often code-switched with her parents, brothers and sisters. The participants were told about their interlocutors' language background prior to testing and they talked together a bit before undertaking the tasks.

The results clearly differentiated pathological from non-pathological mixing. Five of the eight bilinguals with aphasia did not mix their languages at all with the monolingual interlocutor – they only used French, her native language – but they did mix with the bilingual interlocutor. One person did so also with the monolingual but extremely rarely (0.4 German syllables per minute) and this might have been due to stress or fatigue. Finally, two persons mixed their languages quite extensively in the monolingual situation: 6.96 and 17.49 syllables per minute, respectively. It was concluded that of the eight aphasic bilinguals, six of them could still control their language output – monolingual or bilingual – and adapt it to the interlocutor, whereas two could no longer do so.

Are researchers heeding the need to put bilinguals with aphasia into different language modes – monolingual and bilingual – when assessing their languages and finding out whether their intermingling of languages is pathological or not? Paradis (2004) was one of the first neurolinguists to acknowledge the importance of controlling language mode. He wrote that each monolingual test (such as those in Part B of his Bilingual Aphasia Test battery (BAT)) should be administered preferably by a monolingual native speaker of the relevant language. He adds that if the interviewer understands the patient's other language, it is likely that her body language will give her away. The patient will then realize that she can speak that language.

More and more researchers are acknowledging this even though they do not quite go all the way. Thus, for example, Lerman et al. (2019) found that a Hebrew-English aphasic bilingual was about three times more likely to mix languages when his less proficient English was the target language than when it was Hebrew. Their result is of real interest but they do recognize that all testers were bilingual Hebrew–English speakers and the participant was aware of this. They state that it is unclear how this knowledge might have affected their participant's language mixing.

In another study, Goral, Norvik, and Jensen (2019) obtained data from 11 multilingual speakers with aphasia describing a sequence of drawings or cards, and giving a personal narrative. They found that the participants with greater impairment mixed languages more frequently than those with milder impairment, and there was more language mixing when participants were tested in their weaker language. This said, they do point out that the participants were likely aware that their interlocutors were multilinguals who spoke at least two, if not all, of each of the participant's languages. This might have played a role in their findings. Hopefully, in the years to come, bilinguals with aphasia will increasingly be tested in their different language modes by means of stricter procedures. It might be a challenge, though, in environments where most people know several languages but it will be worth doing if at all possible.

References

Albert, Martin L., and Loraine K. Obler. 1978. The Bilingual Brain: Neuropsychological and Neurolinguistic Aspects of Bilingualism. New York: Academic Press.

Bychowski, Zygmunt. 1919. "Über die Restitution der nach einem Schädelschuss verlorengegangenen Sprachen bei einem Polyglotten." *Monatsschrift für Psychiatrie und Neurologie*, 45 (4): 183–201.

Calabria, Marco, Albert Costa, David W. Green, and Jubin Abutalebi. 2018. "Neural basis of bilingual language control." *Annals of the New York Academy of Sciences*, June, 1426 (1). DOI: 10.1111/nyas.13879.

Cargnelutti, Elisa, Barbara Tomasino, and Franco Fabbro. 2019. "Aphasia in the multilingual population." In The Handbook of the Neuroscience of Multilingualism, edited by John W. Schwieter, 533–552. Hoboken, NJ: Wiley Blackwell.

Fabbro, Franco. 2001. "The bilingual brain: Bilingual aphasia." *Brain and Language*, 79: 201–210. DOI: 10.1006/brln.2001.2480.

Fabbro, Franco, Miran Skrap, and Salvatore Aglioti. 2000. "Pathological switching between languages after frontal lesions in a bilingual patient." *Journal of Neurology, Neurosurgery and Psychiatry*, 68: 650–652. DOI: 10.1136/jnnp.68.5.650.

Goral, Mira, Monica I. Norvik, and Bård Uri Jensen. 2019. "Variation in language mixing in multilingual aphasia." *Clinical Linguistics and Phonetics*, 33 (10–11): 915–929.

Green, David. 2000. "Control, activation, and resource: A framework and a model for the control of speech in bilinguals." In The Bilingualism Reader, edited by Li Wei, 374–385. London/New York: Routledge.

Green, David, and Justin Abutalebi. 2013. "Language control in bilinguals: The adaptive control hypothesis." *Journal of Cognitive Psychology*, 25: 515–530.

Grosjean, François. 1985. "Polyglot aphasics and language mixing: A comment on Perecman (1984)." *Brain and Language*, 26: 349–355.

Kuzmina, Ekaterina, Mira Goral, Monica I. Norvik, and Brendan S. Weekes. 2019. "What influences language impairment in bilingual aphasia? A meta-analytic review." *Frontiers in Psychology*, 10: 445, 1–22. DOI: 10.3389/fpsyg.2019.00445.

Lerman, Aviva, Lia Pazuelo, Lian Kizner, Katy Borodkin, and Mira Goral. 2019. "Language mixing patterns in a bilingual individual with non-fluent aphasia." *Aphasiology*, 33 (9): 1137–1153. DOI: 10.1080/02687038.2018.1546821.

L'Hermitte, René, Henri Hécaen, Jean Dubois, Antoine Culioli, and Andrée Tabouret-Keller. 1966. "Le problème de l'aphasie des polyglottes: remarques sur quelques observations." *Neuropsychologia*, 4: 315–329.

Lorch, Marjorie. 2009. "Neurolinguistics and the non-monolingual brain." In Contemporary Applied Linguistics, Volume 2, Linguistics for the Real World, edited by Li Wei and Vivien Cook, 184–201. London: Continuum.

Lorenzen, Bonnie, and Laura L. Murray. 2008. "Bilingual aphasia: A theoretical and clinical review." *American Journal of Speech-Language Pathology*, 17: 299–317.

Marty, Simone, and François Grosjean. 1998. "Aphasie, bilinguisme et modes de communication." *APHASIE und verwandte Gebiete*, 12: 8–28.

Mastronardi, Luciano, Luigi Ferrante, Paolo Celli, Michele Acqui, and Aldo Fortuna. 1991. "Aphasia in polyglots: Report of two cases and analysis of the literature." *Neurosurgery*, 29 (4): 621–623.

Minkowski, Mieczyslaw. 1927. "Klinischer Beitrag zur Aphasie bei Polyglotten." *Schweizer Archiv für Neurologie und Psychiatrie*, 21: 43–72.

Minkowski, Mieczyslaw. 1928. "Sur un cas d'aphasie chez un polyglotte." *Revue Neurologique*, 49: 361–366.

Minkowski, Mieczyslaw. 1963. "On aphasia in polyglots." In Problems of Dynamic Neurology, edited by Lipman Halpern. New York: Grune & Stratton.

Paradis, Michel. 1977. "Bilingualism and aphasia." In Studies in Neurolinguistics, vol. 3, edited by Haiganoosh Whitaker and Harry A. Whitaker, 65–121. New York: Academic Press.

Paradis, Michel. 2001. "Bilingual and polyglot aphasia." In Handbook of Neuropsychology, Vol. 3 Language and Aphasia, edited by Rita S. Berndt, 69–91. Oxford: Elsevier Science.

Paradis, Michel. 2004. A Neurolinguistic Theory of Bilingualism. Amsterdam/Philadelphia, PA: John Benjamins.

Paradis, Michel, Marie-Claire Goldblum, and Raouf Abidi. 1982. "Alternate antagonism with paradoxical translation behavior in two bilingual aphasic patients." *Brain and Language*, 15: 55–69.

Peñaloza, Claudia, and Swathi Kiran. 2019. "Recovery and rehabilitation patterns in bilingual and multilingual aphasia." In The Handbook of the Neuroscience of Multilingualism, edited by John W. Schwieter, 553–571. Hoboken, NJ: Wiley Blackwell.

Perecman, Ellen. 1984. "Spontaneous translation and language mixing in a polyglot aphasic." *Brain and Language*, 23: 43–63.

Pitres, Albert. 1895. "Etude sur l'aphasie chez les polyglottes." *Revue de Médecine*, 11: 873–899.

Ribot, Théodule A. 1882. Diseases of Memory: An Essay in the Positive Psychology. New York: Appleton.

Riccardi, Alessandra. 2012. "Bilingual aphasia and code-switching: Representation and control." In Aspects of Multilingual Aphasia, edited by Martin R. Gitterman, Miral Goral and Loraine K. Obler, 141–157. Bristol/Buffalo/Toronto: Multilingual Matters.

Sasanuma, S., and H. Park. 1995. "Patterns of language deficits in two Korean-Japanese bilingual aphasic patients – A clinical report." In Aspects of Bilingual Aphasia, edited by Michel Paradis, 111–122. Oxford: Pergamon Press.

Part III

Language Use and Language Processing

7

The Bilingual's Languages in Interaction

In their everyday lives, bilinguals have to decide, most often subconsciously, which language they should use at any point in time – this is called the base language – and what role their other language(s) has (have) to play. Should the other language(s) play a part in the interaction or not? In this chapter, we will examine these issues.

Concerning the first topic, traditionally known as language choice, we will see that numerous factors play a role in deciding which language to use. Sometimes the decision is straightforward – the interlocutors only share one language – but very often more than one language can be used, and the reasons that lead to one being chosen as opposed to another are many. We will examine both older sociolinguistic work as well as more recent experimental work dealing with this. We will also concern ourselves with what happens when the wrong language is used, and will evoke situations where the interlocutors are surprised, if not shocked, when someone uses a language they do not expect.

The other question bilinguals have to answer is whether to bring in their other language(s) during the interaction. If they choose to, they can simply change the base language, or mix in the other language in the form of code-switches and borrowings. In the latter cases, the language being spoken remains the same but elements of the other language are brought into the discourse.

These two behaviors – choosing the language to use, and choosing whether to bring in the other language – have led to interesting studies over the years which we will describe. A number of variables have been shown to be important such as the topic of the interaction, how proficient bilinguals are in their languages, the interlocutors' attitude towards language mixing, the formality of the situation and so on.

We will end the chapter with a theoretical framework – the language mode concept– that attempts to account for this dual behavior. It does so in large part by modulating the level of activation of the bilingual's languages. We will also briefly mention the interactional contexts proposed by another framework – the adaptive control hypothesis.

Choosing the Language of the Interaction

Factors Underlying Language Choice

The late psycholinguist, Susan Ervin-Tripp, wrote that a speaker in any language community who enters different social situations normally has a repertoire of speech

The Mysteries of Bilingualism, First Edition. François Grosjean.

alternatives which shift with situation. She presented a number of factors that account for change in code or variety: the participants in the interaction, the setting (time and place) and the situation, the content of discourse, and the function of the interaction (Ervin-Tripp 1968). These same factors can account for language choice, also known as language selection, in bilingual settings. Numerous sociolinguistic descriptive studies in the second half of the last century examined the factors that account for "who speaks what language to whom and when," to take a famous article title by Fishman (1965), and we will quickly review them here.

As concerns participants, the language knowledge and proficiency of the interlocutors are very important. We often consider the language ability of the addressee in choosing between languages. Thus, in answer to the question, "Why did you speak language X to this person?" we often reply that she is more proficient in that language. There is also the history of linguistic interaction between the two participants. Two people may speak a particular language to one another simply because they always have. This habit factor does not need much time to initiate itself, as we will see below when describing recent experimental studies. Age can also play a role, with language choice depending on how old the interlocutor is. In an interesting study of the German–Hungarian community of Oberwart, Gal (1979) reported that younger people mainly spoke German and older people Hungarian. When addressing an older person, a younger person often decided on using Hungarian. Other factors are the socioeconomic status of the participants, the degree of intimacy between the speakers, the participants' attitudes towards a language, and even cultural/ethnical considerations.

As concerns situation, the location of the interaction is an important language choice factor. As argued by Rubin (1968), in bilingual Paraguay one will tend to address someone in the countryside in Guaraní but use Spanish in the cities. Or if one belongs to a language minority in a country, and the minority language is looked down upon by some, one may speak the majority language outside the home, and keep the minority language for the home so as not to stand out. The presence of a monolingual also plays a central role. Bilinguals often accommodate to that person's language so as to include her in the interaction. As soon as the person leaves or has a side conversation, the interlocutors may well revert to the language they usually speak among themselves. The degree of formality is also important: in a formal situation, one language may be used, but in a less formal setting, it might be another. In Switzerland, for example, Swiss German is not usually spoken by members of the Federal government when they are giving a speech on TV (they will use German). But they will speak it as they are getting ready in the studio, and with friends and colleagues afterward.

The content of discourse is another important category. Some topics are simply better dealt with in one language than in another (see Chapter 8 and the Complementarity Principle), and bilinguals speaking among themselves may well change base language when they change topic. In Paraguay again, school, legal, and business affairs are usually discussed in Spanish rather than in Guaraní. Finally, concerning the fourth category, the function of the interaction, we should keep in mind that people often communicate to achieve something and not just to convey information. Thus there are many instances of choosing a particular language to raise one's status, to create a social distance, to exclude someone, to request something, or to give a command.

Usually, several factors taken together explain a bilingual's language choice, and some factors have more weight than others in different communities. In addition, the weighting might change depending on different circumstances, as well as unexpected events or moments of stress.

Recent Studies that Have Looked at Some of These Factors

As bilinguals we are attuned to the many cues linked to people, context, and behavior, which help us choose the appropriate language at the appropriate time. Sociolinguistic work has illustrated this over the years, as we have seen, and more experimental research is now starting to show it too. Thus, Kapiley and Mishra (2018) examined if bilinguals are sensitive to an interlocutor's relative language proficiency when they select a language voluntarily for object naming. In the familiarization phase of their study, Telugu – English bilinguals in India were shown short cartoons representing bilingual interlocutors speaking Telugu and English: two were highly proficient in both languages whereas two others were proficient in Telugu but not in English. In the second experiment of their study, the participants were shown pictures of these interlocutors and then objects the participants had to name (e.g., a banana, a bear, a bone, a box, etc.). They could name them in the language of their choice – Telugu or English – but had to keep in mind who they were addressing. They also had to maintain a balance when choosing a language; in other words, all the naming could not be in Telugu or English only.

The results showed clearly that the bilingual participants took into account the proficiency level of the interlocutors. They named the objects a higher number of times in English when they perceived the cartoon interlocutor as highly proficient in English (mean of 24.41%) compared to the cartoon interlocutor perceived as low proficient in English (mean of 12.08%). The authors concluded that bilinguals take into consideration the language proficiency of their interlocutors. They are sensitive to their language needs and this influences how they plan their language use.

More generally, familiarity with the language background of interlocutors plays a role in bilinguals' processing of language. Molnar, Ibáñez-Molina, and Carreiras (2015) first asked proficient Basque–Spanish bilinguals, who had acquired both languages before the age of three, to familiarize themselves with three types of interlocutors via video recordings: Basque speakers, Spanish speakers, and bilingual Basque–Spanish speakers. The interlocutors introduced themselves and talked about various topics such as their family background, hobbies, work, etc. The Basque and Spanish speakers only spoke their respective language whereas the bilingual speakers used both Basque and Spanish, and code-switched from time to time.

In the second part of the study, the bilinguals participants saw on video each interlocutor produce a word or a made-up word and they simply had to decide whether the item was a real word or not by pressing one of two keys. Seventy-five percent of the time, the Basque and Spanish interlocutors presented words in the language they had spoken during the familiarization phase (the experimenters called this the congruent trials since they corresponded to the language they had used before) and the remainder of the time, they produced words in the other language (the incongruent trials). Thus, these speakers surprised the participants at various points by uttering words in the wrong language. Until this happened, the participants did not know that the interlocutors also spoke the other language. Concerning the bilingual interlocutors, they presented words in the one or the other language equally.

The results showed the importance of interlocutor identity when bilinguals process speech. The participants responded faster to words produced in the language associated with the interlocutors during the familiarization phase (e.g., Spanish words produced by Spanish interlocutors) than to words produced by them in the other language (e.g., Basque words produced by these same Spanish interlocutors). As for the words produced by the bilingual interlocutors, in the one or the other language, they were responded to the slowest.

In a very similar study, Woomans et al. (2015) also examined how familiar faces associated with one language can be used to influence processing. In the familiarization phase, their bilinguals, Spanish–Catalan in one experiment, and Dutch–French in the other, were involved in a simulated Skype interaction with the faces of a number of interlocutors. They had to answer the interlocutors' questions, and each interlocutor spoke only one language. The participants were not aware that their responses did not matter for the rest of the experiment. Then, in a second phase, the participants were asked to generate words semantically related to words presented by familiar and unfamiliar interlocutors, either a verb following a noun (first experiment) or a noun following a noun (second experiment). The familiar faces uttered the words in the same language as during the Skype interactions (congruent trials) or in the other language that was used during the familiarization phase (incongruent trials).

In both experiments, participants produced words faster when they had to respond to familiar faces speaking the same language as in the Skype simulation, compared to the same face speaking the unexpected language. This language priming effect disappeared when it became clear that the interlocutor was actually bilingual and not just the speaker of one language. In other words, the cue was no longer used when it turned out that it was unreliable.

Finally, Zhang et al. (2013) wanted to know if facial characteristics representing cultural identity could lead to language expectation. They asked a number of Chinese students who had been in the United States for about a year to take part in a computer-mediated communication task. The participants viewed the photo of either a Chinese or a Caucasian face of a certain Michael Lee and listened to him on a recording talk with a standard American accent about campus-life topics. The very same recording was played irrespective of the photo. The students then spoke about these same topics in English and were recorded.

When the researchers assessed the participants' verbal fluency and measured their speech rate when speaking to Michael Lee, they found that the students' fluency ratings were lower, as was their objective speech rate, in the Chinese face condition than the Caucasian face condition. Basically, they had expected the Chinese face to speak Chinese and hence their English language output was disrupted when interacting with Michael Lee in English.

In the latter three studies, we have touched upon a "real life" phenomenon experienced by many bilinguals – that of being confronted with a person using the wrong language. Many bilinguals have a story or two of being surprised, if not shocked, when a person suddenly uses a language they did not expect, even though they know it. Some report not understanding what is said at first. There are even threads on the web which refer to this topic. Thus, an American in Japan writes that he gets many shocked looks from Japanese people when he speaks Japanese in front of them for the first time. A Serbian notes that she is very surprised when foreigners in her country speak Serbian. And a teacher in India reports that her eyes nearly popped out when she heard a French student utter something in Hindi. Molnar, Ibáñez-Molina, and Carreiras (2015), Woomans et al. (2015), and Zhang et al. (2013), each in their own way, have confirmed that a language can be deactivated in situations where the other language is primed (see Chapter 8 on selectivity in processing).

What Role for the Other Language?

Bilinguals can bring in the other language (the "guest" or "embedded" language) in various ways (Grosjean 1982, 2010). One of these ways is to code-switch, that is to shift completely to the other language for a word, a phrase, or a sentence. For example, a

French–English bilingual said: "*Va chercher Marc* and bribe him *avec un chocolat chaud* with cream on top" (Go get Marc and bribe him with a hot chocolate with cream on top). Researchers interested in the social aspects of language have concentrated on when and why switching takes place in the social context. Reasons that have been put forward are: to fill a linguistic need, to continue the last language used, to quote someone, to specify the addressee, to exclude someone from the conversation, to qualify a message, to specify speaker involvement, to mark group identity, to convey emotion, to change the role of the speaker, etc. Linguists have sought to study the types of code-switches that occur (single words, phrases, clauses, sentences, etc.) as well as the linguistic constraints that govern their appearance. Although there is still considerable controversy over this latter aspect (Are some constraints general whereas others are language specific? How broad can a constraint be?) it is now clear that switching is not simply a haphazard behavior but that it is, instead, a well-governed process used as a communicative strategy to convey linguistic and social information.

The other way bilinguals can bring in the other, less activated, language is to borrow a word or short expression from that language and to adapt it morphologically (and often phonologically) into the base language (Poplack 2017). Thus, unlike code-switching which is the juxtaposition of two languages, borrowing is the integration of one language into another. Most often both the form and the content of a word are borrowed (to produce what has been called a loanword or more simply a borrowing) as in the following examples taken from French–English bilinguals: "Ca m'étonnerait qu'on ait *code-switché* autant que ça" (I can't believe we code-switched as often as that) and "Maman, tu peux me *tier* /taie/ mes chaussures?" (Mummy, can you tie my shoes?). In these examples, the English words "code-switch" and "tie" have been brought in and integrated into the French sentence.

A second type of borrowing, called a loanshift, consists in either taking a word in the base language and extending its meaning to correspond to that of a word in the other language, or rearranging words in the base language along a pattern provided by the other language and thus creating a new meaning. An example of the first kind of loanshift would be the use of *humoroso* by Portuguese–Americans to mean "humorous" when the original meaning is "capricious." An example of the second kind is the use of idiomatic expressions that are translated literally from the other language, such as "I put myself to think about it" said by a Spanish–English bilingual, based on "Me puse a pensarlo." It is important to distinguish idiosyncratic loans (also called "speech borrowings" or "nonce borrowings"; Poplack 2017) from words which have become part of a language community's vocabulary and which monolinguals also use (called "language borrowings" or "established loans").

It should be noted that there are other classifications of bilingual speech. Thus, for example, Muysken (2000) proposes three categories. First, there are alternations where segments from the two language alternate. He gives a French–Russian example taken from Timm (1978): "les femmes et le vin, *ne ponimayu*" (women and wine, I don't understand). This is similar to code-switching as described above. Second, there are insertions where a lexical item or a constituent is inserted into the base language. This is very much like word borrowing (form and content) as illustrated above. But what is controversial is that Muysken also includes entire constituents such as "in a state of shock" in the following example, "Yo anduve *in a state of shock* por dos dias" (I walked in a state of shock for two days). Finally, Muysken proposes congruent lexicalizations which refer to situations where the two languages share a grammatical structure which can be filled with elements from either language.

Experimental Work on Language Mixing

Although debate continues among experts on how best to characterize bilingual mixed speech, most agree that a number of conditions need to be met for it to take place. Among these we find that the interlocutors must know the two languages in question, they must be open to the languages being used together, the situation must be conducive to mixing languages such as a relaxed atmosphere with no monolingual present, and so on. It is with these conditions in mind that researchers set about doing experimental work on language mixing. We will cover some of this in what follows.

As we will see in the next section, Grosjean (1997, 2001) proposes that bilinguals navigate along a situational continuum ranging from a monolingual to a bilingual language mode. Being in a monolingual mode happens primarily when bilinguals are in situations where they cannot use their other language(s), such as interacting with monolinguals. On the other hand, speakers are in a bilingual mode when they are interacting with other bilinguals who share their two languages and with whom they feel comfortable mixing languages. And speakers can be in any one of a number of intermediate modes such as when, for example, the interlocutor knows the other language but either is not very proficient in it or does not like to mix languages.

In a first study, Grosjean (1990, 1997) wished to investigate two factors that appear to control where the bilingual stands along the continuum – the topic of the exchange, and the person addressed. The method used was to ask French–English bilinguals in the United States to summarize stories they heard in French, as well as to describe cartoons, to persons not actually present. They were were told they were taking part in a "telephone chain" experiment which was being recorded and that the experimenter was interested in the amount of information that could be conveyed from one person to another. The first factor manipulated was the topic of the stories or cartoons that were given to them. Half the stories were in French only (they were monolingual) and concerned situations found in France. As for the accompanying cartoons, they depicted typically French scenes. The other half of the stories and cartoons were bilingual. The stories, in French, concerned typical American activities and hence contained a number of English code-switches. As for the "bilingual" cartoons, they depicted typical American scenes (e.g., Thanksgiving Day) and could not easily be described in French without reverting to code-switching and borrowing.

The second factor manipulated was the person the participants had to speak to. The three persons were described to the participants before the experiment started by means of a short biographical sketch. The first person (referred to as "French" below) had just arrived in the United States to do a post-doc. He could read and write English quite well but had difficulties speaking it. He was still adapting to life in America and spoke French at home. The second person (Bilingual A) had lived in the States for seven years and worked for a French government agency. He taught French and organized French cultural events. His children went to a bilingual school and he only spoke French at home although he was bilingual in French and English. As for the third person (Bilingual B), he too had been in the States for seven years. He worked for a local electronics firm, had French and American friends, and spoke both languages at home. His children went to the local school.

No mention was made of the three persons' practice of language mixing but the answers to a questionnaire filled out by the participants at the end of the experiment clearly showed that they had inferred what this behavior was for each addressee. The French listener was not considered fluent in English and, as a consequence, was not seen as code-switching to a large extent. Bilingual A was considered fluent in English but was also seen as a purist who did not code-switch very much, although slightly more than the French listener. In addition, his attitude towards code-switching was seen as negative. As for Bilingual B, he was seen as being very fluent in English and having a positive attitude towards code-switching, and hence as someone who mixed languages a lot.

The amount of French and English spoken by the participants, and the hesitation pauses they produced, were tabulated for each story and cartoon. The results showed evidence for the importance of the two variables tested. As concerns the topic, bilingual stories and cartoons produced about ten times more English in the form of code-switches and borrowings than monolingual stories and cartoons. As for the second variable, the person being addressed, very few code-switches were used with the French listener but the number of French syllables used, as well as that of hesitation phenomena, were high. The participants had little choice but to try to say everything in French, even though it was more difficult. Bilingual B received the most code-switches and as a consequence fewer French syllables, and fewer hesitation phenomena occurred, in the descriptions related to him. Basically, speakers were totally free to use mixed language as they saw fit. Finally, with Bilingual A, with whom participants did not feel they could code-switch as much because of his purism and his attitude towards code-switching, an intermediary number of code-switches and hesitation phenomena were produced. The information had to be given largely in French, which entailed hesitating more as the participants had to find a way of conveying the information and producing rather lengthy translations of potential code-switches. When this was too demanding, code-switching took place even though the interlocutor was not perceived as appreciating mixed language. This first study, which de Groot (2011) described as "a convincing demonstration" that copied natural communication rather veraciously, was followed by a number of others in which various variables were manipulated.

A second study, conducted by Weil (1990; see Grosjean, 2008, for a full account), replicated the first study but this time Swiss German–French bilinguals addressed three interlocutors whose knowledge of Swiss German ranged from minimal to totally fluent. Since the stories to be retold were in Swiss German, with or without French code-switches, the interesting finding was that the participants changed base language with two of the three interlocutors. In other words, they retold the stories in French, and not Swiss German, so as to resolve the problem of addressing someone in the "wrong language," either because the person could not understand it or because they preferred the other language.

A few years later, Caixeta (2003; also summarized in Grosjean, 2008), involved Brazilian Portuguese–French bilinguals whose knowledge of French was either intermediate or advanced. They spoke in French at different times to two interlocutors who were present, a French monolingual and a Portuguese–French bilingual. The results obtained showed not only that there were more code-switches and borrowings (guest elements) when the bilingual interlocutor was addressed but also that the participants who had an intermediary level of French produced more guest elements than the participants with an advanced proficiency. This confirmed that dominant bilinguals speaking their weaker language will code-switch and borrow more than bilinguals who have a good knowledge of the language, when the situation permits it.

This last study can be compared to the one conducted by Fokke et al. (2007). Two groups of Dutch participants of different English proficiencies (less proficient and proficient) saw cartoons in three different conditions. In the monolingual condition, the cartoon was in Dutch and the experimenter only spoke Dutch to them. In the intermediate condition, the cartoon was also in Dutch but the experimenter switched from time to time to English. Finally, in the bilingual condition, the participants saw the English version of the cartoon and the experimenter also code-switched with them. All participants were asked to retell the cartoon in Dutch.

The results were similar to those in the studies already mentioned: no code-switches into English in the monolingual condition, some in the intermediate condition, and practically a doubling of the amount of code-switching in the bilingual condition. However, the authors did not find any difference in the amount of code-switching produced by the two proficiency groups. This may seem surprising at first when compared with the results obtained in the Brazilian Portuguese–French study just mentioned. However, in that study the participants were speaking in their second language (French) and if their knowledge of it was not sufficient, then they would code-switch, especially if the interlocutor was bilingual. In the Dutch study, the participants were asked to retell the cartoon in Dutch, their first and dominant language. There was therefore much less need to code-switch into English for a word or an expression.

So far, the types of interlocutor and their attitudes towards mixing languages, the topic of the interaction (culturally marked or not), as well as the interlocutor's language proficiency and language dominance, have all been shown to be important factors in communication between bilinguals in a research setting. Dewaele (2001) added another variable to the list: the formality of the situation. He asked university students, trilingual in Dutch, French, and English, to take part in two interactions. In the first, they had one-on-one informal conversations in French with the researcher, who was also their language teacher, in a relaxed atmosphere, where they talked about their studies, hobbies, politics, and so on. In the second, they spoke to him, in French again, but in an oral exam that was aimed at evaluating their proficiency level. The topics were politics, economics, and the students' performance in other exams. Dewaele found a significant difference between the proportion of mixed utterances in the informal situation (mean of 9%) and the formal situation (3%). He also found that speech production was more fluent in the informal than in the formal situation.

A final study, this time undertaken with aphasic patients, confirms the importance of the person being spoken to when deciding whether or not to mix languages. Marty and Grosjean (1998) – described in more detail in Chapter 6 on brain injury and bilingualism – studied spoken language production in eight Swiss German–French bilinguals suffering from aphasia. The patients were asked to undertake various language tasks such as positioning cards on a board, describing postcards, taking part in a topic-constrained interaction and talking freely. The critical independent variable was the patient's interlocutor. The first was a totally monolingual French speaker who did not know any German whatsoever (unlike in other studies involving aphasic patients where the interlocutor knew the other language but pretended not to) and the second was a Swiss German–French bilingual who was used to code-switching. The results clearly differentiated pathological from non-pathological mixing. Five of the eight aphasics did not mix their languages with the monolingual interlocutor and one did so extremely rarely, whereas two did so quite extensively. It was concluded that, of the eight aphasic patients, six of them could still control their language output – monolingual or bilingual – and adapt it to the interlocutor, whereas two could no longer do so.

The Language Mode Concept

We have seen above how bilinguals choose a base language to use in their everyday communication, and also choose whether to bring in their other language. We have also described some of the experimental work that has been done on these topics. Here we will present the language mode concept that attempts to account for this dual behavior.

Ever since his first writings on language mode, Grosjean has maintained, along with many other researchers such as Weinreich (1966), Hasselmo (1970), and Baetens Beardsmore (1986) that bilinguals communicate differently when they are with monolinguals and when they are with bilinguals who share their languages. Whereas they avoid using their other language(s) with monolinguals, they may call upon it (or them) when interacting with bilinguals, either by changing over completely to the other language(s), i.e., code-switching, or by bringing elements of the other language(s) into the language they are speaking, i.e., borrowing.

Grosjean (1997, 2001, 2013) proposes that bilinguals navigate along a situational continuum ranging from a monolingual to a bilingual language mode. To account for different modes, Grosjean calls upon the level of activation of each language and defines language mode as the state of activation of the bilingual's languages and language-processing mechanisms at a given point in time. Figure 7.1 (below) illustrates the concept (to simplify things, we will deal with just two languages at this stage). The bilingual's languages (A and B) are depicted on the vertical axis by squares, and their level of activation by the degree of darkness (black represents an active language and white an inactive one). Only two positions on the continuum are illustrated in the figure but many more are possible between the two and have been entitled intermediate modes (see the previous section for examples). In the two positions depicted here, language A is the most active (it is the base language, i.e., the main language being used) and language B may be active to varying degrees. On the left, language B is either inactive or only very slightly active, and the bilingual is said to be at, or close to, a monolingual language mode. On the right, language B is active, but it is not as active as language A, and the bilingual is said to be in a bilingual mode.

Language mode is made up of two components therefore. The first is the base language chosen (language A in the example) and the second is the comparative level of activation of the two languages – from very different in a monolingual mode to quite similar in a bilingual mode. These two components are usually independent of one another – one can change without affecting the other. Thus, the base language can be changed but not the comparative level of activation of the two languages. This takes

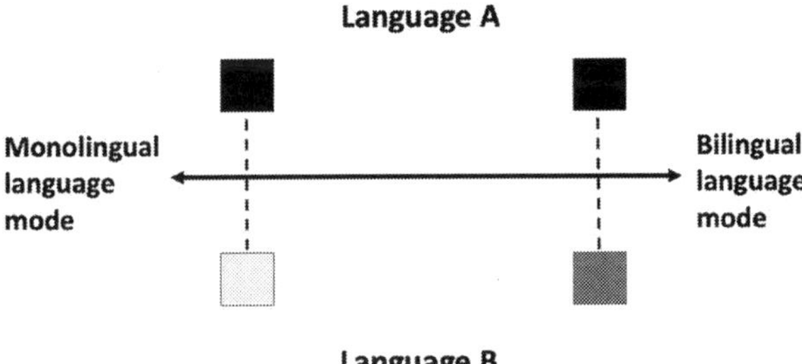

Figure 7.1 The language mode continuum. The level of activation of a language (square) is depicted by the degree of darkness (dark is active, white is inactive).

place, for example, in a bilingual interaction when a bilingual switches over completely to the other language, which becomes the base language (see what happened in the Weil (1990) study described in the previous section). Similarly, there can be a change in the level of activation of the two languages without a change in base language, as in Figure 7.1. Thus, when referring to language mode, both aspects need to be mentioned. For example, a Spanish–English bilingual speaking Spanish to a Spanish monolingual is in a "Spanish monolingual mode"; the same bilingual speaking English to another Spanish–English bilingual, with whom language mixing is possible, is in an "English bilingual mode," and so on.

Movement along the continuum can occur at any time when the factors such as the interlocutors, the situation, and so on, also change. Bilinguals will also differ among themselves as to the extent to which they travel along the continuum. Of course, the particular mode bilinguals are in will have an effect on the amount of use of the other (guest) language. Thus, everything else remaining equal (interlocutor, topic, situation, etc.), being in a monolingual mode prevents a change in base language and limits almost totally the use of code-switches and borrowings from the other language (but interferences may still occur). In the bilingual mode, on the other hand, the other language can be brought in depending on a number of factors.

As we saw in the Caixeta (2003) study in the previous section, it is more difficult for bilinguals who are highly dominant in one language to control language mode in their weaker language. Although they may deactivate their stronger language in a monolingual environment that requires only the weaker language, the latter may simply not be sufficiently developed or active to allow them to stay in a monolingual mode. As for multilinguals, they too can find themselves in various language modes. For example, trilinguals are in a monolingual mode when the people they are interacting with are monolingual in one of their three languages, or when they share only one language with another bilingual or multilingual. But they can also be in a bilingual mode or even in a trilingual mode with other interlocutors with whom they share two or three languages.

Language mode has received support from many empirical studies (see those described in the previous section as well as Dunn and Fox Tree 2014; Khachatryan et al. 2016; Boukadi, Davies, and Wilson 2015, among others; see also Chapter 9 on selectivity). It has also been the object of full length papers by researchers concerned by its importance in language processing, as well as by the role it plays in experimental settings as an independent or a control variable (e.g., Wu and Thierry 2010; Yu and Schwieter 2018). Recently, Gullifer et al. (2021), who mention language mode, have used language entropy as a measure of language balance in various communicative contexts. A low entropy score signifies the use of just one language whereas a high entropy score reflects more language diversity.

At this point, it is worth mentioning another framework that recognizes that bilinguals behave very differently as a function of context. The adaptative control hypothesis does so with its interactional contexts (Abutalebi and Green 2016; Green 2018; Green and Abutalebi 2013). These are included in their model of the control processes needed to account for bilingual speech production. We will not describe the full fledged model as such here but simply concentrate on the interactional contexts proposed, and compare them to Grosjean's different language modes.

Green and Abutalebi agree with past researchers that bilingual speakers use their languages in different ways in different contexts. Thus, according to them, any language control mechanism must be capable of enabling different patterns of language use. Instead of proposing a continuum, as does Grosjean (2001), Green and Abutalebi limit themselves to three interactional contexts: a single-language context, a dual-language context, and a dense code-switching context. According to them, these contexts reflect everyday conversational use of language by bilinguals.[1] Speakers may experience all three contexts to different extents, as in the language mode framework.

Concerning the single-language context, which is quite similar to Grosjean's monolingual mode, the authors state that one language is used in one environment and the other in a second distinct environment. In such a context, frequent switching between languages does not take place. According to the authors, speaking in one language to the exclusion of another is intrinsically linked to a suppressive state, with inhibitory processes being central to the control of interference. Grosjean prefers to think of the other language being deactivated.

In their dual-language context, both languages are used but typically with different speakers. Switching between languages may occur within a conversation but not within an utterance, the authors state. Thus, in a work environment, a speaker may converse in one language to one person and in another language to a different person. Only one language is selected at a time but the control system is in a position to switch languages (Grosjean's change of base language) on detection of an addressee with whom they converse in their other language. In terms of the language mode framework, this interactional context would be a variant of being in a monolingual mode, or could perhaps be the beginning of an intermediate mode.

As for the dense code-switching context, which is similar to Grosjean's bilingual mode, it occurs when speakers routinely interleave their languages in the course of a single utterance and adapt words from their languages in the context of the other. Individuals here may code-switch frequently and intertwine the morphosyntax of their two languages. In such a context, we have a cooperative control process in which the resources of both language networks can be deployed.

In the years to come, it will be interesting to see whether more interactional contexts are added to the adaptive control hypothesis, to become similar in a way, to Grosjean's continuum of different modes. It would be important to involve listening too, as does Grosjean. Also, will the inhibitory control that characterizes this framework, at least for the first two contexts, be maintained as such or will more room be given to activation and deactivation? Grosjean has always preferred different levels of activation of the languages depending on the language mode a bilingual is in.

References

Abutalebi, Jubin, and David W. Green. 2016. "Neuroimaging of language control in bilinguals: Neural adaptation and reserve." *Bilingualism: Language and Cognition*, 19 (4): 689–698.

Baetens Beardsmore, Hugo. 1986. *Bilingualism: Basic Principles*. Clevedon, England: Multilingual Matters.

Boukadi, Mariem, Robert A. I. Davies, and Maximiliano A. Wilson. 2015. "Bilingual lexical selection as a dynamic process: Evidence from Arabic-French bilinguals." *Canadian Journal of Experimental Psychology*, 69 (4): 297–313.

[1] David Green, in an email to me on September 4, 2020, called them "prototypical".

Caixeta, Paulo. 2003. "L'impact de la compétence linguistique du bilingue en L2 sur le mode langagier: une étude de production." Master's Thesis, Institute of Linguistics, Neuchâtel University, Neuchâtel, Switzerland.

de Groot, Annette. 2011. *Language and Cognition in Bilinguals and Multilinguals: An Introduction.* Hove, UK: Psychology Press.

Dewaele, Jean-Marc. 2001. "Activation or inhibition? The interaction of L1, L2 and L3 on the language mode continuum." In *Cross-linguistic Influence in Third Language Acquisition: Psycholinguistic Perspectives,* edited by Jasone Cenoz, Britta Hufeisen, and Ulrike Jessner, 69–89. Clevedon: Multilingual Matters.

Dunn, Alexandra L., and Jean E. Fox Tree. 2014. "More on language mode." *International Journal of Bilingualism,* 18 (6): 605–613. DOI: 10.1177/1367006912454509.

Ervin-Tripp, Susan. 1968. "An analysis of the interaction of language, topic, and listener." In *Readings in the Sociology of Language,* edited by Joshua Fishman, 192–211. The Hague: Mouton.

Fishman, Joshua A. 1965. "Who speaks what language to whom and when?" *La Linguistique,* 1 (2): 67–88.

Fokke, Joke, Imie De Ruyter de Wildt, Ingrid Spanjers, and Janet Van Hell. 2007. "Eliciting code-switches in Dutch classroom learners of English: The language mode continuum and the role of language proficiency." *Poster presented at the 6th International Symposium of Bilingualism, Hamburg, Germany.*

Gal, Susan. 1979. *Language Shift: Social Determinants of Linguistic Change in Bilingual Austria.* New York: Academic Press.

Green, David W. 2018. "Language control and code-switching." *Languages,* 3 (8). DOI: 10.3390/languages3020008.

Green, David W., and Jubin Abutalebi. 2013. "Language control in bilinguals: The adaptive control hypothesis." *Journal of Cognitive Psychology,* 25 (5): 515–530. DOI: 10.1080/20445911.2013.796377.

Grosjean, François. 1982. *Life with Two Languages: An Introduction to Bilingualism.* Cambridge, MA: Harvard University Press.

Grosjean, François. 1990. "The psycholinguistics of language contact and code-switching: Concepts, methodology and data." *Papers for the Workshop on Concepts, Methodology and Data. Network on Code-Switching and Language Contact.* Strasbourg: European Science Foundation.

Grosjean, François. 1997. "Processing mixed language: Issues, findings and models." In *Tutorials in Bilingualism: Psycholinguistic Perspectives,* edited by Annette de Groot and Judith Kroll, 225–254. Mahwah, NJ: Lawrence Erlbaum Associates.

Grosjean, François. 2001. "The bilingual's language modes." In *One Mind, Two Languages: Bilingual Language Processing,* edited by Janet Nicol, 1–22. Oxford: Blackwell.

Grosjean, François. 2008. *Studying Bilinguals.* Oxford/New York: Oxford University Press.

Grosjean, François. 2010. *Bilingual: Life and Reality.* Cambridge, MA: Harvard University Press.

Grosjean, François. 2013. "Bilingual and monolingual language modes." In *The Encyclopedia of Applied Linguistics,* edited by Carol A. Chapelle, 1–9. Hoboken, NJ: Blackwell Publishing.

Gullifer, Jason W., Shanna Kousaie, Annie C. Gilbert, Angela Grant, Nathalie Giroud, Kristina Coulter, Denise Klein, Shari Baum, Nathalie Phillips, and Debra Titone. 2021. "Bilingual language experience as a multidimensional spectrum: Associations with objective and subjective language proficiency." *Applied Psycholinguistics,* 42 (2): 245–278. DOI: 10.1017/S0142716420000521.

Hasselmo, Nils. 1970. "Code-switching and modes of speaking." In *Texas Studies in Bilingualism*, edited by Glen Gilbert, 179–210. Berlin, Germany: De Gruyter.

Kapiley, Keerthana, and Ramesh Kumar Mishra. 2018. "What do I choose? Influence of interlocutor awareness on bilingual language choice during voluntary object naming." *Bilingualism: Language and Cognition*, 22 (5): 1–23.

Khachatryan, Elvira, Flavio Camarrone, Wim Fias, and Marc M. Van Hulle. 2016. "ERP response unveils effect of second language manipulation on first language processing." *PLoS ONE*, 11 (11): e0167194. DOI: 10.1371/journal.pone.0167194.

Marty, Simone, and François Grosjean. 1998. "Aphasie, bilinguisme et mode de communication." *Aphasie et domaines associés*, 12 (1): 8–28.

Molnar, Monika, Antonio Ibáñez-Molina, and Manuel Carreiras. 2015. "Interlocutor identity affects language activation in bilinguals." *Journal of Memory and Language*, 81: 91–104.

Muysken, Pieter. 2000. *Bilingual Speech: A Typology of Code-mixing*. Cambridge: Cambridge University Press.

Poplack, Shana. 2017. *Borrowing: Loanwords in the Speech Community and in the Grammar*. New York: Oxford University Press.

Rubin, Joan. 1968. *National Bilingualism in Paraguay*. The Hague: Mouton.

Timm, Lenora. 1978. "Code-switching in *War and Peace*." In Aspects of Bilingualism, edited by Michel Paradis. Columbia, NV: Hornbeam Press,302–315.

Weil, Sonja. 1990. "Choix de langue et alternance codique chez le bilingue en situations de communication diverses: une étude expérimentale." Master's Thesis, Institute of Romance Studies, Basle University, Basle, Switzerland.

Weinreich, Uriel. 1966. *Languages in Contact: Findings and Problems*. The Hague, Netherlands: De Gruyter.

Woomans, Evy, Clara D. Martin, Charlotte Vanden Bulcke, Eva Van Assche, Albert Costa, Robert J. Hartsuiker, and Woouter Duyck. 2015. "Can faces prime a language?" *Psychological Science*, 26 (9): 1343–1352.

Wu, Yan Jing, and Guillaume Thierry. 2010. "Investigating bilingual processing: The neglected role of language processing contexts." *Frontiers in Psychology*, 1 178: 1–6.

Yu, Ziying, and John W. Schwieter. 2018. "Recognizing the effects of language mode on the cognitive advantages of bilingualism." *Frontiers in Psychology*, 9: 366. DOI: 10.3389/fpsyg.2018.00366.

Zhang, Shu, Michael W. Morris, Chi-Ying Cheng, and Andy J. Yap. 2013. "Heritage-culture images disrupt immigrants' second-language processing through triggering first-language interference." *Proceedings of the National Academy of Sciences*, 110 (28): 11272–11277.

8

What a Bilingual's Languages Are Used For

Bilinguals distribute their languages across different domains of life; in other words, they use their languages across topics, people, and contexts as needed. The well-known Canadian and French writer, Nancy Huston, reveals this with a touch of humor in her own language behavior:

> … I prefer French to English in intellectual conversations, interviews, colloquia – linguistic situations which call upon concepts and categories learned during my adult life. But when I feel like letting off steam, freaking out, swearing, singing, yelling, surfing on the pure pleasure of verbal delirium, I do so in English.(p. 47 of *Losing North* 2002).

The fact that the bilingual's languages serve different purposes become apparent when the wrong language is used. In my book, *Bilingual: Life and Reality* (Grosjean 2010), I give a personal example. When I lived in the United States at the end of the last century, I taught introductory statistics, and I therefore knew the "language of statistics," but only in English. When I came back to Europe and offered to teach a statistics course in French, I suddenly found myself in difficulty. I simply didn't have the vocabulary in French and didn't know how to say such things as "standard distribution," "scattergram," "hypothesis test," and so on. My French is fluent and yet there I was, struggling to get concepts out.

And when one enters the domain of well-learned behaviors such as counting, praying, remembering phone numbers, and so on, doing so in the wrong language is often extremely difficult. Thus, an Arabic–English–French trilingual once reported that he had learned arithmetic in French and that he found that he remembered multiplication tables best in that language. Things become even more apparent with translation. Bilinguals can usually translate simple things from one language to the other but they have real difficulties with more specialized domains, much to the surprise of monolinguals.

In this chapter, we will study the fascinating topic of what a bilingual's languages are used for. We will first call on past research, mainly sociolinguistic, and show how it described the patterns of language use in different domains. We will then discuss recent interest in the phenomenon, mainly in psycholinguistics. This will be followed by a description of approaches used to measure bilingual language use. And we will end with the impact it has on the psycholinguistics and cognition of bilingualism, most notably language perception and production, language acquisition, memory, and mental calculation and mathematics.

The Mysteries of Bilingualism, First Edition. François Grosjean.

What Past Research Has Revealed

One of the fathers of bilingualism research, Uriel Weinreich (1953), wrote that many bilinguals are accustomed to discuss some topics in only one of their languages. He cited an earlier researcher, Georg Schmidt-Rohr, who distinguished nine domains of language use including the family, the school, the church, the press, the administration, and so on. Weinreich added that if a bilingual child studies certain subjects in a monolingual school, she will have difficulties discussing these topics in the other language.

Another well-known linguist from that period, William Mackey (1962, reprinted in 2000), stated that when one describes bilingualism, one has to deal with the question of language functions. What do bilinguals use their languages for? He gives the example of the bilingual technician who normally speaks language A at home, and language B at work. Because of this, when that person talks about his specialty, he will be able to convey his meaning much better in language B than in language A. Mackey also differentiates external and internal functions of languages. External functions are determined by the areas of contact such as the home, the community, the school, the media, etc. As for internal functions, they include non-communicative uses, such as internal speech, which covers counting, praying, cursing, dreaming, note-taking, etc. Another researcher, Dodson (1981), talks of areas of experience and states that bilinguals have a preferred language and a second language for different areas. He notes that some of them operate at preferred and second-language levels in one area of experience, while in another area the status of the two languages is reversed.

Ervin-Tripp (1968), whose work on personality and bilingualism we cover in Chapter 11, gives a fine example of specific language use in bilinguals. In her work, she interviewed Japanese women married to Americans and living in the United States. They had rather isolated lives, and used Japanese in very few situations such as talking with bilingual friends, working in Japanese restaurants (for some), and visiting back to Japan. Ervin-Tripp asked them to explain or describe topics, some associated with English, such as cooking, shopping, and leisure activities, and some associated with Japanese, such as Japanese festivals, Japanese cooking, street story-tellers, and so on. What she found was that when they were instructed to speak English about Japanese topics, they had difficulty doing so. The combination of a Japanese interlocutor and a Japanese topic always demanded the use of Japanese.

Survey studies of bilingual communities during that period also revealed the importance of the functions of languages. Thus, Hoffman (1971), in his research on the language use of young Puerto Rican Spanish–English bilinguals in Jersey City, found that they spoke mainly Spanish to both their parents, although they sometimes spoke English when talking about education and work. They spoke Spanish to their grandparents and to the parents of their girl/boy friends, but English with their siblings. Both languages were used with their friends, at school and when they went shopping. They used English only for all official matters outside the home as well as at church. And at work, everything was done in English. Thus, the two languages were distributed across the domains of life; some domains were covered by one language only, some by the other, and some by both.

It is interesting to note that in a study of another Puerto Rican community, conducted some forty years later, Schrauf (2009) confirmed this bilingualism by domain. Even though this time he concentrated on older individuals, he corroborated many aspects of the earlier study such as that his participants used more English in the public domain, at work for example, and more Spanish in the private domain, with their spouses and their close friends. Because their children were more acculturated to American life, they spoke more English with them, but retained Spanish for their families of origin, their in laws, and friends their age.

Of course, bilingualism by domain exists in every country of the world, in particular where there are minority language communities. One that received some interest in the second part of the last century is in Santa Caterina, Brazil. Heye (1979) reported on language behavior in this small town founded by German immigrants from Pomerania in Germany. Both German, more precisely, East Pomeranian, and Portuguese are spoken by a majority of the population. In some situations, only Portuguese is used such as with the authorities, in clubs, for sport, and for writing, and in others, only German is used (e.g., at church). In other situations still, both languages are employed such as at work, in stores, at home, and with friends. Thus, here too the languages are distributed across the domains of life.

Recent Interest in Bilingual Language Use

As I was preparing my first book on bilingualism, *Life with Two Languages,* I was fascinated by this sociolinguistic work that I reported on extensively. It greatly influenced me, and a few years later, in an article on the holistic nature of the bilingual person (Grosjean 1985), I talked of the different needs that bilinguals have for their languages. Some ten years later, in Grosjean (1997), I called this phenomenon the Complementarity Principle which I defined as follows: "Bilinguals usually acquire and use their languages for different purposes, in different domains of life, with different people. Different aspects of life require different languages." To visualize the principle, I have used the kind of illustration shown in Figure 8.1, which shows the domains covered by a bilingual's three languages.

Each quadrilateral represents a domain of life such as work/studies, home, family, shopping, leisure, administrative matters, holidays, clothes, sports, transportation, health, politics, etc. As can be seen, the person depicted uses language a (La) in seven

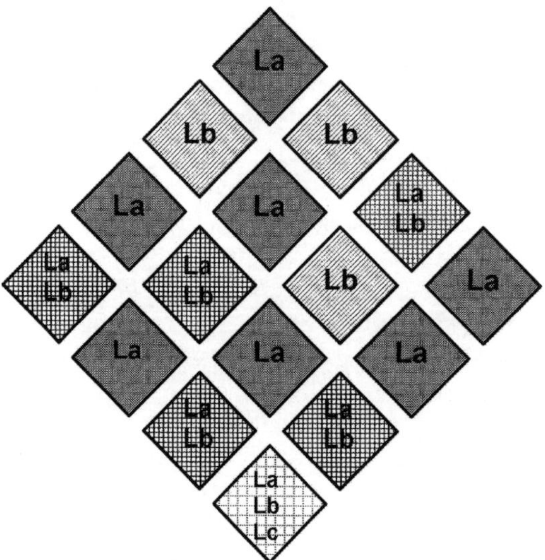

Figure 8.1 The domains covered by a bilingual's three languages.

domains of life, Lb in three, both La and Lb in five, and all three languages (La, Lb and Lc) in just one domain. Some domains, therefore, are specific to one language (ten in all), and others are shared by two or three languages (six in all). Extra quadrilaterals can, of course, be added for internal domains such as thinking, counting, praying, talking to oneself, and so on.

In Grosjean (1997, 2016), I discussed the impact the principle has on the proficiency of bilinguals in their two or more languages and proposed that the level of proficiency attained in a language (more precisely, in a language skill) will depend on the need for that language and will be domain-specific. If reading and writing skills are not needed in a language, they will not be developed. If a language is spoken with a limited number of people in a reduced number of domains, its proficiency may be less. If a language is never used for a particular purpose, it will not develop the linguistic properties needed for that purpose (specialized vocabulary, stylistic variety, some linguistic rules, etc.).

The distribution of languages by domains also has a direct impact on language dominance. Dominance is a very complex issue that has been difficult to define: is it based on language proficiency, language use, the first language acquired, the ability to read and write a language, facility in processing or, more probably, a combination of these? Whichever way one defines dominance, the domains of language use have to be taken into account, as do Silva-Corvalán and Treffers-Daller (2016) in their own definition (see Chapter 1). Thus, the bilingual depicted in Figure 8.1 would appear to be globally dominant in La (13 domains counting shared domains), but there are three domains in which she uses Lb exclusively. With adequate assessment tools, it would be fairly easy to show that this bilingual is dominant in Lb in these domains. Hence, one can be globally dominant in a specific language but be dominant in the other language for particular domains of life.

The principle also explains why regular bilinguals are usually not very good translators or interpreters. They may simply not have the necessary translation equivalents or the stylistic varieties needed in the target language, not to mention the pragmatic competence required in that language. Over the years, I have compiled a lot of information on the Complementarity Principle and the impact it has on the bilingual's everyday life, and I present it in Grosjean (2016).

In the last 20 years, an increasing number of researchers, from all areas of the language sciences, have shown interest in bilingual language use, some of them adopting the Complementarity Principle label I have proposed. Thus, Carroll and Luna (2011) in their work on lexical access, state that bilinguals learn from an early age to deal with certain content areas in a particular language. For them, language accessibility depends on the domain being discussed. Chiaro (2009), interested in the interaction within bilingual couples, examines which language are used in different domestic domains. Planas and Setati (2009) studied how immigrant bilingual students in Catalonia use their two languages – Spanish and Catalan – during the learning of mathematics in the classroom. And Montanari et al. (2018), investigating the development of vocabulary during the first four years of school, stress that a language, spoken in a reduced number of domains and with limited number of people, will develop at a lesser rate than a language used in more domains and with more people.

We will return to these studies later on in this chapter but we should end this part with a mention of the theoretical position espoused by researchers at McGill University working on this phenomenon. It is very similar to what I have defended over the years. In the presentation of their language entropy work, first proposed in Gullifer and Titone (2019), Gullifer et al. (2021) state that bilinguals distribute their use of particular languages differentially depending on the communicative context in question and the topics of conversation that occur. Because of this, proficiency for a given language may develop uniquely in some contexts. They give as an example a French–English bilingual who uses French at home. This person may have difficulty accessing words in English for concepts that typically occur in the home. As for Tiv et al. (2020), who are also interested in how bilinguals use languages differentially across different communicative context, they stress that bilinguals vary in meaningful ways regarding the social use of language.

Measuring Bilingual Language Use

In this part, we will review a few approaches used by researchers to measure bilingual language use. This is important if one wants to capture the phenomenon numerically as well as prepare future studies. The first approaches looked at the distribution of languages in terms of percentages or scale values. The later ones employed more complex methodologies: language entropy and network analysis.

Language Use in Terms of Percentages or Scale Values

We will start with work that was done in my laboratory by Gasser (2000) and Jaccard and Cividin (2001). Since this work was done in French at the time, I discuss it extensively in Grosjean (2016). One of its aims was to find empirical evidence for the Complementarity Principle, and more precisely, to show that the languages of bilinguals are distributed as a function of topic and activity. Gasser worked with English–German bilinguals in Basle, and Jaccard and Cividin with Italian–French bilinguals in the French-speaking part of Switzerland. They used the same approach and so I will spend a bit more time on the Gasser study.

The bilinguals Gasser worked with had all grown up speaking English, and had moved to Switzerland as adults. At the time of the study, they averaged 22 years of English–German bilingualism. They were asked to fill in an extensive questionnaire pertaining to their biography (who they were, where they had lived, etc.), their language history, how they rated their oral comprehension and production of both languages, and with whom they spoke which language. They were also asked about their language use for different topics and in different activities. Examples of the topics proposed were: work/studies (in general), work/studies (specific topics indicated by each participant), immediate family (with whom you live), distant family (or ancestors), house-related matters (cooking, cleaning, etc.), shopping, leisure (in general), leisure (specific activities indicated by each participant), administrative matters, holidays/trips, evenings out, etc. (The complete list is given in Grosjean 2016.)

For each topic they indicated how often they talked about it (daily, a few times a week, a few times a month, a few times a year, and never). They also indicated the extent to which each language was involved by giving a percentage for that language. For example, talking about politics could be marked a few times a week, and the percentages could be 70% for English and 30% for German. (The percentages for German and Swiss–German were combined during the data analysis.)

The instructions for activities were similar (frequency of use and importance of each language). The activities concerned were: writing (at work), writing mail (letters, email), note-taking, attending local circles/clubs, speaking colloquially, counting, calculating, expressing one's feelings, singing alone, praying, swearing, speaking to oneself, other (specified by each participant).

The percentages obtained were organized in grids by participant, topic and activity, and language. Five percentage classes were chosen (0–19, 20–39, 40–59, 60–79 and 80–100) and the different topics and activities were inserted into them. This allowed one to visualize the distribution of topics (or activities) across languages. Thus, for example, concerning topics, a particular participant (Bilingual 14) talked about his family (immediate), family (distant), home and love, only in English (all these topics were given 100% and were inserted in the 81–100% class). For German, three topics received 100% also: leisure, shopping and administration. In the 61–80% class, one found holidays (80%) and evenings out (70%) for English, and politics and clothes, both 80%, for German. The 40–80 range, where topics were discussed in both English and German, only had one entry: work with 60% in English, 40% in German. And so on down the range of percentage classes.

The results for the activities were represented in the same manner. For this same bilingual, seven activities were in the 81–100 class in just one language (English): note-taking, expressing feelings, praying, calculating, counting, writing at work, and writing mail. This is not surprising for a late English–German bilingual who started doing these activities in his first language.

To obtain a measure of bilingual language use for topics and activities, a Complementarity Index (CI) was developed. It ranged from 0% (all topics or activities were covered equally by the two languages) to 100% (topics or activities were language specific; none were covered by both languages). Fifty percent meant that basically half the topics or activities were covered by the two languages and half by just one language. For the 20 participants in Gasser's study, the mean CI for topics was 79.45% with a range that extended from 29.41% to 100%. As for activities, the mean CI was 81.24% with a range that went from 36.36% to 100%. When we combined the above results (topics and activities) and worked out a grand mean, it came to 80.35%.

Clearly for this group of English–German bilinguals, many topics or activities were language specific; that is, they were covered mainly (or totally) by one language. To illustrate this further, we looked at the items that fell in the 81–100% class within the whole group for a particular language. As concerns topics, English was clearly preferred when talking about love, family (both immediate and distant) and spending an evenings out. German came out top when discussing shopping, transportation, administration, health, and sports. As for activities, almost all were covered by English. There was one exception where German was preferred just slightly – attending clubs. In sum, as the Complementarity Principle states, different aspects of life and different activities required different languages.

Jaccard and Cividin (2001) undertook a replication of this research with second-generation Italian–French bilinguals in the Swiss French part of Switzerland. The results they obtained were similar to those reported by Gasser. The mean CI value for topics was 60.58% with a range that extended from 12.5% to 100%. As for the activities, the mean value was 73.46% with a range extending from 40% to 100%. The grand mean, combining topics and activities, was 67.02%. Thus, even though this percentage was lower than the one found in Basle (grand mean of 80.35%), more than half of the topics and activities were covered, to varying degrees, by just one language in the Swiss French study. This, of course, is exactly what the Complementarity Principle would predict.

Before moving on to recent approaches, it is worth mentioning two studies by others, one using percentages and the other scale values to get at bilingual language use. Chiaro (2009) asked bilingual couples representing a number of different language pairs to state which languages they spoke in various domains and activities. She found that a number of activities received very high single-language percentages: 74% for counting,

88% for doing sums and calculating, 81% in prayer and worship, and 73% for talking to oneself. Other domains were shared between the two languages such as work, arguing, food, etc.

In the second study, Carroll and Luna (2011) asked their Spanish–English bilingual participants in Boston, all highly proficient in their two languages, to rate their language use on a seven-point scale (with "never" on one end and "always" on the other). They did this for three different domains: home, family and friends, and work. For home, Spanish was the dominant answer (5.93 vs. 4.03 for English); for family and friends, Spanish again came out on top (5.87 vs. 3.67); and for work, English was the dominant answer (6.30 vs. 3.17). All these differences were significantly different.

Up to now, the distribution of language use has been measured in rather straightforward ways with simple statistics (percentages or scale values). Recent work has brought real advances in methodology and is mentioned below.

Language Use in Terms of Language Entropy and Network Analysis

Following on Gullifer and Titone (2019), Gullifer et al. (2021) used language entropy as a measure of language use. Their study was aimed at depicting the bilingual experience of French–English bilingual speakers in Montreal, Canada, as a function of variables such as timing of language exposure, amount of L2 exposure, language proficiency, as well as language use. In what follows, we will only concentrate on their approach to get at language use via language entropy. They define the latter as being a flexible measure of language balance in various communicative contexts. A low entropy value signifies that only one language is used and a high entropy value that several languages are used.

To obtain values of language entropy, the researchers first asked their participants about their language use in three communicative contexts. The first pertained to conversations in different social contexts. Here the participants had to "estimate the percent of conversations that take place in each of your languages, and what percentage of that is with the following people." The latter were family members, friends, classmates, and coworkers. The second context related to inner thoughts and expressing emotion. Here they had to indicate on a 1 to 7 scale how often they used their languages for the following activities: doing arithmetic, remembering numbers, dreaming, thinking, talking to yourself, and expressing anger or affection. And the third context involved passive language use. The participants were asked to "estimate the total number of hours each day that you spend engaged in the following activities, and indicate what percentage of that time you spend engaged in that activity in each of the languages that you know." The activities were: listening to the radio or watching the TV, reading for fun, reading for work, reading on the internet, writing e-mails to friends, and writing articles or papers.

For each of these communicative contexts, they computed the language entropy (H) using Claude Shannon's well-known entropy formula. The first author of the study kindly sent me a table of their entropy results and it is clear that some contexts/activities are mainly in one language, such as writing articles or papers, reading for work, speaking with classmates, etc. There are also cases where two languages are involved, such as writing e-mails to friends, speaking with coworkers, remembering numbers, dreaming, thinking, and talking to yourself. The authors conclude the part dedicated to getting entropy values by stating that bilinguals differentially distribute their use of particular languages depending on the communicative context in question and the topics of conversation that occur in that context.

Another approach to get at differential language use is proposed by Tiv et al. (2020). They use network analysis to gain a better understanding of language use across varying communicative contexts. French–English bi- or multilinguals, also from Montreal, were divided into two groups based on a question which asked them to indicate the language they were most fluent in (the authors called this their dominant language) and also the second language they were most fluent in (the non-dominant language). They were then asked which language they used when speaking about a number of conversational topics, e.g., cultural, emotional, intimate, chit chat, daily activities, family activities, gossip, hobbies, personal history, sports, work, etc. There were 21 topics in each of a number of contexts: work, family, home, school, and social. The authors give as an example the home where one may discuss emotional topics only in one's dominant language but then discuss chit chat in both the dominant and non-dominant language.

The data they obtained were used to build five web-like context networks, one for each of the contexts, and two language networks, for the two levels of dominance. For each network, the researchers calculated the network size (the larger they are, the more variability there is), network strength (the higher it is, the more topics are used together in more contexts/languages) and network density (this captured the number of edges, i.e., the connections or relationships between the nodes).

The networks they obtained, presented in different hues, are not only visually appealing but also tell us a lot about differential language use in bilinguals. Thus, for the five context networks, the researchers found that the work context displayed low network size, suggesting fewer topics discussed at work, and low weight or strength distributions, suggesting that fewer languages are use in this context. On the other hand, the social context network benefited from high network size (more topics are discussed in social interactions) and high weight or strength distributions (more languages are used in this context). The other communicative contexts (school, home and family) displayed patterns somewhere in between these two. As for the two language networks (dominant, non-dominant), the dominant language network showed greater network size, strength and density than the non-dominant network, suggesting that more topics are used in a wider variety of contexts in the dominant language.

This visualization approach, along with the one that uses language entropy, will certainly encourage other researchers to study differential language use in novel ways and confirm its importance in the study of bilinguals.

Impact of Bilingual Language Use

As we have seen, different language use is prevalent in the life of bilinguals, and so it is only normal that it impacts on the psycholinguistics and cognition of bilingualism, most notably language perception and production, language acquisition, memory, and mental calculation and mathematics. One or two examples of studies will be described in each domain.

Language Perception

In the domain of language perception, Carroll and Luna (2011) investigated how the recognition of words depends on how they are used by bilinguals in everyday life. They proposed that words will be more accessible, and hence better recognized, when the language in which they are coded is the language that is typically used to discuss a particular content area. Having shown that certain topics are discussed more readily in a particular language by their Spanish–English bilinguals (see the preceding part), they conducted a visual word recognition task in both English and Spanish (this is Study 1 of their article). One group did a lexical decision task on English words that matched the "work" content area spoken about in English by their participants, and they did the same task on Spanish words that matched the Spanish-language "friends and family" content area. The other group did the same lexical decision task but this time on English words that did not match the English-language content area (that is, on English words pertaining to friends and family) and on Spanish words that did not match the Spanish-language content area (that is, on Spanish words pertaining to work).

The results obtained showed how important differential language use is during language processing. When words were shown in Spanish and they belonged to the Spanish-language content area (family and friends, therefore), they were recognized faster than the same words shown in English. And when words were shown in English and they belonged to the English-language content area (work), they too were recognized faster than the same words shown in Spanish. Having controlled for both word frequency and length (two important variables in word recognition), the authors concluded that words in the language used in the words' content areas (work for English, friends and family for Spanish) are more accessible than similar words in the other language. This is exactly what one would expect of differential language use.

Since Carroll and Luna (2011) were interested in researching the language used in advertisements targeting bilingual individuals, they did another study bearing on this issue (Study 2 of their paper). They found that when an ad that is shown in a particular language, and the ad's content belongs to the domain most associated with that language, then ad evaluations are higher than when there is a mismatch between the language of presentation and the content of the ad. They theorized that this occurs because knowledge relevant to the ad content is more accessible in the language typically used in that content area.

Language Production

Gasser (2000), who worked alongside Jaccard and Cividin (2001) on the Complementarity Principle, wanted to see what would happen if her bilingual participants talked about a topic in the wrong language. By this was meant a topic normally talked about in the other language. More precisely, if they talked about the topic while in a bilingual mode situation, that is, with a bilingual interlocutor with whom they felt free to mix their languages, would they code-switch and borrow more than when using the right language, i.e., a topic associated with that language? In what follows, we will refer to a topic as "strong" if it was characterized by high use in the language in question (see the previous part) and as "weak" if it was in the low use category. Gasser worked out for ten of her bilingual participants, and each of their two languages, the strong and the weak topics. Thus, for example, she found for a particular bilingual the following topics in each category: strong English topics: home, family (distant); weak English topics: leisure, shopping; strong German topics: sports, education; and weak German topics: holidays, evenings out.

Gasser prepared questions for the strong/weak parts of the English interviews, and other questions for the strong/weak parts of the German interviews. The questions took into account the culture linked to each language, a British or American culture for English, and the Swiss German culture for German. These questions served as a starting point for a semi-guided interview that took place in a quiet room, very often in the bilinguals' homes. The participants were told that they should feel free to talk about any aspect related to the questions, the only restriction being that they were to stay in the base language set at the beginning of each section. They could code-switch if they wanted to, however, as the experimenter knew both languages.

The variable examined during the data analysis stage was the amount of language mixing that took place, that is, instances of the language not being spoken at that time, such as code-switches and borrowings. There were two different dependent measures. The first was the number of mixed syllables per minute. The other, that took into account the speaker's speech rate, was the percentage of mixed syllables per condition (see Grosjean 2016, for details). The results obtained were very similar for each measure and clearly showed that differential language use is a factor in bilingual speech production. There were significantly fewer mixed syllables per minute in the strong language condition than in the weak language condition. As for the percentage of mixed syllables, the percentage was significantly lower in the strong language condition as opposed to the weak language condition.

Jaccard and Cividin (2001) used exactly the same approach with their Italian–French second-generation bilinguals in the French-speaking part of Switzerland. Their results were even more marked in that the amount of mixed language increased more than fourfold when bilinguals went from a strong topic in a language to a weak topic. Thus, in both studies, bilinguals showed that language mixing depended on whether the bilinguals talked about a strong language topic or a weak language topic. If, for example, they had to talk about a topic in the "wrong language" (a weak language topic), they brought in their other language to help themselves out since they were in a bilingual language mode. This happened much less when they were speaking about a topic in the "right" language (a strong language topic). Thus both studies showed the very real impact that regular bilingual language use has on language behavior.

Language Acquisition

Bilingual language use in different domains also plays a large role in language acquisition in bilinguals children. We will illustrate this with two studies, both of them on the development of vocabulary in the school language and the family language. Bialystok et al. (2010) examined the receptive vocabulary of a large number of children between the ages of three and ten: 772 were English monolingual speakers, and 966 were bilingual speakers. The latter were educated in English at school but they spoke a non-English language at home with family members. Their parents reported that they were fluent in both English and their family language, and also said that they used both languages on a daily basis. All the children, monolingual and bilingual, were given the English version of the Peabody Picture Vocabulary Test where they have to point to one of four pictures that best represents a word spoken by the experimenter. Younger children were allowed to respond by pointing to the picture, and older children responded by either saying the number corresponding to the picture or by pointing to it.

The results showed that monolingual children outperformed bilingual children at every age comparison. This simply confirmed what had been found in other studies. But the researchers did not leave things at that. They reasoned that since bilingual children primarily used English at school, and the non-English language at home, it could be that these contexts selectively disadvantage certain portions of the English vocabulary. So they conducted an item analysis and classified the words on the basis of their primary context of use: home or school. In the home category, they put food and household items (e.g., squash, camcorder), culture-specific items (e.g., canoe, camper), and words that were unlikely to occur in a classroom context (e.g., horrified). In the school category they put items dealing with professions (e.g., astronaut), animals or plants (e.g., raccoon), shapes (e.g., rectangle), musical instruments (e.g., harp) and words reflecting school experiences (e.g., writing).

An analysis of receptive vocabulary in terms of these primary contexts was applied to 161 children between the ages of 6;0 to 6;11. The results obtained are a fine example of differential language use. The difference found between monolinguals and bilinguals was maintained in the home domain. This is normal: the bilingual children used their other language at home and hence did not know English home words as well. However, in the school domain, a domain where English is used by both groups, the monolingual and bilingual children showed similar results. In sum, as with adults, the vocabulary of bilingual children will be in a given language for certain domains, in the other language for other domains, and in both languages for some shared domains (Grosjean 2016).

Of course, as bilingual children spend more and more time in school, and with their friends outside, their family language may lose some of its importance. This is what Montanari et al. (2018) showed in their study. Basing themselves on the Complementarity Principle, they hypothesized at the onset of their paper that when a language is spoken in a reduced number of domains and with a limited number of people, it will develop at a lesser rate than a language used in more domains and with more people. They examined vocabulary development in Russian–German bilinguals, aged 6;0 to 10;11, in Germany. All children had at least one parent or caregiver who spoke Russian as a first language, and close to two thirds of the children received Russian language support at school and/or in a parents' association.

All children did an expressive vocabulary task in which they named objects or actions that were presented on photos (sometimes they also had to name the opposite). Both languages were assessed in this way. The results showed a rapid development of the vocabulary of the majority language from Grades 1 to 4 whereas that of the family (heritage) language hardly increased at all. In addition, concerning the items named in the family language *only*, the mean declined from 53.2% in Grade 1 to 23.4% in Grade 4.[1]

What happened to doublets is revealing also. This concerns concepts that have a label in both languages (they are also called translation equivalents). In past research, Pearson, Fernández, and Oller (1995) found that 30.8% of words in bilingual children were doublets, and more recently Poulin-Dubois et al. (2013) reported a very similar percentage (37.4%). In Montanari et al.'s study, the percentage of doublets went from 38.7% in Grade 1 to 55.8% in Grade 4, thereby showing an increasing overlap of the two vocabularies. The authors explain this by the fact that teaching contents in the first years of schooling are linked to everyday experiences which, at first, could have been favored in the family language vocabulary. They added that in 60% of the families, the school language is also used in the family domain.

In sum, in terms of different language use, it is to be expected that the vocabulary in the majority language will develop more quickly than in the family (heritage) language. As the authors write, the school domain offers particularly rich input and various possibilities for use of the majority language. As for the family language, it is not used more intensively as time goes by and stagnates.

[1] The authors had originally given the results in naming values; they kindly converted them into percentages for this chapter.

Memory

Memory is also influenced by bilingual language use. Marian and Neisser (2000) found that bilinguals remember things better when the language that is used for recall matches the language used at the time of the event in a particular domain. In interviews they conducted with Russian–English bilinguals, both in English and in Russian, they gave them English prompt words in the English part of the study, and Russian translation equivalents in the Russian part. The English prompt words included items such as "summer," "neighbors," "birthday," "cat," and "doctor." The bilinguals were asked to describe an event from their own life that the prompt word brought to mind. The researchers also asked the participants, after the interview, to indicate the language in which they had been spoken to, or they had spoken, or they had been surrounded by, at the time that each recalled event took place. If the event prompted by the word "cat," for example, took place in Russian, the researchers called this a Russian memory; if it took place in English, then it was an English memory.

Marian and Neisser found that their bilingual participants accessed more Russian memories when interviewed in Russian than when interviewed in English, and more English memories when interviewed in English than when in Russian. They concluded that bilinguals are more likely to retrieve memories that occurred in a particular language if that same language is also used in the retrieval setting. They called this language-dependent recall. In sum, bilingual language use manifests itself, at least indirectly, in the recall of events that took place in the bilingual's different languages – which, as we have seen, are often linked to different domains.

Mental Calculation and Mathematics

In one of her *Psychology Today* posts, "What languages do bilinguals count in?" (also in Grosjean 2021), Aneta Pavlenko writes:[2]

> It is often said that bilinguals continue using their first language for simple arithmetic operations, such as addition or multiplication, long after they shifted to the second language in other domains. I am not an exception to this phenomenon. After two decades in the United States, I live, lecture, and write in English, but when it comes to balancing my checkbook, calculating a tip, or counting the number of reps at the gym, I often switch to Russian. Do others also count in their first language while living in the second, and if so, why? And what does this adherence mean for kids who study math in a second language or shift languages mid-way through the schooling process?

Work on bilingual language use is well on the way to answering the two questions she asks. On the topic of which language one counts in, Dewaele (2007) analyzed the answers to a questionnaire given to some 1,454 bi- and multilinguals and found that 65.6% state that their first language is their preferred language for mental calculation. He proposes that this preference may be linked to the fact that this specific cognitive operation has most probably been learned in that language, and that it is typically also the dominant language. He examined the factors that can account for which language is used for mental calculation, and the very first predictor he found was frequency of

[2] https://www.psychologytoday.com/intl/blog/life-bilingual/201504/what-languages-do-bilinguals-count-in.

general use of the language. A constant use of a language can make that language become the inner language used for cognitive operations. Among some of the other predictors he found were socialization in the language, context of acquisition, and age of onset of acquisition. More recently, a meta-analysis study by Garcia et al. (2021) on number processing ease in bilinguals confirms that the privileging of the first language is not uniform, as indicated by Dewaele, but varies by bilingualism onset, proficiency, language of early schooling, and language-specific characteristics.

As for the second question, what this means for children who study mathematics in a second language, an interesting study by Planas and Setati (2009) gives us elements of an answer. They examined how young immigrant bilingual students, who had arrived in Catalonia from South American countries, used their two languages, Spanish, their home language, and Catalan, their school language, during mathematical activities. The students, who were 12 years old on average, and who took part in small working groups made up of bilingual students like them, tended to use the two languages for different purposes, in different domains of mathematical practices, and in relation to social settings within the classroom. Thus, Catalan was used when the students were becoming familiar with the task asked of them and with the new mathematical vocabulary. As for Spanish, it was used when they started to reflect on solving the tasks and developing mathematical explanations. Of course, during whole group discussions, they used Spanish, the language of teaching and learning.

In sum, differential language use is certainly one of the most pervasive aspects of individual bilingualism. And, as we have just seen, there is increasing empirical evidence for its impact on the psycholinguistics and cognition of bilingualism.

References

Bialystok, Ellen, Gigi Luk, Kathleen F. Peets, and Sujin Yang. 2010. "Receptive vocabulary differences in monolingual and bilingual children." *Bilingualism: Language and Cognition*, 13 (4): 525–531.

Carroll, Ryall, and David Luna. 2011. "The other meaning of fluency: Content accessibility and language in advertising to bilinguals." *Journal of Advertising*, 40 (3): 73–84.

Chiaro, Delia. 2009. "Cultural divide or unifying factor? Humorous talk in the interaction of bilingual, cross-cultural couples." In *Humor in Interaction*, edited by Neal R. Norrick and Delia Chiaro, 211–231. Amsterdam/Philadelphia, PA: John Benjamins.

Dewaele, Jean-Marc. 2007. "Multilinguals' language choice for mental calculation." *Intercultural Pragmatics*, 4 (3): 343–376.

Dodson, Carl J. 1981. "A reappraisal of bilingual development and education: Some theoretical and practical considerations." In *Elements of Bilingual Theory*, edited by Hugo Baetens Beardsmore, 4–27. Brussels: Vrije Universiteit Brussel.

Ervin-Tripp, Susan. 1968. "An analysis of the interaction of language, topic, and listener." In *Readings in the Sociology of Language*, edited by Joshua Fishman, 192–211. The Hague: Mouton.

Garcia, Omar, Nafiseh Faghihi, Akash R. Raola, and Jyotsna Vaid. 2021. "Factors influencing bilinguals' speed and accuracy of number judgments across languages: A meta-analytic review." *Journal of Memory and Language*, 118: 104211. DOI: org/10.1016/j.jml.2020.104211.

Gasser, Christine. 2000. "Exploring the Complementarity Principle: The case of first generation English-German bilinguals in the Basle area." Master's Thesis, English Linguistics, University of Basle, Switzerland.

Grosjean, François. 1985. "The bilingual as a competent but specific speaker-hearer." *Journal of Multilingual and Multicultural Development*, 6: 467–477.

Grosjean, François. 1997. "The bilingual individual." *Interpreting*, 2 (1/2): 163–187.

Grosjean, François. 2010. *Bilingual: Life and Reality*. Cambridge, MA: Harvard University Press.

Grosjean, François. 2016. "The Complementarity Principle and its impact on processing, acquisition, and dominance." In *Language Dominance in Bilinguals: Issues of Measurement and Operationalization*, edited by Carmen Silva-Corvalán and Jeanine Treffers-Daller, 66–84. Cambridge: Cambridge University Press.

Grosjean, François. 2021. *Life as a Bilingual: Knowing and Using Two or More Languages*. Cambridge, UK: Cambridge University Press.

Gullifer, Jason W., and Debra Titone. 2019. "Characterizing the social diversity of bilingualism using language entropy." *Bilingualism: Language and Cognition*, 1–12. DOI: 10.1017/S1366728919000026.

Gullifer, Jason W., Shanna Kousaie, Annie C. Gilbert, Angela Grant, Nathalie Giroud, Kristina Coulter, Denise Klein, Shari Baum, Nathalie Phillips, and Debra Titone. 2021. "Bilingual language experience as a multidimensional spectrum: Associations with objective and subjective language proficiency." *Applied Psycholinguistics*, 42 (2): 245–278. DOI: 10.1017/S0142716420000521.

Heye, Jürgen B. 1979. "Bilingualism and language maintenance in two communities in Santa Caterina, Brazil." In *Language and Society*, edited by William C. McCormack and Stephen A. Wurm, 401–422. The Hague: Mouton.

Hoffman, Gerard. 1971. "Puerto Ricans in New York: A language-related ethnographic summary." In *Bilingualism in the Barrio*, edited by Joshua Fishman, Robert Cooper, and Roxana Ma, 13–42. Bloomington, IN: Indiana University Press.

Huston, Nancy. 2002. *Losing North: Musings on Land, Tongue and Self*. Toronto: McArthur & Company.

Jaccard, Roxane, and Vanessa Cividin. 2001. "Le principe de complémentarité chez la personne bilingue: Le cas du bilinguisme français-italien en Suisse Romande." Master's Thesis, Language Pathology Program, University of Neuchâtel, Switzerland.

Mackey, William. 1962; 2000. "The description of bilingualism." *Canadian Journal of Linguistics*, 7: 51–85. Reprinted in *The Bilingualism Reader*, edited by Li Wei, 26–54. London/New York: Routledge.

Marian, Viorica, and Ulric Neisser. 2000. "Language-dependent recall of autobiographical memories." *Journal of Experimental Psychology: General*, 129: 361–368.

Montanari, Elke G., Roman Abel, Barbara Grasser, and Lilia Tschudinovski. 2018. "Do bilinguals create two different sets of vocabulary for two domains?" *Linguistic Approaches to Bilingualism*, 8 (4): 502–522.

Pearson, Barbara Z., Sylvia Fernández, and D. Kimbrough Oller. 1995. "Cross-language synonyms in the lexicons of bilingual infants: One language or two?" *Journal of Child Language*, 22: 345–368.

Planas, Núria, and Mamokgethi Setati. 2009. "Bilingual students using their languages in the learning of mathematics." *Mathematics Education Research Journal*, 21 (3): 36–59.

Poulin-Dubois, Diane, Ellen Bialystok, Agnes Blaye, Alexandra Polonia, and Jessica Yott. 2013. "Lexical access and vocabulary development in very young bilinguals." *International Journal of Bilingualism*, 17: 57–70.

Schrauf, Robert W. 2009. "English use among older bilingual immigrants in linguistically concentrated neighborhoods: Social proficiency and internal speech as intracultural variation." *Journal of Cross-Cultural Gerontology*, 24: 157–179.

Silva-Corvalán, Carmen, and Jeanine Treffers-Daller. 2016. *Language Dominance in Bilinguals: Issues of Measurement and Operationalization*. Cambridge: Cambridge University Press.

Tiv, Mehrgol, Jason W. Gullifer, Ruo Ying Feng, and Debra Titone. 2020. "Using network science to map what Montréal bilinguals talk about across languages and communicative contexts." *Journal of Neurolinguistics*, 56 (November). DOI: 10.1016/j.jneuroling.2020.100913.

Weinreich, Uriel. 1953. *Languages in Contact: Findings and Problems*. New York: Publications of the Linguistic Circle of New York 1.

9

Is Language Processing in Bilinguals Selective or Non-selective?

One of the questions researchers have asked themselves concerning the perception and production of language by bilinguals is whether processing is selective or non-selective when only one language is being used. In other words, When they perceive and comprehend just one language, is only that language involved in the processing, or do(es) the other(s) intervene?; and, When they are speaking a single language, without code-switching or borrowing, do they call on just that language or do(es) the other(s) play a role?

Until recently, many researchers have opted for non-selectivity. Thus, for example, Costa (2005) wrote concerning production that there is wide agreement in assuming that the conceptual system activates the two languages of a bilingual simultaneously and that this supports the notion that the activation flow from the conceptual system to the lexical system is language non-selective. A few years later, Bialystok et al. (2009) stated that it is now well documented that both languages of a bilingual are jointly activated even in contexts that strongly bias towards one of them. Green and Abutalebi (2013) went along with this when they said that substantial experimental evidence indicates that in bilingual speakers, both languages are active even when only one is being used. Finally, and quite recently, Marian (2019), writing about word recognition, stated that not only do the words we hear activate other, similar-sounding words, but the translations of those words in other languages become activated. And that same year, Paap (2019) stated that there is considerable evidence that during reading, listening, and speaking, words in the non-target language become coactivated and create conflict that needs resolution.

Thus, to the question of whether processing in bilinguals is selective or non-selective when just one language is being used, many researchers have opted for non-selectivity. But this opinion is starting to change as more research is conducted.

In this chapter, we will study selectivity in language perception and comprehension first of all, be it written or oral, and then in spoken language production. We will describe studies that have found non-selectivity, but also studies that have shown selectivity, and we will try to understand why it is that they come to different conclusions. We will also show that many different factors are involved such as language proficiency, language dominance, the context and the people present, the type of stimuli being produced or perceived, as well as the experimental task bilinguals are asked to do. We will end with a brief summary of two accounts of what happens when a bilingual is speaking just one language – that of the language mode framework, and that of the adaptive control hypothesis.

The Mysteries of Bilingualism, First Edition. François Grosjean.

Language Perception and Comprehension

In this first part, we will examine a few studies that show non-selectivity as well as some that show the reverse. We will then consider some factors that seem to play a role in whether just one language is involved or all languages play a role.

Examples of Studies that Show Non-selectivity

Paulmann et al. (2006) asked their German–English bilingual participants to do a visual lexical decision task whilst they measured event-related brain potentials (ERPs). They presented interlingual homographs, that is words written in the same way in two languages but that have different meanings, and often a different pronunciation. They wanted to know whether a visual homograph presented in English as a prime, such as "chef," would activate the German meaning of "chef," which is "boss." The English word "boss" was presented as the target following the word "chef" and the participants had to say whether it was a word or not. Another example was "bald" as a prime and "soon" as a target ("bald" means "soon" in German). The interlingual homograph always served as the prime and the target always reflected the German meaning of the interlingual homograph.

The researchers also changed the global language context by showing a film either in German or in English before the experiment which always took place in English. They argued that if the expectation caused by the English film was not sufficient to close out German, and the participants showed the presence of activation in their German, then a non-selective view could be supported.

Their participants were German speakers who had started learning English between the ages of ten and 11, who had spent a mean of 17 months in an English-speaking country, and who were proficient in English. The experiment was conducted in English and the instructions, also in English, asked the participants to read the two words on the screen, presented one after the other, and to decide whether the second word was a word or not, that is, make a lexical decision. After some practice, and before the actual experiment started, the English or German version of the short film was presented to the participants.

In the results obtained, the reaction times showed no language context effect. That is, whether the film had been in English or German, the participants responded in the same amount of time to the target following a homograph. The language version of the film did not seem to play a role, therefore. As for the ERP measurements, the priming effects were the same regardless of the language of the film. The researchers concluded that there was an automatic, parallel activation of both the first and second language lexical entries during the presentation of interlingual homographs. They argued that the bilinguals were not able to consciously or unconsciously suppress the influence of the first language in a second-language task preceded by a global second language setting.

As we will see often in this chapter, various external factors were present and may explain, in part at least, the results obtained. Among top-down factors, the experiment took place in a German laboratory and German was the language used daily by all concerned. I contacted the senior author in 2020 and she told me that they had greeted their participants in German, and that the debriefing had also taken place in that language. Could German really have been fully deactivated during the experiment, at least in those who saw the English version of the movie? One can have doubts especially if some (or all) had known from others that this was a study related to their bilingualism, and hence both their languages might come in useful. Another factor, more bottom-up this time, is that the participants saw language ambiguous words during the experiment such as "chef" and "bald," among many other interlingual homographs. This, along with seeing the meaning of these words presented as targets ("boss" and "soon," respectively) might well have kept their two languages active. I have called this being in a "bilingual language mode" (Grosjean 2001). As Wu and Thierry (2010) have written, "... stimuli with a special status in the two languages of a bilingual speaker, such as cognates, and interlingual homographs, create a dual-language processing context which ... raises the participants' explicit or implicit awareness of the bilingual context of testing."

Another study which also proposed that language processing is non-selective was conducted by Spivey and Marian (1999) with Russian-English bilinguals. They used a head-mounted eye tracker which allows the experimenter to see where the participants are looking while speech comprehension is taking place. Their bilingual participants were asked to look at a 3 by 3 board that contained a number of objects. For example, a stamp was in the bottom right-hand square, a marker (or a ruler) in the top left-hand square, and two filler objects in the top-right and bottom-left squares.

In the Russian part of the study, the participants were given instructions in Russian to displace the target object on the board to the middle square. For example, "Poloji marku nije krestika" (Put the stamp below the cross). In the interlingual competitor condition, an object on the board had an English name that shared initial phonetic characteristics with the onset of the name of the Russian target object. Thus when the target object was a stamp ("marku"), the interlingual competitor object was a marker, an object whose English name shares the same word beginning as "marku." The researchers examined the eye movements made to this interlingual competitor object as compared to a control object, in exactly the same position, such as a ruler. In this condition, the object's name bore no phonetic similarity with the name of the target object ("marku").

The results obtained showed that the participants made significantly more eye movements to the interlingual competitor object (32%) than to the control object (7%). Why was that? It would seem that the word onset of the target object (e.g., "marku") not only activated Russian words in the Russian lexicon but also English words in the English lexicon that began in a similar way ("marker" is very similar to "marku"). This happened through bottom-up processing, that is, the processing of the speech input. Based on this, the authors concluded that processing is non-selective.

This study, among many others, reinforced the non-selectivity position of researchers such as those quoted in the introduction. But during the same time, and especially in the last years, those who believed in selectivity were working on the topic. In addition, some of those who believed in non-selectivity were redoing their experiments and controlling certain factors. As we will see below, the results they obtained were quite different.

Examples of Studies that Show Selectivity

A few years after their first study, Marian and Spivey (2003) came back to the question. They thought that several things may have activated the other language such as the fact that the bilinguals knew they were taking part in an experiment on bilingualism (as might have been the case in the Paulmann et al. 2006 study), that they were tested by bilingual experimenters fluent in both languages, and that the two languages were tested in adjacent experimental sessions. We could add that the bilingual participants probably knew that the laboratory was doing bilingual research (in part, at least), and that they may have received reports from other participants who had taken part in the experiment. In short, there were enough factors present to produce the results obtained.

So as to put their participants in a situation that deactivated the other language as best as possible, the authors undertook a new study in which they used different experimenters who posed as monolingual speakers for the Russian and then the English sessions. (Note that we will concentrate here on the Russian session once again.) And during testing, they used only the language of the session, and participants only took part in one or the other session. The results they obtained were quite convincing. The participants looked at interlingual English competitor objects in only 8% of the trials as opposed to 5% for the control object, a non-significant difference. It should be recalled that in their first study, the percentages had been 32% and 7%, respectively. Now that the other language had been totally "closed out," processing had become selective.

Other researchers who showed selective processing were Dunn and Fox Tree (2014). Like Paulmann et al. (2006) they used a lexical decision task in English but did not measure ERP. They made sure that their Spanish–English bilingual participants were unaware that their bilingualism was of interest to them. Along with a group of monolingual English speakers, they were greeted by non-Latino research assistants in English. All sessions were also scheduled so as to avoid that they encounter any known bilingual or Latino participants or students. And the English written words that were presented in the experiment contained no homographs or cognates. The results were clear. The reaction times were similar for bilinguals and monolinguals, both for words and for non-words. Clearly, processing was selective and the bilingual's knowledge of Spanish did not intervene in anyway in their processing of English.

What is interesting is that the experimenters then showed a Pink Panther video to their participants and asked them to retell the story. For half the bilinguals, however, and prior to viewing the video, a Latina experimenter entered the room and revealed her ability to speak and understand Spanish. She asked those participants to retell the story in Spanish, providing the cover story that Spanish retellings would enrich their database. All participants then did a second lexical decision task. The results were now different for the bilingual subgroup that had retold the story in Spanish. They took longer to reject English non-words in the study. The researchers explain this by the fact that they had both their languages competing during the processing of non-words, that is, they were in a "bilingual mode," to use the language mode terminology (see Chapter 7). This raises the possibility that bilingual listeners will be sensitive to factors that will result in processing being selective at times and non-selective at other times, as we will see below.

Factors that Affect Whether Perception Is Selective or Not

An important factor that plays a role in selectivity is language proficiency. If a study is done in the dominant or first language, and the other language is less well-known, then a more selective process will emerge. And the reverse occurs when the weaker language is used. In the first of two studies undertaken by Weber and Cutler (2004; Studies 3 and 4), Dutch–English bilinguals were presented with spoken words in their second language, English. The visual display from which they had to select a target included a distractor item of which the Dutch name, but not the English name, made it a potential competitor. Thus, for example, they heard, "Click on the kitten. Now put it on top of the diamond," whilst they also saw a visual competitor whose name in Dutch ("kist," which means "chest") overlapped phonemically with the beginning of the target ("kitten"). The proportion of fixations obtained showed that the Dutch competitors were activated when the bilingual participants did the study but not when a control group of monolingual American speakers responded. They concluded, like Spivey and Marian (1999), that non-native listeners experienced spurious competition from native language candidates, that is, that processing was non-selective.

However, Weber and Cutler then asked themselves what would happen when bilinguals listened to their first language. They therefore changed the language of the experiment, and of the test items, and ran a second group on the new stimuli. The result was clear: they found no activation of the English competitors! Their conclusion was that for listeners who use their second language less frequently than their native language, competition when listening to the native language is not increased by second language candidates.

Another factor that affects the activation of the other language is the bottom-up information heard by participants. Ju and Luce (2004) tested highly proficient Spanish–English bilinguals in Spanish using an eye-tracking task like Spivey and Marian (1999). They manipulated primarily the Voice Onset Time (VOT) of the first consonant of the Spanish target words, that is, the brief delay between the release burst and glottal pulsing, and replaced it with its English counterpart. For example, the Spanish /p/ of the word "playa" (beach) was basically replaced with the English /p/ sound (the two differ in VOT but also in aspiration). This was enough to attract eye movements to the interlingual competitor object (a picture of "pliers") when the participants were asked to click on the picture that corresponded to the target word ("playa" said with the English /p/ sound). Thus, even a subtle phonetic cue from the other language is enough to activate it.

Lexical information can also play a role. Lagrou, Hartsuiker, and Duyck (2011) presented interlingual homophones with almost complete overlap between Dutch and English (e.g., Dutch "lief" (sweet), English "leaf" /li:f/). They asked dominant Dutch–English bilinguals to decide whether these words pronounced in English were words or non-words. Only 10% of the stimuli were interlingual homophones and yet despite being buried among other words, the homophones were recognized more slowly than control words and produced more errors.

In a later study, Lagrou, Hartsuiker, and Duyck (2013) preceded these words with low constraining sentences (e.g., "When you walk in the forest, there is a chance that you find a leaf") and high constraining sentences (e.g., "When the fall is coming in September most trees are losing more than one leaf"). They still found a homophone effect, but it was far weaker in the high-constraining sentences. Thus, when the semantic context points to words in the language being used in the study, cross-lingual interactions are reduced.

This was also clearly shown by Chambers and Cooke (2009) who again used an eye-tracking technique and who asked English-French bilinguals to listen to French sentences. They preceded the target words (e.g., "poule" (chicken)) with non-restrictive and restrictive sentences. In the former case, such as in "Marie va décrire la poule" (Marie will describe the chicken), there was very little prior semantic constraint on the target word (here "poule") but in the restrictive case (e.g., "Marie va nourrir la poule" (Marie will feed the chicken)), the predicate constrained the noun. The competitor object was the picture of an interlingual homophone (a picture of a "pool" in our example).

The researchers found that consideration of the interlingual competitor object was greatly reduced when the context sentence was restrictive. But why was the number not reduced to zero? Quite simply because homophones were used in the study and participants were activating both the French lexicon and the English lexicon in a bottom-up manner. Can cross-language competition be removed totally during sentence comprehension? A study by Shook et al. (2015) would seem to show that it can. They observed no eye movements to cross-linguistic competitors in their eye-tracking study when targets were at the end of sentences. These sentences had activated the language being used and deactivated the other language.

To study whether processing is selective or non-selective, researchers have used experimental tasks and stimuli, and put participants in particular contexts, which can at times push the results one way or the other, as discussed by Grosjean (1998, 2001). Among the top-down factors which can lead a participant to activate the language not being overtly used, we have the knowledge that the study relates to bilingualism, a laboratory that works on bilingual research, a bilingual university environment, reports from other bilingual participants who have just been in the study or who will do it soon an experimenter who is bilingual, the task that is used and/or the instructions that are bilingual, the languages used in the experimental sessions, and so on. As for bottom-up factors, there is the presence of cross-language homophones or cognates, as well as shared word onsets in phonetically similar languages, among others. In sum, just one factor, or a combination of factors, may well activate the language not being used and trigger non-selective processing.

Researchers such as Wu and Thierry (2010) have repeated Grosjean's words of warning and have even given researchers questions they should consider before doing their studies, such as: Do the experimental tasks require explicit retrieval of representations from one or the two languages? Do the experiments involve stimuli from those languages or stimuli that are ambiguous? Is there any (...) contextual information that might draw the participants' attention to one language in particular? etc. Yu and Schwieter (2018) have reiterated similar warnings and they too list a number of variables that can make processing selective or non-selective.

To end this part, what can we say about the selectivity of processing in bilinguals in monolingual speech perception and comprehension? The bottom-up, phonetic, information that is heard is processed by the language(s) that contain(s) elements of that input and this can lead to non-selective processing, such as when the words that are used have similar word beginnings in the other language, or when homophones, homographs, and cognates are involved, as studies have shown repeatedly. Of course, if the input only contains elements of one language, then only one language will process it. Top-down factors such as the interlocutor and the context will also play a role as we have seen. Things are further complicated by the proficiency bilinguals have in their different languages. If, for example, the weaker language is being processed, then the stronger language may be active and may influence the processing that is taking place. However, if the stronger language is being processed, then the weaker language will not be activated as much, or at all. This might even lead some listeners in everyday life to be surprised, sometimes even shocked, to hear the interlocutor say something in the weaker language. As bilinguals, we have all found ourselves in situations where we simply can't process, at least momentarily, something said in the "wrong" language. So, is processing selective, or not selective, during the perception and comprehension of just one language? As Grosjean (2013) wrote, the answer is quite simply that it depends – it will be selective at times and non-selective at other times.

Spoken Language Production

The topic of selectivity has also been studied in language production, that is when the bilingual is speaking just one language. The question remains the same: Is the other language involved or not when the bilingual is speaking just one language with no code-switching or borrowing?

A Study that Showed non-selectivity

Hermans et al. (1998) asked Dutch–English bilinguals to do a picture-word interference task. They had to name pictures presented on a computer screen as quickly as possible while ignoring auditorily presented words, called distractors. In Experiment 2, the bilinguals named the pictures (e.g., of a mountain) in English, their second language, and were told to ignore the accompanying Dutch words presented orally. The latter were either phonologically related to the English name (e.g., Dutch "mouw" which means "sleeve" when the name of the picture was "mountain"), semantically related to it (e.g., Dutch "dal" which means "valley"), unrelated to it (e.g., Dutch "kaars" which means "candle") or – and this is important – phonologically related to the Dutch name of the picture (e.g., Dutch "berm" which means "verge," the Dutch name of the picture being "berg"). These phono-translations were called Phono-Dutch by the authors.

The time interval between the auditory words and the presentation of the pictures (the stimulus onset asynchrony or SOA) was varied, from minus values, meaning that the words were presented before the pictures, to positive values, meaning that the words were presented after the pictures. The crucial result concerns the latency to name the picture (e.g., "mountain") in the Phono-Dutch condition, that is, when the Dutch word ("berm" in our example) was phonologically related to the Dutch name of the picture. It was compared to the latency to name the picture when the unrelated word was heard (i.e., "kaars").

The authors found that at negative and zero SOAs, the latency to name "mountain" when "berm" was presented was slowed down significantly. Their explanation was that the auditory word "berm" probably activated the Dutch word "berg" in the participants' internal lexicon and hence made it harder to select the English word "mountain." They concluded that in the initial stages of word selection, bilingual speakers do not appear to be able to prevent their first language from interfering with the production of their second language.

Even though this study has been referred to often by those who defend non-selectivity, other researchers have pointed out a number of methodological issues with this kind of research. An important one is that tasks that call on the bilingual's two languages, as is the case here, will activate both languages in the bilingual. This becomes a very real problem when the question being studied pertains to such issues as selective versus non-selective processing (Grosjean 1998). Costa, La Heij, and Navarette (2006) stated something very similar: one should assess whether there is activation of the non-response language in experimental circumstances in which such a language is not called into play at all. These words of warning started to be heeded by researchers and new studies were undertaken.

Studies that Show Selective Processing

Boukadi, Davies, and Wilson (2015) used the same task as Hermans et al. (1998), the picture-word interference task, but made sure that in the first of their two experiments, the language setting was entirely monolingual. Tunisian Arabic–French bilinguals named pictures in French while ignoring French auditory distractors. They were of the same type as in the Hermans et al. study – phonologically related, semantically related, unrelated, and phono-translations. Concerning the latter, the participants would see, for example, the picture of a candle (a "bougie" in French), which they had to name, and they heard at the same time the French word "chapeau." If non-selectivity occurred, this distractor might activate /ʃamʕɑ/ which is the Tunisian Arabic name for "bougie." The two words also share the first two phonemes. Were that to happen, then this should be reflected in slower naming latencies as compared to the unrelated distractor.

When this first experiment took place, the participants only communicated with the experimenter in French. They were never informed that the research was related to bilingualism, all experimental instructions and stimuli were presented in French and, as we saw, the naming of the pictures took place in French. The results obtained were clear: the phono-translations did not affect naming latencies unlike in the Hermans et al. study. The experimenters took this absence of an interference effect as an indication that lexical selection proceeded in a language-specific way, that is that processing was selective in a monolingual context.

A second experiment was then conducted. Here the participants named the picture in French again, but all the auditory distractors were in Arabic. Thus, in the crucial phono-translation condition, the picture was that of a candle ("bougie" in French) and the spoken Tunisian Arabic distractor was /ʃabka/ which means "net." Here it was thought that the distractor might boost the activation of /ʃamʕɑ/ (they share the same first two phonemes) which is the Arabic name for a "bougie." The two words, "bougie" and /ʃamʕɑ/, would compete for lexical selection during naming, reflected in slower naming latencies as compared to the unrelated distractor.

When the experiment was run, the participants were told that the research was on bilingualism, they were allowed to speak their native language (Tunisian Arabic), the experimenter switched willingly between French and Tunisian Arabic while explaining the nature of the experiment and giving instructions, and so on. The results were as expected: all distractors interfered with the picture naming, including the phono-translations. This showed that the non-target language names of the pictures were activated and competed for selection during naming. The researchers concluded that the participants had to be in a bilingual context, or mode, for the phono-translations to interfere. In a monolingual mode, as in their first experiment, only the target language was activated. They concluded that lexical selection in bilinguals is a dynamic process modulated by factors like language similarity, language proficiency, and the experimental language context.

Hermans et al. (2011) also showed that when participants are in a monolingual context, processing is selective, but when they are in a bilingual context, then it is non-selective. (Note that this is the same senior author who had argued for non-selectivity in 1998; see above). In their first experiment, they asked Dutch–English bilinguals to look at pictures on a computer screen followed by a letter representing a phoneme. They had to decide whether the phoneme was part of the English name of the picture presented just before. There were three possibilities. First, the phoneme could be part of the English name of the picture. For example, /b/ or /t/ are phonemes of the word "bottle" corresponding to the picture of a bottle presented on the screen. The answer would be "yes" therefore (they called this the affirmative condition). Second, the phoneme could be the first consonant of the Dutch name of the picture being presented (e.g., /f/ is part of "fles," the Dutch translation equivalent of "bottle"). Here the answer would be "no" (they called this the cross-language condition). And finally, the phoneme could be part of neither the English nor the Dutch name (e.g., /p/ is not part of "bottle" or "fles").

The pictures were divided up into two categories: half the pictures were used in the experimental condition where there was an English name and a noncognate translation equivalent in Dutch. Examples are: "bottle" ("fles" in Dutch); "pillow" ("kussen" in Dutch), and so on. The other half were used in the filler condition. It is in this condition that the experiments differ from one another. In the first experiment, all the filler pictures had noncognate names in Dutch and English. (The authors defined cognates as translation equivalents that have similar orthographic and phonological forms in both languages, e.g., English "apple" and Dutch "appel.") Examples of noncognates would be English "money" and Dutch "geld"; English "present" and Dutch "cadeau," etc. The results the authors obtained showed that there was no difference between the cross-language condition and the unrelated condition, be it in response latencies or in accuracy scores. They concluded from this that the Dutch name of the picture was not phonologically activated during phoneme monitoring in the bilinguals' second language. Processing was selective therefore, as in the Boukadi et al. study.

In the second experiment, all the authors did was to change the filler stimuli. The fillers now contained cognate names in English and Dutch, such as "moon" and Dutch "maan," "mouse" and "muis," and so on. This time the two critical conditions (cross-linguistic and unrelated) did produce different response latencies and accuracy scores. It took the participants more time to do the task in the cross-linguistic condition than in the unrelated condition, and they were also less accurate. Processing had become non-selective therefore. In their third experiment, the authors simply replicated the second experiment with 25% of the fillers that were cognate and 75% that were not cognate. They obtained results similar to those of the second experiment.

Despite many other factors that could have been changed, Hermans et al. (2011) concentrated just on the composition of the stimulus list in their study. According to them, if the list contains filler pictures that have noncognate names exclusively, then the Dutch names of the pictures are not activated when monitoring takes place in English (see the first experiment in this study). However, when the stimulus list contains filler pictures that do have cognate names in Dutch and English (this was the case in the second and third experiments), then the phonological representations of the Dutch picture names are activated and they slow down the response regarding the presence of a phoneme in the English name.

Based on these findings, we can only agree with the authors who concluded that the bilingual language production system is indeed dynamic and that it too can operate in different activation states. Grosjean (2013) listed a number of factors that could create these states when bilinguals speak. Among these we find the languages involved (including proficiency, dominance, recency of use, etc.), the general context (a bilingual or monolingual environment, the interlocutors), the context of the study (a study relating to bilingualism or not, the use of two languages in the experiment), other people (the presence of bilinguals or not), the topic, the stimuli used (the use of cognates, homophones and homographs, code-switches or borrowings), the experimental task (does it call on both languages or not), etc.

A Brief Summary of Two Theoretical Frameworks

As we have just seen, the spoken language production systems of bilinguals can be in different states, all the way from a state where just one language is being produced to a state where two of more languages are produced, separately or in an intermingled manner, as when bilinguals code-switch and borrow. Grosjean (2001) has called this being in different language modes. Another framework, that of Green and Abutalebi (2013), is the adaptive control hypothesis and it too accounts for monolingual as well as bilingual speech production. In what follows, we will concentrate just on monolingual speech production in bilinguals, and describe rapidly how the two frameworks talk about it.

Language mode: As we have already seen in Chapter 7, Grosjean (2001) defines language mode as the state of activation of the bilingual's languages and processing mechanism at a given point in time. According to him, bilingual speakers navigate along a situational continuum ranging from a monolingual to a bilingual language mode. They differ among themselves as to the extent they travel along the continuum; some rarely find themselves at the bilingual end (for example, bilinguals who rarely code-switch, sometimes on principle) whereas others rarely leave this end (for example, bilinguals who live in communities where mixed language is the norm).

Being in a monolingual mode happens primarily when bilinguals are in situations where they cannot use their other language(s) such as interacting with monolinguals or being forbidden to use another language. In this particular mode, bilinguals deactivate their other language(s), most often subconsciously, so that it is (they are) not produced. This in turn prevents changing the base language – the language of the interaction – as well as producing code-switches or borrowings. However, and this is important, dynamic interferences may still take place, that is ephemeral intrusions in the language being spoken due to the influence of the other deactivated language(s). As Grosjean (2012) stated, research will have to explain at what point, and how, such interferences occur in the speech production process despite the fact that the speech produced is monolingual. Models such as those of De Bot (1992, 2004) have not done so adequately.

Grosjean (2001) also discusses bilinguals who are highly dominant in one language. They may simply not be able to control language mode in the same way as less dominant or balanced bilinguals. Although they may deactivate their stronger language in a monolingual environment that requires only the weaker language, the latter may simply not be developed enough or active enough to allow them to stay in a monolingual mode.

The adaptive control hypothesis: Green and Abutalebi (2013) also take into account in their framework the interactional context bilinguals find themselves in. But instead of proposing a continuum of states, as does Grosjean (2001), they propose three interactional contexts: a single-language context, a dual-language context, and a dense code-switching context. These contexts reflect everyday conversational use of language by bilinguals. Speakers may experience all three contexts to different extents, as in the language mode framework.

As stated in Chapter 7, in the single-language context one language is used in one environment and the other in a second distinct environment. Hence, frequent switching between languages does not take place. To stay in this context, and avoid cross-language intrusions, speakers maintain the current language goal using the goal maintenance process. It is not totally clear how intrusions are avoided but a control process, interference suppression, intervenes. According to the authors, speaking in one language to the exclusion of another is linked to a suppressive state, with inhibitory processes being central to the control of interference.

To conclude this chapter, whether language processing in bilinguals is selective or non-selective when only one language is being used, be it in perception and comprehension, or in production, depends on different aspects. There is definitely no unique answer since the final outcome is governed by many internal as well as external factors.

References

Bialystok, Ellen, Fergus Craik, David Green, and Tamar Gollan. 2009. "Bilingual minds." *Psychological Science in the Public Interest*, 10 (3): 89–129.

Boukadi, Mariem, Robert A. I. Davies, and Maximiliano A. Wilson. 2015. "Bilingual lexical selection as a dynamic process: Evidence from Arabic-French bilinguals." *Canadian Journal of Experimental Psychology*, 69 (4): 297–313.

Chambers, Craig, and Hilary Cooke. 2009. "Lexical competition during second-language listening: Sentence context, but not proficiency, constrains interference from the native lexicon." *Journal of Experimental Psychology: Learning, Memory, and Cognition*, 35 (4): 1029–1040.
Costa, Albert. 2005. "Lexical access in bilingual production." In *Handbook of Bilingualism: Psycholinguistic Approaches*, edited by Judith Kroll and Annette de Groot, 308–325. Oxford/New York: Oxford University Press.
Costa, Albert, Wido La Heij, and Eduardo Navarette. 2006. "The dynamics of bilingual lexical access." *Bilingual: Language and Cognition*, 9 (2): 137–151.
De Bot, Kees. 1992. "A bilingual production model: Levelt's 'speaking' model adapted." *Applied Linguistics*, 13 (1): 1–24.
De Bot, Kees. 2004. "The multilingual lexicon: Modeling selection and control." *The International Journal of Multilingualism*, 1 (1): 17–32.
Dunn, Alexandra L., and Jean E. Fox Tree. 2014. "More on language mode." *International Journal of Bilingualism*, 18 (6): 605–613. DOI: 10.1177/1367006912454509.
Green, David W., and Jubin Abutalebi. 2013. "Language control in bilinguals: The adaptive control hypothesis." *Journal of Cognitive Psychology*, 25 (5): 515–530. DOI: 10.1080/20445911.2013.796377.
Grosjean, François. 1998. "Studying bilinguals: Methodological and conceptual issues." *Bilingualism: Language and Cognition*, 1 (2): 131–149.
Grosjean, François. 2001. "The bilingual's language modes." In *One Mind, Two Languages: Bilingual Language Processing*, edited by Janet Nicol, 1–22. Oxford: Blackwell.
Grosjean, François. 2012. An attempt to isolate, and then differentiate, transfer and interference. *International Journal of Bilingualism*, 16(1): 11–21.
Grosjean, François. 2013. "Speech production." In *The Psycholinguistics of Bilingualism*, edited by François Grosjean and Ping Li, 50–69. Malden, MA/Oxford: Wiley-Blackwell.
Hermans, Daan, Theo Bongaerts, Kees de Bot, and Robert Schreuder. 1998. "Producing words in a foreign language: Can speakers prevent interference from their first language." *Bilingual: Language and Cognition*, 1 (1): 213–229.
Hermans, Daan, Ellen Ormel, Ria van Besselaar, and Janet van Hell. 2011. "Lexical activation in bilinguals' speech production is dynamic: How language ambiguous words can affect cross-language activation." *Language and Cognitive Processes*, 26 (10): 1687–1709. DOI: 10.1080/01690965.2010.530411.
Ju, Min, and Paul Luce. 2004. "Falling on sensitive ears: Constraints on bilingual lexical activation." *Psychological Science*, 15 (5): 314–318.
Lagrou, Evelyne, Robert J. Hartsuiker, and Wouter Duyck. 2011. "Knowledge of a second language influences auditory word recognition in the native language." *Journal of Experimental Psychology: Learning, Memory, and Cognition*, 37 (4): 952–965.
Lagrou, Evelyne, Robert J. Hartsuiker, and Wouter Duyck. 2013. "The influence of sentence context and accented speech on lexical access in second-language auditory word recognition." *Bilingualism: Language and Cognition*, 16 (3): 508–517.
Marian, Viorica. 2019. "The language you speak influences where your attention goes." *Scientific American*, December 5.
Marian, Viorica, and Michael Spivey. 2003. "Competing activation in bilingual language processing: Within- and between-language competition." *Bilingualism: Language and Cognition*, 6: 97–115.
Paap, Kenneth R. 2019. "Bilingualism in cognitive science: The characteristics and consequences of bilingual language control." In *The Cambridge Handbook of Bilingualism*, edited by Annick De Houwer and Lourdes Ortega, 425–465. Cambridge: Cambridge University Press.
Paulmann, Silke, Kerrie E. Elston-Güttler, Thomas C. Gunter, and Sonja A. Kotz. 2006. "Is bilingual lexical access influenced by language context?" *NeuroReport*, 17 (7): 727–731.

Shook, Anthony, Matthew Goldrick, Caroline Engstler, and Viorica Marian. 2015. "Bilinguals show weaker lexical access during spoken sentence comprehension." *Journal of Psycholinguistic Research*, 44 (6): 789–802.

Spivey, Michael, and Viorica Marian. 1999. "Cross talk between native and second languages: Partial activation of an irrelevant lexicon." *Psychological Science*, 10: 281–284.

Weber, Andrea, and Anne Cutler. 2004. "Lexical competition in non-native spoken-word recognition." *Journal of Memory and Language*, 50 (1): 1–25.

Wu, Yan Jing, and Guillaume Thierry. 2010. "Investigating bilingual processing: The neglected role of language processing contexts." *Frontiers in Psychology*, 1 (178): 1–6.

Yu, Ziying, and John W. Schwieter. 2018. "Recognizing the effects of language mode on the cognitive advantages of bilingualism." *Frontiers in Psychology*, 9: 366. DOI: 10.3389/fpsyg.2018.00366.

Part IV

Biculturalism and Personality

10

Bilinguals Who Are also Bicultural[1]

Individuals can be bilingual and bicultural, but also bilingual and monocultural, monolingual and bicultural, as well as monocultural and monolingual, as clearly indicated by James Soffietti (1960) more than 50 years ago. Many people are indeed bilingual without being bicultural such as members of diglossic communities, inhabitants of countries with lingua francas or different school languages, foreign language learners who then use their second language regularly, etc. And, conversely, some people are monolingual but bicultural as in the case of speakers of a language who move to a different country where the same language is used, or of members of a minority culture who no longer know the minority language but who retain other aspects of the culture. Thus, bilingualism and biculturalism are not coextensive.

We will concentrate here on bilinguals who are also bicultural, often called bicultural bilinguals. We will first examine how they are described in the literature and how researchers sometimes diverge on how to do so. We will then evoke how one becomes bicultural and will examine the evolution of biculturalism over time. A discussion of how biculturals adapt different behaviors in different situations will then follow with a section dedicated to experimental work. Finally, the complex topic of bicultural identity will be evoked.

Since research on bilingualism has now amassed a knowledge base that is quite impressive, and much larger than that of biculturalism, we will allow it to guide us throughout this chapter. Thus, we will begin the presentation of each topic with a paragraph or two on what is known about it in the field of bilingualism before delving into that of biculturalism. This will allow us to show that bilingualism can sometimes give us a filter through which biculturalism can be better observed.

Describing Biculturals

We will start with a few words from the domain of bilingualism. As we saw in Chapter 1, some early researchers had a tendency to define bilinguals in terms of language fluency/proficiency; as did Bloomfield (1933), who wrote that bilingualism is the native-like

[1]This chapter has been inspired in part by an article I wrote a few years ago: Grosjean, F. (2015). Bicultural bilinguals. *International Journal of Bilingualism*, 19(5): 572–586.

The Mysteries of Bilingualism, First Edition. François Grosjean.

control of two languages. In fact, if one were to count as bilingual those who pass as monolinguals in each language, one would be left with no label for the vast majority of people who use two or more languages regularly but who do not have native-like fluency in each language. So, in the last century, researchers opted for language use as the main defining factor of bilingualism. Weinreich (1968) and Mackey (1962) both stated that it is the alternate use of two (or more) languages and, similarly, Grosjean (1982, 2010) wrote that bilinguals as those who use two or more languages (or dialects) in their everyday lives.

Of course, fluency, which is increasingly referred to as language proficiency, remains an important descriptive factor of bilingualism as do other variables such as age of acquisition of the two or more languages, language history, language dominance, and so on. One variable that is coming back to the fore is language function, that is the fact that bilinguals usually acquire and use their languages for different purposes, in different domains of life, with different people. Different aspects of life often require different languages. Grosjean (1997, 2016) has called this the Complementarity Principle and has shown its impact on fluency, dominance, memory and translation abilities (see Chapter 8).

Turning to biculturals, can one find the cultural equivalents of language fluency, language use and maybe even the Complementarity Principle? This appears to be the case. Among the definitions of the bicultural person, one does indeed find a dichotomy between cultural competence or knowledge, on the one hand, and behavior, on the other. For example, Luna, Ringberg, and Peracchio (2008) appear to put the emphasis on the equivalence of fluency when they write that biculturals have two distinct and complete sets of knowledge structures, one for each culture. Padilla (2006) goes along with this and states that the completely bicultural person is equally at ease with members of either culture and can easily switch from one cultural orientation to the other, and does so with native-like facility. Hong and Khei (2014) are a bit less extreme but do state that bicultural or multicultural individuals are those who acquire and internalize multiple shared cultural knowledge systems associated with multiple groups.

Other researchers, though, put the emphasis on behavior, without denying the importance of knowledge, as there is no behavior without it. Thus, Grosjean (1983, 2008, 2015) characterizes biculturals by at least three traits. First, they take part, to varying degrees, in the life of two or more cultures. Second, they adapt, at least in part, their attitudes, behaviors, values, languages, etc. to these cultures. And third, they combine and blend aspects of the cultures involved. Certain characteristics (attitudes, beliefs, values, behaviors, etc.) come from the one or the other culture whereas other characteristics are blends based on these cultures. In this latter case, it becomes difficult to determine the cultural origin of a particular characteristic since it contains aspects of both cultures. It should be noted that it is rare that the two cultures have the same importance in the life of biculturals. One culture often plays a larger role than the other. One can therefore speak of "cultural dominance" just as one speaks of "language dominance" in bilinguals.

Nguyen and Benet-Martinez (2007), quite independently, define biculturals in a very similar manner. According to them, biculturals are those who have been exposed to and have internalized two cultures (this is quite close to Grosjean's first characteristic). They add that biculturalism also entails the synthesis of cultural norms from two groups into one behavioral repertoire (this is quite similar to Grosjean's third characteristic). And they state that biculturalism entails the ability to switch between cultural schemas, norms and behaviors in response to cultural cues (see Grosjean's second characteristic). Although neither Grosjean nor Nguyen and Benet-Martinez mention explicitly a cultural equivalent of the Complementarity Principle in biculturalism, it is not excluded from their definitions.

Other criteria have been put forward in the definition of the bicultural person and it is worth stopping for a moment on one of them: identifying with both cultures. Thus, Szabó et al. (2020) state that biculturalism is the integration of multiple cultural streams into one's behavioral repertoire, value system, and *identity* (our italics). And West et al. (2017) propose that multiculturals are people who identify with more than two cultures. As for Schindler et al. (2016) they state that biculturals identify with both cultures to some degree. We will deal with the complex issue of cultural identity a bit later on in this chapter, but we can already say that some biculturals only identify with one or the other culture, and sometimes neither, even though they are bicultural according to the characteristics given above. Ying-yi Hong, a leading researcher on biculturalism, addressed this issue with me via email quite recently.[2] She stated that biculturalism can be divided into a cognitive process (the bicultural mind) and an identity process (the bicultural self). According to her (see also Hong and Khei 2014), the bicultural mind refers to the acquisition of the cultural meaning systems of two (or more) cultures, and the utilization of these systems subsequently. As for the bicultural self, it refers to categorizing oneself into the cultural groups and developing an attachment to the groups. These two processes can be independent, she proposes, as in the example of local Hong Kong people who have acquired a bicultural mind (they know a lot about Eastern and Western cultures) but do not have a bicultural self (they have not acquired a Western identity).

Over the years, I have found other criteria proposed when evoking bicultural people, such as accepting one's bicultural status, that is that one is bicultural only if one acknowledges that this is indeed the case. However, one often meets people who are clearly bicultural but who do not recognize their biculturalism. It should be noted that something similar is found in bilinguals. People may recognize using two or more languages in their everyday lives but may not accept to be labeled bilingual. Another criterion is the manner in which a person has become bicultural. Some maintain that one must have grown up with both cultures to be defined as bicultural when, in fact, one can become bicultural at different moments in life, as we will see below. A similar requirement can be found regarding bilingualism. For example, both in France and Switzerland, many people assume that bilinguals have grown up using two or more languages. This is unfortunate as one can become bilingual at any stage of one's life.

A fourth criterion concerns how well one knows the two cultures. Some maintain that one must know them perfectly to be called bicultural (see, for example, the Luna, Ringberg, and Peracchio (2008) definition given above). But this is in fact rarely the case, just as knowing two languages perfectly is quite rare. Most biculturals have a cultural dominance due to the fact that they have greater contact with, and spend more time in, one culture than the other, but this in no way makes them less bicultural. Among other criteria mentioned we find: feeling at ease in both cultures (it is unfortunately not always the case); being recognized as bicultural (this is still quite rare); being accepted fully by the two cultures in question, etc. All of these criteria are questionable and it explains why they have not been added to the defining characteristics proposed by either Grosjean or Nguyen and Benet-Martinez. This said, some researchers have included some of them in the past when describing bicultural competence (e.g., LaFromboise, Coleman, and Gerton 1993).

One important aspect of being bicultural, that needs to be underlined, is the fact that it also involves the combining and blending of features of the cultures involved. We

---

[2] Email received on March 7, 2021.

observe in biculturals an aspect that is adaptable and controllable (it allows them to adapt to the situation, context, etc.) and another aspect that is more static; here, the blend of features from the two cultures is not easily adapted to given situations. This is important as it means that not all behaviors, beliefs, and attitudes can be modified according to the cultural situation the bicultural person is in. This blending component, also called hybridizing, is far less obvious in the languages of bilinguals. Although combining languages in the form of code-switches and borrowing is frequent, the actual blending of languages is far rarer in individual bilinguals. It takes place over generations in groups of speakers (see the literature on pidginization and creolization) but more rarely in individuals.

West et al. (2017) discuss hybridizing, also called hybridization. It occurs, according to them, when biculturals mix their cultures to create an end product that is distinct from its cultural raw materials. It is a recombination process with a unique outcome. To illustrate this, they propose the analogy of baking a cake. It is not enough to simply add the ingredients together. They have to be combined in a particular way, such as mixing the dry ingredients together before slowly adding the wet ingredients. The mixture must then be heated in an oven before ending up as a cake. They point out that other researchers have used other terms such as fusion, synergy and blendedness to describe the same phenomenon. A likely result over time, according to West et al. (2017), may be the emergence of a third culture that bridges the source cultures.

What we have said so far has put the stress on the "bi" in biculturalism when in fact many people take part in the life of more than two cultures. This has been recognized for bilinguals who are seen as those who use two or more languages (or dialects) in their everyday lives, and who may receive labels such as "trilingual," "quadrilingual," and even "plurilingual" or "multilingual." As concerns biculturalism, I have always been careful to include more than two cultures in my description of the bicultural person (Grosjean 2010). However, many researchers have restricted themselves to just two cultures. This is the case for Luna, Ringberg, and Peracchio (2008) who refer to "two distinct and complete sets of knowledge structures," Padilla (2006) who refers to "two social persona," as well as Nguyen and Benet-Martinez (2007) who state that biculturals have been exposed and have internalized two cultures, and who refer to the cultural norms of two groups. More recently, definitions of biculturalism are slowly reflecting the fact that some people do indeed take part in the life of more than two cultures and that they adapt to each of these cultures, as well as combine and blend aspects of several cultures (see, for example, Meca et al. 2019; Szabó et al. 2020).

Becoming Bicultural and the Evolution of Biculturalism over Time

As in the preceding section, we will begin with a few words on bilingualism. Why does about half the world's population use two or more languages in everyday life? In Chapter 2, we saw that one reason is that some countries house numerous languages, and some have lingua francas, all of which leads to language contact between the inhabitants, and hence bilingualism. Another reason is that people have always traveled for trade, commerce, business, employment, religion, politics, conflicts, and so on. Migrants usually acquire the language of their host country but there is also the case of the original inhabitants of that country acquiring the language of the newcomers when the causes of the arrival are military or political. Education and culture are also important reasons. Many students pursue their studies in a region or country with another language and hence become bilingual. Other events, such as intermarriage or professional opportunities – diplomacy, business, foreign journalism, language learning, and so on – lead to language contact and bilingualism.

All this explains why one can become bilingual at any time during one's life (Grosjean 2010). Some children acquire two languages simultaneously, but they are far rarer than children who acquire their languages successively. In fact, the majority of child bilinguals start monolingually. They first acquire a home language and then, usually when they start going to school, they learn a second language, most often the majority language. Then, depending on the country, they may start learning a third (and even a fourth) language as a school subject. Older children, young adolescents as well as adults may also become bilingual for all the reasons given above. The main factor that leads to the acquisition and development of a second language is the need for that language – the need to interact with others, to study or work, to take part in social activities and so on.

Are things much different when one examines the reasons that lead to biculturalism? Not really. People become bicultural because they are in contact with two (or more) cultures and have to live, in part at least, with these cultures. They can move to a new country or region which has another culture, they might live in multicultural societies and take part in the life of two or more cultures, they may have parents or family members from different cultural backgrounds, they may themselves belong to a cultural minority and have regular interactions with the cultural majority, they might marry someone from another cultural background, and so on. All this can take place in early childhood (e.g., a child who is born within a bicultural family or has daily contact with two cultures from birth) and can continue throughout life, just as with people who are bilingual.

It is interesting to note that researchers working on biculturalism have concentrated for a long time on acculturation in adult migrants and in their children. Literally thousands of studies have described future migrants' idealization of the cultures they wish to emigrate to. Those studies have listed the adaptation stages which the migrants experience once they have moved into their new society: culture shock, isolation, turning in on oneself; but also, over-adaptation at times, more or less rapid acculturation according to the size and concentration of the migrant group and the presence of children, the "host" society's attitude towards the group, etc. The literature also mentions the migrants' idealization of their home country, their way of talking about it, the "return shock" they experience when they see that the reality does not match their dreams, and a more or less permanent acceptance of their migratory status sometimes accompanied by a reasoning that they are doing so "for the sake of the children who were born here."

The Canadian and French writer, Nancy Huston, reflects on these stages clearly in her book, *Losing North* (2002, 14, 69 & 70):

> Those to whom you feel close are far away. For the first few years, you think of them all the time and are affected by everything that happens to them. By writing letters, making phone calls, buying newspapers from back home, you do your best to reduce the gulf that has opened up between you.... As time goes by, your communications with "back home" become fewer and farther between. Imperceptibly, your friends from there are replaced by friends from here.... And the day comes when you're forced to recognize that you no longer share the values of the people who brought you into the world, talked and sang to you as a child, cuddled and fed you in the warmth and comfort of the family home.

It is only recently that biculturalism has started to be seen as a natural consequence of migration. For a long time, one evoked the passage from one monoculturalism in the first culture to a form of monoculturalism in the new culture. Migrants were not viewed as people who tended to blend and synthesize aspects of their two or more cultures but rather as those who no longer belonged to culture A and had not yet become members of culture B. Depending on who was studying the phenomenon, the solutions advocated were integration or assimilation into the new culture, or a return to the original culture, but rarely the intertwining of two cultures in the form of biculturalism as discussed here.

Synchrony and Asynchrony of Bilingualism and Biculturalism

As we have just seen, people can become bilingual and bicultural at any time during their lives. Sometimes both components develop at the same time (the person becomes bilingual and bicultural over the same time span), but there are also other possibilities which one must not overlook. For example, a person can acquire two languages first and only after some years start becoming bicultural. A case in point can be found in diglossic societies where two languages or two varieties of a language are employed, each language having a very precise domain of use. The example of Swiss German and German, in the German part of Switzerland, is a case in point. Very early on, Swiss German children, whose mother tongue is Swiss German, start acquiring German, which becomes the main school language over the years. By the time they reach adolescence they are bilingual in the two varieties, which are mutually incomprehensible, but unless they have a German or Austrian parent they remain monocultural. It is only later that they may become bicultural if they go and live in Germany or Austria.

The opposite may also happen, that is starting off bicultural and only later becoming bilingual. For example, a Jewish family in France may be monolingual in French although bicultural in most aspects of life. After a number of years, one of the children, having become an adult, may decide to migrate to Israel and with time he or she will become bilingual in French and Hebrew. Thus, one must leave open the possibility that the linguistic and cultural components of the bicultural bilingual person may develop at different times.

The Evolution of Biculturalism over Time

Even though less studied than the evolution of bilingualism, a person's biculturalism can evolve in sometimes quite amazing ways. For reasons such as moving to another country or region, starting school, getting a job, settling down with a spouse, moving again, losing a family member, etc., biculturalism can evolve and restructure. A person's cultural dominance may change with the possibility that the first culture may no longer be the stronger culture after many years in another cultural environment. In addition, cultural forgetting (culture loss or attrition) may start taking place. As with language, this occurs when contact with one of the cultures is considerably reduced, if not quite simply absent, and this for a long stretch of time. In this case, biculturals may even lose their ability to adapt their attitudes, behavior, values, etc. to the weaker culture, and the blends of the two cultures will be made in favor of the now dominant culture. This can happen several times during a lifetime.

Since the evolution of biculturalism has not been studied academically to any great extent, aside from the literature on acculturation, it is through individual memoirs that one can get an idea of how complex it can be. Grosjean's (2019) own life story is a good example of how languages and cultures can wax and wane over a lifetime. He spent his early years in a small village just outside Paris and, until the age of 7 1/2, he was a normal

French boy, both linguistically and culturally. But then he moved to an English-speaking boarding school in Switzerland, learned English, and acculturated into both English and American cultures. His English side was consolidated by four years of boarding school in England and by the age of 18 he was basically English, despite his very French name and the nationality indicated on his passport. He moved back to France for his university studies – a land he no longer knew – and went through culture shock and another acculturation process. His adaptation to French culture was slow and difficult, and he rejected momentarily his English background. Then, ten years later, he emigrated to the US, with his family, and went through yet another adaptation process. By the end of their stay, 12 years later, the children were totally American and the family was English-speaking. But then they came back to Europe and settled down in Switzerland and the author went through one more period of cultural restructuring. As he writes, after this long journey in cultures and languages, "The four cultures I came into contact with and lived in all found their place in a mosaic of cultures that characterize me."[3]

Acting Biculturally

To help us understand how acting biculturally may take place, we will once again start by reminding ourselves how bilinguals use their different languages. In their everyday lives, they find themselves at various points along a situational continuum which induce different language modes (Grosjean 2001; see Chapter 7). At one end of the continuum, they are in a totally monolingual mode in that they are interacting with monolinguals of one – or the other – of the languages that they know. They adopt the language of the interlocutor(s) and deactivate their other language(s). But sometimes they produce interferences, that is speaker-specific deviations from the language being spoken due to the influence of the other "deactivated" language.

At the other end of the continuum, bilinguals find themselves in a bilingual language mode in that they are communicating with bilinguals who share their two (or more) languages. First they adopt a language to use together, what is known as the base language (also the "host" or "matrix" language). This process is called language choice and is governed by a number of factors: the interlocutors involved, the situation of the interaction, the content of the discourse, and the function of the interaction. Once the base language has been chosen, they can bring in the other language, the "guest" or "embedded" language, either by code-switching, i.e., shifting completely to the other language for a word, a phrase, or a sentence, or by borrowing a word or short expression from the other, less activated language. In between the two end points, intermediary modes exist where some language intermingling may take place.

Moving over to biculturalism, is it possible to adapt the language mode concept to account for how biculturals behave in their everyday lives? It has not been done so far – work on cultural frame switching comes the closest to it (see the next section) – so what follows is tentative. Biculturals also find themselves at various points along a situational continuum – but cultural this time – that requires different types of behavior and attitude depending on the situation. At one end they are in a monocultural mode, since they are with monoculturals or with biculturals with whom they share only one culture.

[3] F. Grosjean, "Keeping my four cultures alive." Psychology Today blog post: https://www.psychologytoday.com/intl/blog/life-bilingual/201912/keeping-my-four-cultures-alive.

In this situation they must deactivate as best they can their other culture(s). At the other end of the continuum they are with other biculturals who share their cultures. With them, they will use a base culture to interact in (the behaviors, attitudes, beliefs of that culture) and they will bring in the other culture(s), in the form of cultural switches and borrowings, when they choose to. Movement along the situational continuum, and the behavioral and attitudinal consequences that follow, may at times be voluntary and conscious whereas at other times they are automatic and unconscious.

In the monocultural mode, biculturals usually attempt to apply the motto, "When in Rome, do as the Romans do." If their knowledge of the culture in question is sufficient (a bit like having sufficient knowledge of the language that has to be used), and they manage to deactivate, at least to a large degree, their other culture(s), then they can behave appropriately. Nancy Huston states this nicely when she writes,[4] "Consciously or not, you observe the prevailing codes, adapt to them and gradually begin to censor the gestures and postures which are inappropriate in your new context..." Many biculturals will know how to adapt their cultural behavior in order to welcome monocultural acquaintances at home, hold a meeting at work, deal with relatives who belong to just one culture, do business with the local administration, dress according to the context, and so on.

However, because of the blending component in biculturalism, certain behaviors, attitudes, and feelings may not be totally adapted to a situation and may instead be a mixture of the person's two (or more) cultures. An example is evoked by Daniel Schweimler, a British journalist based in Argentina who writes[5] that Argentines like to get much closer than he is accustomed to. While in queues at the supermarket checkout for instance, he reports that he has elbowed elderly ladies as he stooped to sign his credit card slip since they were standing too close to him!

This form of cultural interference is a differentiating factor between bilingualism and biculturalism: bilinguals can usually deactivate one language and use the other exclusively in particular situations, whereas biculturals cannot always deactivate certain traits of their other culture when in a monocultural environment. Other examples of cultural interference can be found in greeting behaviors (e.g., shaking someone's hand on departure when it is not expected), body language, eye contact, keeping to a schedule or being on time, the amount of space you leave between yourself and others (as we have just seen), what you talk about (in some cultures, for example, you do not talk about salaries with people you don't know), how much you tip, and so on.

At the other end of the continuum, biculturals are with other biculturals like themselves with whom they use a cultural base within which to interact (the behaviors, attitudes, beliefs, etc., of one culture) – the equivalent of language choice on the linguistic side of things. They may then bring in the other culture in the form of cultural switches and borrowings when they choose to do so. This can correspond to a shift in behavior, for example, from the base behavior chosen for the interaction to the behavior usually used within the other culture, sometimes simply to mark their belonging to both cultures.

It can happen that two bicultural people interacting may choose a different cultural base from one another – what is called non-accommodation in research on bilingualism – and this can have an effect on the interaction. Here is an example. During the

[4] Nancy Huston, *Losing North*, p. 20.

[5] Sealed with an Argentine kiss. Daniel Schweimler. BBC News. 28/5/07.

May' 68 events in Paris, I served as a contact person for the English-speaking media since I was an Anglo–French bicultural bilingual who knew firsthand what the problems were. One notable reporter who came to us was Olivier Todd, also an Anglo-French bicultural bilingual, who at that time worked for the BBC. I remember vividly that one day he was interviewing me and the camera was rolling. He asked me about the street violence the night before and I replied that it had indeed taken place, in what I thought was a subdued British tone. He stopped the camera, told me to be a bit more emphatic and upset à la française, and then signaled to restart the camera. Sharing the same languages and cultures, both Todd and I should have been on the same wavelength. However, he was letting his French side react, and wanted a strong reaction, whereas I was thinking of those who would see me on the BBC and was letting my English side speak. I was therefore more restrained.

Leaving aside instances such as these, being in a bicultural mode with other biculturals are precious moments as one can relax and not have to worry about getting things right each time. Bicultural people often state that their good friends (or their "dream" partners) are people like them, with whom they can be totally at ease about going back and forth between their cultures, and their languages if they are also bilingual.

Experimental Work

For all of us biculturals who have to adapt to a cultural context, a situation, and different interlocutor(s), we would expect that extensive descriptive and experimental research has been done on the behavior of biculturals in terms of body position and language, eye contact, space used, topics discussed, voice volume and pitch, etc. and this in different physical real-life situations, such as greeting or leaving people of different cultures, cooking and having a meal together, doing a business transaction, etc. However, such research is relatively rare. Here is an example of a study of this type.

So (2010) wished to examine the extent to which exposure to two cultures affects the gesture frequency of Chinese–American bicultural bilinguals when speaking each of their languages. Chinese culture is reported to be relatively low-gesture whereas American culture is said to be a relatively high-gesture culture. The participants tested were Chinese–English bicultural bilinguals at the National University in Singapore. Not only were they totally fluent in Chinese and English, but they were also in daily contact with the Chinese and American cultures in Singapore. Two groups of monolingual monoculturals were also tested: English-speaking students at the University of Chicago, and Chinese-speaking students at the University of Nanjing (China). They were all asked to retell stories based on short cartoons that they saw. The monolinguals did so to monolingual speakers in their respective countries, and the bicultural bilinguals did so twice, once in Mandarin Chinese to a native Chinese experimenter, and once in English to a native English experimenter.

Two types of gestures were examined: representational and non-representational. Representational gestures can be iconic (e.g., a hand is shaped in the form of a pipe) or abstract deictic (e.g., a finger points to a space left by a character). They communicate a specific meaning, and represent movements, actions, properties, entities, and so on. Non-representational gestures are made up of speech beats, emblems (e.g., the OK sign), and concrete deictic gestures (e.g., pointing to something on a screen). The results So obtained showed that, when speaking English the bicultural bilinguals resembled the English speaking monoculturals regarding the frequency of both representational and non-representational gestures. And, when speaking Chinese they produced a similar number of non-representational gestures to the Chinese monoculturals, but more representational gestures. The author concluded that the bicultural bilinguals had learned the gestural characteristics of each of the cultures, to a large extent at least. We could add that there was a slight dominance for the American cultural gestures which can be seen in the number of representational gestures when speaking Chinese.

Despite studies of this type, most of the experimental research on acting biculturally is much more cognitive in nature and involves what is termed "cultural priming" or "cultural frame-switching." Ying-yi Hong founded this research and is at the forefront of it. In Hong and Khei (2014), among other works, she describes the underlying premise, which is termed the dynamic-constructivist approach. Culture is internalized within individuals in the form of a network of domain-specific knowledge structures. Individuals can acquire more than one cultural knowledge system, and the context, environment, and objects (e.g., icons) can cue one set of cultural knowledge and render it salient.

Hong and her colleagues developed cultural priming to validate these ideas, and Hong and Khei (2014) tell us how it works. It involves three experimental conditions. For example, if one is interested in Chinese–American biculturals, the conditions would be: a Chinese culture priming condition, an American culture priming condition, and a control condition. The biculturals would be randomly assigned to one of the three conditions. Those in the Chinese culture priming condition would be exposed to Chinese cultural icons (e.g., Confucius, The Great Wall of China), those in the American culture priming condition would be exposed to American cultural icons (e.g., Abraham Lincoln, the Statue of Liberty), and participants in the control condition would be exposed to culturally neutral stimuli (e.g., geometric figures, clouds, etc.). After the priming conditions, the participants' responses on some relevant measure would be assessed. Thus, for example, they could be asked to interpret an ambiguous event such as a picture of a fish swimming in front of a school of fish. Their responses, such as the fish in front is a leader, or the fish is being chased by a group of fish behind him, would then be compared with those typically found among Chinese versus American monocultural participants. In several experiments conducted by Hong and her colleagues, bicultural participants in the Chinese culture priming condition responded in ways that are typical of Chinese people, and participants in the American culture priming conditions responded in ways that are typical of Americans. In sum, the biculturals shifted between interpretive frames in response to various cultural situations.

It is worth describing a concrete study to see how culture priming functions and how it can actually influence behavior. Wong and Hong (2005) focused on the cooperative behavior towards friends and strangers among Chinese-American bicultural individuals. They wanted to see if they were more likely to cooperate with friends, as opposed to strangers, when their Chinese cultural knowledge was activated, as opposed to their American cultural knowledge. North Americans seem to feel less sense of duty towards in-group members such as friends whereas Chinese value interdependence among friends more. Would this be apparent in the behavior of their bicultural participants when they were primed accordingly?

They asked Hong Kong bicultural students, who had been exposed extensively to both Chinese and American cultures, to do two things. First, to look at slides which would prime them culturally, and second to play a social dilemma game entitled The Prisoner's Dilemma. For the presentation of the slides, the students were divided into three groups. One group was exposed to slides of Chinese cultural icons (e.g., a Chinese dragon, a person performing kung fu), a second saw American cultural icons (e.g., the

American flag, a scene from an American football game), and the third group was exposed to neutral primes (geometric figures). To make sure they paid attention to the slides, they were required to answer questions about them, or to trace the outline of the figures for the neutral primes.

They were then asked to play the Prisoner's Dilemma game with two types of partners that were assigned to them: either five friends or five strangers. To get them to understand the game, they were told that a fictitious character, Ben, had to cross two rivers, and in each of the crossings, he would have a partner who would cross the river at the same time. The reward Ben and his partner could gain from crossing the rivers depended on the mode of transportation they chose *individually*. If both of them chose to ride in a sailing boat, both would be rewarded with three points as they could assist each other to sail the boat. So they would be cooperating. If Ben chose to ride in a sailing boat but his partner chose a speedboat, Ben would receive no points as he was not strong enough to make the sailing boat go fast enough. However, his partner would receive four points as the speedboat was very fast. And if both chose the speedboat, then they would only receive one point because the weight of the two of them would slow the boat down. Basically, they could cooperate (use the sailing boat) and get a certain number of points, or not cooperate (use the speed boat) and possibly win more points, but this depended on whether the other had decided to cooperate or not. Recall that the decision was taken separately by each person. When the participants played, they were asked to imagine themselves crossing the rivers like Ben. The frequency with which they chose to cooperate was taken as an indication of their cooperative behavioral tendency.

The results clearly showed that priming one cultural knowledge versus the other had an effect on behavior. When the partners were friends, Chinese primes elicited significantly more cooperation (76.9%) than American primes (53.0%). That is, participants showed more cooperation towards friends when Chinese cultural knowledge was activated than when American cultural knowledge was activated. However, when the partners were strangers, participants in the Chinese and in the American priming conditions had a similar likelihood of cooperation (62.9% for Chinese primes and 58.5% for American primes, a non-significant difference). Here, the participants showed a similarly low level of cooperation towards strangers after both Chinese and American culture priming. In sum, cultural priming can indeed have an effect on behavior.

Many studies of this type have been done over the years and clearly cultural priming is a rich paradigm to get at cultural frame switching (see also the next chapter for its use in personality research). What remains unclear though is whether participants are in a monocultural mode when they take part in them or in a bicultural mode. They clearly adopt the cultural response that has been primed, a bit like choosing the appropriate language in a study dealing with bilingualism. But where are they positioned on the situational continuum described at the beginning of this section? It would be worth making the situation and interlocutor either monocultural or bicultural to see what the effects would be on the results obtained.

Bicultural Identity

We will start this last part by first saying a few words concerning identity in bilinguals, and then moving on to identity in biculturals. Identity is not a central characteristic of bilingualism. Admittedly, as we saw in Chapter 1, some bilinguals who hold an older view of what it means to be bilingual – i.e., it is the equal and perfect knowledge of two languages – may not label themselves as bilingual even though they use their languages in their everyday lives. When this happens, they usually choose to say that they are speakers of language A and that they also know to some extent languages B, C, etc. Some may even belittle their knowledge of all their languages, but this phenomenon is relatively rare. Reaching a point where one accepts one's bilingualism may take time but it is made easier by the fact that the scholarly definition of bilingualism (the use of two or more languages or dialects in everyday life) is slowly making its way into the layperson's world. Hence, one will find more and more bilinguals accepting that they are indeed bilingual.

Identity is much more central in the life of biculturals and is much more complex. As I have written over the years (e.g., Grosjean 2010), a bicultural person may have to go through a long, and sometimes trying, process to be able to reach the point of saying, "I am indeed bicultural, a member of culture A and of culture B" (or even of cultures A, B and C). Different factors are taken into account. An important one is the reaction, overt or covert, of the members of the cultures involved. The latter take into account the bicultural's kinship, language, physical appearance, nationality, education, attitudes, etc. The outcome can be straightforward, and sometimes quite categorical: X is judged to belong solely to culture A or solely to culture B. But it can also be contradictory: X is categorized as a member of culture A by members of culture B, and as a member of culture B by members of culture A. For many years in my youth, this is exactly what happened to me. The French considered me to be British, and the British saw me as French. It is still rare that cultures accept you as both, i.e., as bicultural, having roots in cultures A and B. Hong and Zhan (2019) have a very good discussion of the reactions of others on the bicultural individual's identity.

Faced with this double, sometimes contradictory, labeling, biculturals have to reach a decision on their own cultural identity. To do this they take into account this exterior perception and bring in other factors such as their personal history, their identity needs, their knowledge of the languages and cultures involved, and as Benet-Martínez (2012) adds, their own coping skills, tolerance for ambiguity (vs. rigidity) and other individual factors. The outcome of this process is, in general terms, to identify solely with culture A, to identify solely with culture B, to identify with neither culture A nor culture B, or to identify with both culture A and culture B. These categories share some similarities with Berry's (1990) acculturation positions: assimilation, separation, marginalization, and integration.

Research on bicultural identity has made great progress since the turn of the century and there are now many fuller descriptions, proposals, and models. Since there is no room in this chapter to review them all, we have opted to describe a recent study by Comănaru, Noels, and Dewaele (2018) which explored the various ways that people from an immigrant background describe their own bicultural identity. The identity orientations that emerge from this research appear to fit all types of biculturals, not just those who have immigration backgrounds. The authors made use of existing bicultural identity instruments such as the Benet-Martinez and Haritatos (2005) Bicultural Identity Integration (BII) scale, the Noels and Clément (2015) scale, etc. as well as phrasings taken from focus groups. With this, they constructed a new bicultural identity instrument, the Bicultural Identity Orientation Scale (BIOS).

The authors isolated five interrelated orientations of bicultural identity, many of which have been found in previous research, but sometimes with a different terminology. There was the *monocultural* orientation where participants identify with only one of the two cultures (only A or only B above). This involves being loyal to one cultural group and being uncomfortable in situations that takes into account both cultures. Other terms that have been used in the field are "assimilation" and "separation." They also found a *conflicted* orientation where there is perceived discord between the two cultural identities and hence a sense of discomfort and distress attached to belonging to two cultures (neither A nor B above). Terms used by others are "marginalization" and "deculturation." A third orientation was the *complementary* orientation where there is a perception that both cultures, though different, are compatible and complementary (A *and* B above). Terms by others include "integration," "acculturation," and "multiculturalism." The authors also found the *hybrid* orientation which reflects the idea of mixing or blending of the two cultures. In the field, we find terms like "hybridity," "fusion," and "blended." And finally, the authors revealed an *alternating* orientation with a shifting of identities according to the cultural context. This means there is variability and flexibility depending on the situation and the people involved. Others have called this "alternation" or "situational alternation."

The authors tested the newly developed identity scale on first and second generation Canadians by means of an online questionnaire. The results showed that both generations more strongly endorsed the hybrid and the complementary orientations than the other three. They also endorsed the alternating orientation more strongly than the monocultural and the conflicted orientations. In addition, the first generation group reported more conflicted, monocultural and alternating identities than did the second generation group, and the second generation group reported more complementary and hybrid identities than the first generation group. The authors concluded that their study provides a more comprehensive understanding of the diversity of identity experiences of bicultural persons, and that it offers an instrument to assess these orientations.

Hong and Zhan (2019) end their chapter on multicultural identities by stating, "It is ever more pressing to understand how people navigate among cultures, form bi- or multi-cultural identities, and adapt to new cultural environments cognitively and biologically, and the challenges and barriers they face." We can only applaud this and hope that all types of bicultural identities are fully accepted in the years to come, and that bicultural persons themselves are serene with the one(s) they choose to have.

References

Benet-Martínez, Verónica. 2012. "Multiculturalism: Cultural, personality, and social processes." In *Handbook of Personality and Social Psychology,* edited by Kay Deaux and Mark Snyder. Oxford/New York: Oxford University Press.pp. 623–648.

Benet-Martinez, Verónica, and Jana Haritatos. 2005. "Bicultural Identity Integration (BII): Components and psychosocial antecedents." *Journal of Personality,* 73: 1015–1049.

Berry, John. 1990. "Psychology of acculturation." In *Nebraska Symposium on Motivation, 1989: Cross-cultural Perspectives, Current Theory and Research in Motivation,* edited by John J. Berman, vol. 37, 201–234. Lincoln, NE: University of Nebraska Press.

Bloomfield, Leonard. 1933. *Language.* New York: Holt, Rinehart and Winston.

Comănaru, Ruxandra-Silvia, Kimberly A. Noels, and Jean-Marc Dewaele. 2018. "Bicultural identity orientation of immigrants to Canada." *Journal of Multilingual and Multicultural Development,* 39 (6): 526–541. DOI: 10.1080/01434632.2017.1404069.

Grosjean, François. 1982. *Life with Two Languages: An Introduction to Bilingualism.* Cambridge, MA: Harvard University Press.

Grosjean, François. 1983. "Quelques réflexions sur le biculturalisme." *Pluriel*, 36: 81–91.
Grosjean, François. 1997. "The bilingual individual." *Interpreting: International Journal of Research and Practice in Interpreting*, 2: 163–187.
Grosjean, François. 2001. "The bilingual's language modes." In *One Mind, Two Languages: Bilingual Language Processing*, edited by Janet Nicol, 1–22. Oxford: Blackwell.
Grosjean, François. 2008. "The bicultural person: A short introduction." In *Studying Bilinguals*, edited by François Grosjean, 213–220. Oxford/New York: Oxford University Press.
Grosjean, François. 2010. *Bilingual: Life and Reality*. Cambridge, MA: Harvard University Press.
Grosjean, François. 2015. "Bicultural bilinguals." *International Journal of Bilingualism*, 19 (5): 572–586.
Grosjean, François. 2016. "The Complementarity Principle and its impact on processing, acquisition, and dominance." In *Language Dominance in Bilinguals: Issues of Measurement and Operationalization*, edited by Carmen Silva-Corvalán and Jeanine Treffers-Daller, 66–84. Cambridge: Cambridge University Press.
Grosjean, François. 2019. *A Journey in Languages and Cultures*: The Life of a Bicultural Bilingual. Oxford: Oxford University Press.
Hong, Ying-yi, and Mark Khei. 2014. "Dynamic multiculturalism: The interplay of socio-cognitive, neural and genetic mechanisms." In *The Oxford Handbook of Multicultural Identity: Basic and Applied Psychological Perspectives*, edited by Verónica Benet-Martinez and Ying-yi Hong, 11–34. Oxford/New York: Oxford University Press.
Hong, Ying-yi, and Siran Zhan. 2019. "Multicultural identities." In *The Handbook of Culture and Psychology*, edited by David Matsumoto and Hyisung C. Hwang, 615–639. Oxford/New York: Oxford University Press.
Huston, Nancy. 2002. *Losing North*. Toronto, Ontario: McArthur & Co.
LaFromboise, Teresa D., Hardin L. K. Coleman, and Jennifer L. Gerton. 1993. "Psychological impact of biculturalism: Evidence and theory." *Psychological Bulletin*, 114 (3): 395–412.
Luna, David, Torsten Ringberg, and Laura A. Peracchio. 2008. "One individual, two identities: Frame switching among biculturals." *Journal of Consumer Research*, 35 (2): 279–293.
Mackey, William. 1962. "The description of bilingualism." *Canadian Journal of Linguistics*, 71: 51–85.
Meca, Alan, Kyle Eichas, Seth J. Schwartz, and Rachel J. Davis. 2019. "Biculturalism and bicultural identity development: A relational model of bicultural systems." In *Youth in Multicultural Societies: New Directions for Future Research and Interventions*, edited by Peter F. Titzmann and Philipp Jugert. New York: Routledge. pp. 41–57.
Nguyen, Angela-MinhTu D., and Verónica Benet-Martinez. 2007. "Biculturalism unpacked: Components, measurement, individual differences, and outcomes." *Social and Personality Psychology Compass*, 1 (1): 101–114.
Noels, Kimberly A., and Richard Clément. 2015. "Situational variations in ethnic identity across immigration generations: Implications for acculturative change and cross-cultural adaptation." *International Journal of Psychology*, 50 (6): 451–462.
Padilla, Amado M. 2006. "Bicultural social development." *Hispanic Journal of Behavioral Sciences*, 28 (4): 467–497.
Schindler, Simon, Marc-André Reinhard, Martin Knab, and Dagmar Stahlberg. 2016. "The bicultural phenomenon: The interplay of group prototypicality and cultural identity switching." *Social Psychology*, 47 (5): 233–243. DOI: 10.1027/1864-9335/a000276.

So, Wing Chee. 2010. "Cross-cultural transfer in gesture frequency in Chinese–English bilinguals." *Language and Cognitive Processes*, 25 (10): 1335–1353. DOI: 10.1080/01690961003694268.

Soffietti, James. 1960. "Bilingualism and biculturalism." *The Modern Language Journal*, 44: 275–277.

Szabó, Ágnes, Colleen Ward, Alan Meca, and Seth J Schwartz. 2020. "Testing the construct validity and empirical distinctiveness of the Multicultural Identity Styles Scale (MISS) and the Bicultural Identity Integration Scale (BIIS-2)." *Psychological Assessment*, 32 (7). DOI: 10.1037/pas0000825.

Weinreich, Uriel. 1968. *Languages in Contact*. The Hague, The Netherlands: Mouton.

West, Alexandria L., Rui Zhang, Maya Yampolsky, and Joni Y. Sasaki. 2017. "More than the sum of its parts: A transformative theory of biculturalism." *Journal of Cross-Cultural Psychology*, 48 (7): 963–990.

Wong, Rosanna Yin-mei, and Ying-yi Hong. 2005. "Dynamic influences of culture on cooperation in the Prisoner's Dilemma." *Psychological Science*, 16 (6): 429–434.

11

Change of Language, Change of Personality?

Of the many questions that intrigue both monolinguals and bilinguals when talking about bilingualism, the one concerning personality never wanes: do bilinguals change personalities when they change language? Over the years, I have collected testimonies in favor of the change from a variety of bilinguals. Here are a few:

> My personality changes no matter where I am or who I am with whenever I change my language. My sister has commented many times that it's very eerie and seems like I'm not even the same person.
>
> Trying to observe myself as objectively as possible, I still have the impression that I do feel a shift in my personality depending on language.
>
> I find when I'm speaking Russian I feel like a much more gentle, "softer" person. In English, I feel more "harsh," "businesslike."
>
> My father was from Hungary and came to Sweden in 1956.... He talked Swedish with me and my brother... He had a different personality in Hungarian. I think I never got to know him totally.... Who was he in Hungarian?

In what follows we will first review opinions and beliefs that would appear to give credence to a change of personality when there is a change of language. We will then describe some pioneering studies by Susan Ervin-Tripp that produced experimental evidence that also seemed to go along with this view. This will be followed by a description of more recent studies that examine why it is that some bilinguals feel different when using different languages. Do some variables such as the bilingual's age, education level, age of onset of bilingualism, frequency of use of a language, and so on, help explain this feeling?

We will then narrow in on actual studies that explore personality traits and examine the ratings obtained when bilinguals use the one or the other language. We will compare these results with those of monolinguals in different social contexts. And we will end with an explanation that calls upon the fact that bicultural bilinguals adapt to different cultural situations, and call upon different cultural representations, in their everyday lives as users of two or more languages.

The Mysteries of Bilingualism, First Edition. François Grosjean.

Opinions and Beliefs

In addition to the testimonies of bilinguals who report that their personality changes when they change language, there is an old Czech saying that goes in the same direction: "Learn a new language and get a new soul." Bilingual intellectuals and writers also have something to say about the issue. For example, the famous anthropologist, Robert Lowie (1945), who was born in Austria but then emigrated to the United States, wrote: "The popular impression that a man alters his personality when speaking another tongue is far from ill-grounded." In his book on bilingualism, Adler (1977) asserts that bilingualism can lead to a split personality. As for Julian Green, a French-born American writer, he relates the difficulties he had translating one of his books from French into English. It was as if he had become a different person. He finally gave up and wrote an entirely new book. Other writers express similar feelings. Even in the domain of research, the titles of certain articles evoke the possibility of a change of personality: "Is personality modulated by language?," "Two languages, two personalities...?," or "One individual, two identities...."

It is therefore not surprising that the general media have picked up on the issue. Thus, for example, in 2008, Reuters entitled a news item, "Switching Languages Can Also Switch Personality: Study." It then reported on research that supposedly showed that "people who are bicultural and speak two languages may unconsciously change their personality when they switch languages." A few years later, in 2014, The New Republic had an article with the enticing title, "Multilinguals Have Multiple Personalities." And that same year, the IESE Blog Network had a piece entitled, "Multilingualism: Multiple Personalities or Just a Diverse One?"

Pioneering Research on the Question

Susan Ervin, who later became Susan Ervin-Tripp, did a number of studies in the second half of the last century in an attempt to understand whether personality is modified when there is a change in language. In a first study, Ervin (1964) recorded bilinguals telling different stories in each language when asked to relate what they saw on Thematic Apperception Test (TAT) cards. These are cards that show pictures with ambiguous content. When describing them, participants are presumed to be projecting their feelings, attitudes, and motives... in a word, their personalities. Ervin called on French adults who were bilingual in French and English and who had lived in the United States for an average of 12 years. Most were married to Americans, and spoke both languages fluently. They were asked to describe a number of cards that showed various scenes mainly involving male and female figures, adults and children. There were two sessions, six weeks apart. In the first one, one of the languages was used; in the second, it was the other language.

Participants were given instructions to tell what was happening in each scene, what had happened in the past, and what would happen in the future. In addition, they had to say what the characters were thinking and feeling. Ervin-Tripp (2011) tells us that, for this study, she had scoured the literature on French culture to identity elements that would be different in the two countries. She finally analyzed what the participants had said in terms of nine personality themes such as achievement, verbal aggression, guilt, recognition of others, domination, autonomy or withdrawal, and so on.

Importantly for our discussion, Ervin found no differences for six of the nine personality themes when the languages changed. Thus, for example, there was not more emphasis on recognition by others in English, there was not more domination by elders in French, nor was there more verbal aggression towards parents in English, and so on. She did find, however, different results for three themes, and it is these that are underlined in the many accounts given of her study. For women, there was a greater achievement need in English. And more generally, there was more withdrawal and autonomy in French, and more verbal aggression towards peers in this language.

To illustrate these positive findings, Ervin gives a 27-year-old French woman's responses in French and English to a TAT card representing a man turning away from a woman who is grabbing his shoulders:

> French version: She seems to beg him, to plead with him. I don't know if he wants to leave her for another woman or what.... I think he wants to leave her because he's found another woman he loves more.... I don't know whose fault it is but they certainly seem angry. Unless it's in his work, and he wants to go see someone and he wants to get in a fight with someone, and she holds him back and doesn't like him to get angry.
>
> English version: In the past, well I think it was a married couple, average, and he got out of the Army and got himself a job or something like that or has decided he would go to college. He's decided to get a good education.... He keeps on working and going to college at night some of the time.... He'd have to give something up, and he's very discouraged and his wife tries to cheer him up.... He'll probably keep on working his way through and finally get his diploma and get a better job and they will be much happier and... well, his wife will have helped him along.

Ervin observes that in French the picture elicited a variety of themes of aggression and striving for autonomy, whereas in English the heroine supports her husband in his achievement strivings.

The study ends with possible explanations for the differences in content. Here are the first four Ervin proposes: the participants may have interpreted the instructions to speak a particular language as a request to tell a story appropriate to that language; bilinguals had different recall of past experience in two languages; their responses may be reflecting the respective mass media; and the differences were due to the verbal preoccupations and values expressed verbally in the two cultures. Ervin's fifth explanation is the one that I quote in my book *Life with Two Languages* (Grosjean 1982): "This is a result no more surprising than any other shift in behavior with social context. It happens that bilinguals have available an additional dimension of potential variation in behavior in comparison with the alternative roles available to monolinguals." She concludes nevertheless with, "Do these findings mean that our subjects have two personalities? The answer seems to be yes, at least to the extent that personality involves verbal behavior and perhaps further."

Ervin-Tripp pursued this research with Japanese–American women this time. They were married to Americans and were generally isolated from the American Japanese minority group. In Ervin-Tripp (1968) she reports on how they reacted to sentence completion tests. When they were given sentences to finish (each sentence was offered in English and Japanese), Ervin-Tripp found that they often proposed different endings. She gives the following three examples from one woman's responses:

When my wishes conflict with my family...
  Japanese: it is a time of great unhappiness.
  English: I do what I want.
I will probably become...
  Japanese: a housewife.
  English: a teacher.
Real friends should...
  Japanese: help each other.
  English: be very frank.

In her later comments on the study (Ervin-Tripp 2011), she states that those who shifted story content with language, as in these examples, typically had close American friends. Basically they were bicultural. It is interesting that she does not call on a shift in personality here.

Finally, in a third publication, Ervin-Tripp (1973) relates that she also tested a 27-year-old Japanese American who was born in the United States but who lived in Japan between the ages of eight and fourteen. He was thus fully bilingual and bicultural. She showed him a picture of a boy lying down with someone bending over him, and he provided the following descriptions in Japanese and English:

Japanese: A son comes home ill and dies before his mother, who goes mad with grief.
English: A young man was invited in off the highway when he was lost by a hypnotist, who robbed him.

Another picture showed a figure sitting on the floor and facing away, with the head resting on a couch or bench:

Japanese: A woman weeps over her lost fiancé and thinks of suicide.
English: A girl tries to complete a sewing project for class.

Ervin-Tripp observed that there was much more emotion in the Japanese responses; these involved members of the family and dealt with love, unfaithfulness, and loss of loved ones. In the English responses the relationships were formal, the people abstract and cold. Once again, in her later comments on the study, Ervin-Tripp (2011) does not call on a personality shift as the reason for the different responses. Instead, she states that speakers may shift thematic focus with language in a way consistent with cultural differences.

Based largely on Ervin-Tripp's studies, and the last reason she gives to explain her first study, I proposed in Grosjean (1982) that bilinguals choose a language according to the situation, the interlocutor, the topic, and the intent of the conversation. These factors trigger different attitudes, impressions, and behaviors. Thus, what is seen as a personality change due to language shift may really be a shift in situation and interlocutor. In a word, it is the environment and the culture as a whole that cause the bilingual to change attitudes, feelings and behaviors, along with language – and not language as such.

How has research since then resolved the change of language, change of personality enigma? Two lines of research, working in parallel, have furthered our knowledge of the issue. The first examines why bilinguals feel different when using different languages. And the second examines whether personality rating values change when there is a change of language. Each will be taken up in turn.

Feeling Different When Using Different Languages

In 2001, Jean-Marc Dewaele and Aneta Pavlenko set up a web questionnaire entitled, "Bilingualism and emotions." It was maintained on the Birkbeck College (University of London) website from 2001 to 2003. It contained 34 questions in all including one open-ended question which is of particular interest to us: "Do you feel like a different person sometimes when you use your different languages?"

Pavlenko (2006) analyzed the answers obtained and published the results. A total of 1039 bi- and multi-linguals were included, whose mean age was 35.6 years. A full 65% of the participants offered an affirmative response, that is, they did feel like a different person when they used a different language. Of the remaining participants, 26% gave a negative responses, 6% an ambiguous response, and 3% did not answer. Among those who answered positively, some gave a linguistic or cultural explanation of the type, "... you conform yourself to the way the native speakers talk and express themselves..." or "... the use of a certain language demands that you act according to the behavioral norms of the corresponding culture...."

Others, such as immigrants, expatriates and people who learned their languages in distinct contexts, stressed how they had acquired their languages. Here is an example: "If you pick up the language from living in (a country) where it is spoken then you pick up the traits and habits of those people." There were also those who invoked the feeling that the first language is "real" and "natural" while later learned languages are "fake" and "artificial." Pavlenko gave this example: "I feel less myself when speaking any language other than German but not in a bad sense. I feel more like I am acting a persona...."

As for those who gave a negative response, that is, did not feel like a different person, they often stressed that they simply adapted to the culture, and that the changes did not affect the core of who they are. For example, "I feel that the two cultures (i.e., French vs American) are so different that the language is just a way to express these cultural differences, but using a different language doesn't change the core of who I am." Another person stated, "Different languages allow me different thought structures and possibly different ways of feeling too. But these changes do not affect me deep within where I remain the same person." Participants such as these appeal to an unchangeable core of who a person is, while adapting to the situations and interlocutors. This is something we will return to in what follows.

The fact that two thirds of the respondents answered positively and that about a quarter did not raises an interesting question: Could it be that not everyone is equally apt at judging that they "feel different" when they change language? Ożańska-Ponikwia (2012) examined this very issue. She asked some 100 bilinguals made up of people who had grown up speaking two languages, immigrants who acquired their second language later on in life, as well as students who had stayed in a foreign country for an extended period of time, to give answers to two personality questionnaires and to give scale values to statements such as, "I feel I'm someone else while speaking English," or "Friends say that I'm a different person when I speak English."

What she found was that only people who are emotionally and socially skilled are able to notice feeling different. According to her, some people do not report changes in their behavior as well as in their perception or expression of emotions when changing language, not because they do not exist, but because they are unable to notice them. She speculates that it is people with an above-average level of social and emotional skills who can notice that they adapt aspects of their personality and behavior when using another language.

The results reported by Pavlenko led to a series of follow-up studies by Jean-Marc Dewaele and members of his team at Birkbeck College. Dewaele (2016), using the answers obtained with the Bilingualism and Emotions Questionnaire, examined a number of variables that might explain feelings of difference. He found that age correlated positively with the results, although weakly, suggesting that older bi- and multilinguals may be more likely to feel different when changing language. One explanation put forward is that younger people report more code-switching which could account for a weakening of feelings of difference. Another variable which showed a significant effect was education level. More educated participants reported a greater feeling of difference. A third variable was foreign language anxiety. The author found a positive correlation, again rather weak, between feelings of difference and foreign language anxiety in oral interactions with colleagues and in phone conversations, in the second (L2) and third (L3) languages. In other words, some participants who felt more anxious also felt more different when changing language.

Dewaele examined many other variables but did not find any link between them and the feeling of difference. They were early versus late bilingualism, female versus male, number of languages known, language dominance, age of onset of the LX (L2, L3, L4 or L5), context of acquisition of the LX, self-perceived proficiency in the LX, and frequency of use of the LX. In his conclusion, Dewaele remarked that many participants who reported feeling different when changing language also reported a change in the context in which they used the language(s). He agreed with the position I have held that these changes in environment and interlocutors might cause the difference in feeling different, rather than the language change itself.

In a follow-up study, Panicacci and Dewaele (2018) examined the feeling of difference when changing language with different interlocutors: strangers, colleagues, friends, family, and partner. They also looked at the topics of the conversation: neutral, personal, and emotional. Their participants were 468 Italian migrants mostly born in Italy who were highly multilingual. About a third said that they felt different when using the LX with different interlocutors – mainly with strangers, colleagues, and friends, less so with the family and the partner. The feeling of difference increased, therefore, when the interlocutors were less familiar. As for topics, emotional topics elicited the greatest feeling of difference, followed by personal topics and then neutral topics. Participants often indicated a strong emotional mismatch as the main reason of their sense of feeling different when using English. The authors concluded that situational changes are involved once again in a participant's feeling of difference.

Finally, it is worth mentioning a study by Dewaele and Nakano (2012) which examined what participants mean by "feeling different." The authors offered multilinguals a number of questions for each of their languages such as "How logical ... do you feel in this language?," "How serious...?," "How emotional...?" and "How fake...?," and the participants had to give a rating on a 5-point scale ranging from 1 (feel the same) to 5 (feel very different). The results showed a systematic shift on most scales across the four languages (L1, L2, L3 and L4) with participants feeling gradually less logical, less serious, less emotional and increasingly fake (although values here were much less high) when using the L2, L3 and L4. The first and second languages (L1 and L2) seemed to belong to the category of languages where shifts were more clearly perceived. One possible reason the authors give is that the other languages (L3, L4) are used too infrequently, and are not mastered well enough to experience a difference when changing over to these languages. The exception is feeling emotional, where the value for the L4 is significantly lower than that for the L3.

As in the other studies, a number of participants did not report feeling different. The authors suggest that within communities of bilinguals who code-switch, the feeling of differences would be minimal because the context remains unchanged.

Is a Change of Personality Involved When Changing Languages?

To introduce this section, it is worth giving a few definitions of personality. The American Psychological Association's (APA) states:[1] "Personality refers to individual differences in characteristic patterns of thinking, feeling and behaving." The APA Dictionary of Psychology gives a longer version of the definition:[2] "The enduring configuration of characteristics and behavior that comprises an individual's unique adjustment to life, including major traits, interests, drives, values, self-concept, abilities, and emotional patterns." Many general dictionary definitions of personality choose to stress what is unique in a person. Thus the Merriam-Webster Learner's Dictionary[3] definition is: "The set of emotional qualities, ways of behaving, etc., that makes a person different from other people," and the British English Collins Dictionary definition under Psychology[4] is: "The sum total of all the behavioral and mental characteristics by means of which an individual is recognized as being unique." Even though it concerns another language, the French Academy's Dictionary (9th edition) takes this uniqueness aspect one step further and defines personality as: "The mental structure which constitutes the deeper nature of a person and which is the base of their uniqueness."

For many years, personality has been measured by means of ratings given to personality traits. One of the best known instruments, the Big Five Inventory, is a self-report inventory designed to measure five broad dimensions: Openness to experience, Conscientiousness, Extraversion, Agreeableness, and Neuroticism. Each dimension is linked to a number of correlated and more specific factors or traits. Thus, for example, among the traits linked to Extraversion we find sociable, forceful, energetic, adventurous, enthusiastic, and outgoing. It is to these traits that participants give numerical ratings to when judging their personality in sentences such as: "I see myself as someone who... is talkative/... is full of energy/... generates a lot of enthusiasm."

There have been several studies that have examined how bilinguals assess their personality traits. For example, Chen and Bond (2010), in the first study of their paper, asked Hong Kong Chinese–English bilinguals to rate *themselves* using the Big Five Inventory (John 1990; John and Srivastava 1999). They were university students who had not experienced a physical relocation from one culture to another, and they had spent most of their time on campus using both Chinese and English. Of the 213 participants they used, 105 completed the English version of the inventory, and 108 the Chinese version. Responses to the sentences were anchored on a 5-point scale, ranging from 1 (strongly disagree) to 5 (strongly agree).

The results showed great similarities in the ratings in the one and the other language. Thus, for example, the mean Extraversion self-perception rating in Chinese was 2.82 as compared to 2.92 in English, a difference of only 0.10 on a 5-point scale! The mean

---

[1] https://www.apa.org/topics/personality.

[2] https://dictionary.apa.org/personality.

[3] http://www.learnersdictionary.com/definition/personality.

[4] https://www.collinsdictionary.com/dictionary/english/personality.

Openness to experience rating was 3.05 in Chinese and 3.17 in English, a difference of 0.12. Over the five factors, the mean of the absolute differences was only 0.124. Basically, the participants were giving themselves similar ratings in Chinese and in English.

Is this replicated in the participants' perception of the personality of the two cultural groups? Chen and Bond examined this by asking the bilinguals to give ratings for "typical native speakers of Chinese" and "typical native speakers of English." Here, the ratings were much more different. If one takes the mean absolute difference between the ratings given to the Chinese and to the English native speakers, over the five personality traits, it was 0.692. In other words, the bilingual participants saw personality differences between speakers of Chinese and speakers of English, as would be expected when comparing people of different cultures, but this did not carry over to the perception of themselves.

Ramírez-Esparza et al. (2006) conducted a study which, this time, clearly used bicultural bilinguals (it is unclear whether the Hong Kong participants were fully bicultural). Their participants were three groups of Spanish–English bicultural bilinguals. The first group was from Austin, Texas, the second group from the US and Mexico, and the third group from the San Francisco area. Their aim was "to test whether bilinguals switch their personality when they switch the language they are using when they respond to a questionnaire." They too used the Big Five Inventory, in its English and in its Spanish versions.

When the data of the three groups were analyzed, very similar results to the Hong Kong study were obtained. Even though three of the five factors produced statistically significant differences, it is the magnitude of the differences that is of interest here. Thus, the mean difference for Extraversion was a mere 0.097 between the ratings in English and Spanish (in Chen and Bond it was 0.10); the mean difference for Openness to experience was 0.07 as compared to 0.123 for Chen and Bond, and so on. The grand mean difference for all five factors was 0.116, a value that was highly similar to Chen and Bond's 0.124. These are extremely small variations for a 5-point scale.

This led me to look for studies *within just one language* that ask whether personality ratings can be modulated depending on the situation/context the participant is put into. If that is the case, and if the modification is greater than that found when there is a change of language, then headway can be made on the change of personality issue in bilinguals. Such studies were done by Donahue and Harary (1998) and by Robinson (2009). We will review the latter. Robinson used an adapted version of the Ten-Item Personality Inventory (TIPI) with the same five dimensions as the Big Five Inventory: Openness, Conscientiousness, Extraversion, Agreeableness, and Emotional Stability/Neuroticism.

His participants were given pairs of items such as "extraverted, enthusiastic," "dependable, self-disciplined," and "sympathetic, warm," and they had to judge how strongly they felt these applied to them in three different situations: with their parents, with their friends, and with their work colleagues. To do so, they had to write a number down from a scale of 1 (disagree strongly) to 7 (agree strongly).

Robinson regrouped the results under the five personality dimensions tested, and showed that the ratings were strongly influenced by context. Thus, the mean rating for Extraversion was 4.72 with work colleagues, 5.18 with parents, all the way up to 5.78 with friends. For Agreeableness, the corresponding mean ratings were 4.88, 4.54 and 5.17 respectively. The other three traits showed similar variation. The author concluded that the majority of people adapt or modulate their personality to "fit in" to social situations they are put into.

It is now worth comparing Robinson's results with those obtained in the two personality studies we reviewed above in which bilinguals were asked to give ratings in their different languages. First, we took for each dimension in Robinson's study, the absolute difference between the highest rating and the lowest rating across the three contexts (e.g., for Extraversion, 5.78 – 4.72 = 1.06). We then took the mean of these differences, and converted it from a 1 to 7 scale to a 1 to 5 scale. The result we found was a difference of 0.45! In other words, *within language* personality ratings variation in monolinguals in various social situations was practically four times larger than personality ratings variation due to language in bilinguals (0.124 in Chen and Bond and 0.116 in Ramírez-Esparza et al.). If a change in language had induced a real change in personality, we would have expected the opposite, with much greater variation between languages than within a language!

An Explanation

So, where do we stand on the proposal that bilinguals, more specifically, bicultural bilinguals, change their personality when they change language? Is there any truth to the Czech proverb, "Learn a new language and get a new soul"? As mentioned above, I proposed in Grosjean (1982) that what is seen as a change in personality in bilinguals is simply a shift in attitudes and behaviors corresponding to a shift in situation or context, independent of language. Bilinguals use their languages for different purposes, in different domains of life, with different people. Different aspects of life often require different languages. Thus, what is seen or felt as a personality change is probably an adaptation to the social situation/context the bilingual is in, and to the interlocutor(s) being spoken to, and may have nothing to do with the language itself.

Many bilingual testimonies that I have collected over the years put their finger right on this. Here are two examples:

> Many times I have experienced a feeling of "not being the same person" when I express myself in English, since my native language is French. When I try to analyze these situations, I realize that it is more a matter of context. I obviously tend to associate one language with its context.
>
> I don't really know if my personality changes when I change language. The main reason for this uncertainty is that I use the two languages in different situations and therefore I would act differently even if it was in the same language.

Lowie (1945), whom we cited at the beginning of this chapter, also comes up with this explanation:

> When I speak German to Germans, I automatically shift my orientation as a social being, I spontaneously adapt myself to the atmosphere characteristic of their status, outlook, prejudices.

Thus, different interlocutors can make one feel and behave differently, whether one is using one language or several languages. We should think of the way we speak to our best friend, and the behavior and attitudes we adopt with him or her. Then we should compare this with more formal interactions we have with people such as an employer or a religious authority.

The environment and the situation one is in can also change our attitudes, feelings, and behaviors, along with language. Language itself is not the cause. A trilingual puts it very nicely when she writes:

> When talking English, French, or German to my sister, my personality does not change. However, depending on where we are, both our behaviors may adapt to certain situations we find ourselves in.

Testimonies from bilinguals are important but so are the opinions of researchers in the field, as well as the results of observational studies and experimental studies. Dr. Jennifer Fayard, a personality specialist, wrote the following to me:

> I tend to agree with you that what we're seeing (in bilinguals) is not actual personality change, but different aspects of personality, attitudes, behaviors, etc. shifting in response to environmental pressures. I'd argue that all of those different manifestations are still the person's personality, it's just that some are highlighted in some situations, and others are more prominent in other situations.

This opinion goes well with the results of the Robinson study we described above and it does too with the "feeling different" studies. Dewaele (2016) stated that many of his participants who reported feeling different when changing language also reported a change in the context (environment, interlocutors) in which they used their languages. And Panicacci and Dewaele (2018) wrote that reports from their participants confirmed the position that feelings of difference are linked to situational changes.

Concerning observational studies, Di Pietro (1977) himself bilingual in Italian and English, wrote that in an Italian American store in Washington, D.C., the butcher's style differs with the language being spoken. In English he is rather matter-of-fact and formal, whereas in Italian he often carries on a light banter of jokes. Mkilifi (2014) reported that in Tanzania, when discussing such notions as agnosticism and democracy, a bilingual might hold slightly varying views depending on whether the discussion is in English or Swahili. And Gallagher (1968) reports that in North Africa, when an Arabic-French bilingual is enjoying himself with French friends, his attitude, indeed his whole character, is quite distinct from that expressed by his more robust joking in Arabic. In the latter examples, the contexts and interlocutors were certainly quite different.

Finally, experimental studies bring evidence to our position. We have already evoked Ervin-Tripp's (2011) change of emphasis when she was asked to look back on her studies many years after having done them. She stressed that bilinguals shifted thematic focus – she no longer mentioned personality – in a way consistent with cultural differences. Closer to the present time, a number of researchers have examined cultural frame switching in bicultural bilinguals. Hong et al. (2000) explain that individuals shift between interpretive frames rooted in different cultures in response to cues in the social environment. Contexts or symbols that are psychologically associated with one culture, or the other, may trigger frame-switching. Benet-Martínez et al. (2002) add that people switch between culturally appropriate behaviors depending on the context. (See Chapter 10 for a more extensive discussion of frame-switching and how it is researched.)

Luna, Ringberg, and Peracchio (2008) set about obtaining additional experimental evidence for frame switching in bicultural bilinguals. For them, the content of culture can be seen as a collection of mental frames that are internalized through individuals' socialization and participation in a cultural group. Bicultural individuals with extensive experience in two cultures seem to access different culture-specific cognitive structures, or mental frames, depending on the sociocultural context.

Luna and his colleagues asked Hispanic American bilingual women students to perform several tasks. In one study, they had to interpret target advertisements, first in one language and then, six months later, in another. (We should note the uncanny resemblance with Ervin-Tripp's original studies although the authors do not mention them.) The ads contained fictitious brands and images of women. For example, the Nature ad showed a woman sitting atop a hill overlooking a lagoon. The ad was for a resort hotel and the major headline stated, "For those who rarely find themselves at a loss for words, prepare to be left speechless." The ad added that the scenery is "too unbelievable to describe," with pristine beaches, towering mountains, and peaceful deserts.

The participants were asked questions like, "What is the woman in the ad doing?" "How does she feel?," "What do you think might have have happened before and after this snapshot in this woman's life?" and finally, "Try to imagine yourself in this ad. Where would you be? What would you do? And what would you feel?" The researchers found that in the Spanish sessions, informants perceived women in the ads as more self-sufficient (strong, intelligent, industrious, ambitious) as well as extroverted. In the English sessions, however, they voiced a more traditional, other-dependent and family-oriented view of the women. For the authors, the results provide qualitative evidence for frame switching triggered by sociocultural cues.

In a second study, the subjects were given a timed categorization task that showed that the associations between the category "masculine" and the category "other-dependent," on the one hand, and the categories "feminine" and "self-sufficient," on the other, were stronger in Spanish than in English, thereby bringing converging evidence for the results of the first study. In an email conversation we had concerning his study, David Luna told me that he thought of language as a very strong contextual cue. For him, frame-switching is a cultural phenomenon that can also be triggered by language.

We will end with a study by Rodríguez-Arauz et al. (2017) which concentrated on self-schemas, that is, views of the self. These are memories that summarize a person's experiences, attitudes, and beliefs in various domains. The authors give the following definition: "Self-schemas are defined as those constructs that are chronically accessible and that direct an individual to focus on certain aspects of their life. Self-schemas influence how an individual perceives, remembers, and feels about life experiences." They asked a large number of Mexican–American bicultural bilinguals (193 in all) to describe their personality in each of their languages, English and Spanish, leaving one week between the two. The instructions were as follows: "Personality has been defined as an individual's characteristic traits, behaviors, and attitudes. For the next 15 minutes, describe your personality."

The authors then extracted the most frequently used content words in each language, over all the participants, which they inserted into a factor analysis so as to observe how they clustered together. The clusters obtained can be thought of as underlying self-schemas that guide word choices in each language. For both languages, a self-schema appeared for bicultural identity but was expressed slightly differently. In English the words referred to student identity (e.g., graduate student, education, reliable, busy) while in Spanish the words referred more towards general introspection or appreciation of the bicultural identity (e.g., think, feel, identity, roots, mind, love, respect).

The authors concluded that when bicultural bilinguals changed languages, they shifted to the cultural values more associated with the priming language. As concerns whether this is a change of personality, one of the authors, Nairán Ramírez-Esparza, clarified things for me in an email message by stating that it is not that bilinguals change their personalities when they are switching between languages; it is just that the language primes a part of the self that becomes active and de-activates the other part of the self. This is very much akin to behaving biculturally: that is, adapting, at least in part, one's attitudes, behaviors, values, along with languages, to the respective cultures (see Chapter 10).

This hopefully puts to rest the change of language, change of personality myth that has persisted for so long. And it makes research into bicultural bilinguals all the more fascinating and valuable.

References

Adler, Max K. 1977. *Collective and Individual Bilingualism: A Sociolinguistic Study.* Hamburg: Helmut Buske Verlag.

Benet-Martínez, Verónica, Janxin Leu, Fiona Lee, and Michael. M. Morris. 2002. "Negotiating biculturalism: Cultural frame switching in biculturals with oppositional versus compatible cultural identities." *Journal of Cross-Cultural Psychology*, 33 (5): 492–516.

Chen, Sylvia Xiaohua, and Michael Harris Bond. 2010. "Two languages, two personalities? Examining language effects on the expression of personality in a bilingual context." *Personality and Social Psychology Bulletin*, 36 (11): 1514–1528.

Dewaele, Jean-Marc. 2016. "Why do so many bi- and multilinguals feel different when switching languages?" *International Journal of Multilingualism*, 13 (1): 92–105.

Dewaele, Jean-Marc, and Seiji Nakano. 2012. "Multilinguals' perceptions of feeling different when switching languages." *Journal of Multilingual and Multicultural Development*, 34 (2): 107–120. DOI: 10.1080/01434632.2012.712133.

Di Pietro, Robert. 1977. "Code-switching as a verbal strategy among bilinguals." In *Current Themes in Linguistics: Bilingualism, Experimental Linguistics, and Language Typologies*, edited by Fred Eckman, 3–13. Washington, DC: Hemisphere Publishing.

Donahue, Eileen M., and Keith Harary. 1998. "The patterned inconsistency of traits: Mapping the differential effects of social roles on self-perceptions of the Big Five." *Personality and Social Psychology Bulletin*, 24 (6): 610–619.

Ervin, Susan. 1964. "Language and TAT content in bilinguals." *Journal of Abnormal and Social Psychology*, 68 (5): 500–507.

Ervin-Tripp, Susan. 1968. "An analysis of the interaction of language, topic, and listener." In *Readings in the Sociology of Language*, edited by Joshua Fishman, 192–211. The Hague: Mouton.

Ervin-Tripp, Susan. 1973. "Identification and bilingualism." In *Language Acquisition and Communicative Choice*, edited by Anwar Dil, 45–61. Stanford, CA: Stanford University Press.

Ervin-Tripp, Susan. 2011. "Advances in the study of bilingualism: A personal view." In *Language and Bilingual Cognition*, edited by Vivian Cook and Benedetta Bassetti, 219–261. New York/Hove: Psychology Press.

Gallagher, Charles. 1968. "North African problems and prospects: Language and identity." In *Language Problems in Developing Nations*, edited by Joshua Fishman, Charles Ferguson, and Jyotirindra Das Gupta, 129–150. New York: Wiley.

Grosjean, François. 1982. *Life with Two Languages: An Introduction to Bilingualism.* Cambridge, MA: Harvard University Press.

Hong, Ying-yi, Michael W. Morris, Chi-yue Chiu, and Verónica Benet-Martínez. 2000. "Multicultural minds: A dynamic constructivist approach to culture and cognition." *American Psychologist*, 55 (7): 709–720.

John, Oliver P. 1990. "The Big Five factor taxonomy: Dimensions of personality in the natural language and in questionnaires." In *Handbook of Personality: Theory and Research*, edited by Lawrence A. Pervin, 66–100. New York: Guilford.

John, Oliver P., and Sanjay Srivastava. 1999. "The Big Five trait taxonomy: History, measurement, and theoretical perspectives." In *Handbook of Personality: Theory and Research*, edited by Lawrence A. Pervin and Oliver P. John, 102–138. New York: Guilford.

Lowie, Robert H. 1945. "A case of bilingualism." *Word*, 1 (3): 249–259.

Luna, David, Torsten Ringberg, and Laura A. Peracchio. 2008. "One individual, two identities: Frame switching among biculturals." *Journal of Consumer Research*, 35 (2): 279–293.

Mkilifi, Abdulaziz M. H. 2014. "Triglossia and Swahili-English bilingualism in Tanzania." In *Advances in the Study of Societal Multilingualism*, edited by Joshua Fishman, 129–150. The Hague: De Gruyter Mouton.

Ożańska-Ponikwia, Katarzyna. 2012. "What has personality and emotional intelligence to do with 'feeling different' while using a foreign language?" *International Journal of Bilingual Education and Bilingualism*, 15 (2): 217–234.

Panicacci, Alessandra, and Jean-Marc Dewaele. 2018. "Do interlocutors or conversation topics affect migrants' sense of feeling different when switching languages?" *Journal of Multilingual and Multicultural Development*, 39 (3): 240–255. DOI: 10.1080/01434632.2017.1361962.

Pavlenko, Aneta. 2006. "Bilingual selves." In *Bilingual Minds: Emotional Experience, Expression, and Representation*, edited by Aneta Pavlenko, 1–33. Clevedon: Multilingual Matters.

Ramírez-Esparza, Nairán, Samuel D. Gosling, Verónica Benet-Martínez, Jeffrey P. Potter, and James W. Pennebaker. 2006. "Do bilinguals have two personalities? A special case of cultural frame switching." *Journal of Research in Personality*, 40: 99–120.

Robinson, Oliver C. 2009. "On the social malleability of traits: Variability and consistency in big 5 trait expression across three interpersonal contexts." *Journal of Individual Differences*, 30 (4): 201–208.

Rodríguez-Arauz, Gloriana, Nairán Ramírez-Esparza, Norma Pérez-Brena, and Ryan L. Boyd. 2017. "Hablo Inglés y Español: Cultural self-schemas as a function of language." *Frontiers in Psychology*, 8: 885. DOI: 10.3389/fpsyg.2017.00885.

Index

a

The Mysteries of Bilingualism, First Edition. François Grosjean.

k

l

Manufactured by Amazon.ca
Bolton, ON